Heal Using Intuition
And Energy

Discover Mental and Emotional Roots of Health Issues

Carrie Suwal

First edition August 2022

Cover design by Aaftab Sheikh

Edited by Ioana (Aya) Gheorghiu

This publication contains the opinions and ideas of its author and is designed to provide useful information in regard to the subject matter covered. This publication is not intended to provide a basis for action in particular circumstances without consideration by a competent professional. The author/publisher expressly disclaim any responsibility for any liability, loss, or risk, personal or otherwise, which is incurred as a consequence, directly or indirectly, of the use and application of any of the contents of this book.

ISBN 978-1-7782038-2-4 (*paperback*)

ISBN 978-1-7782038-3-1 (*hardcover*)

ISBN 978-1-7782038-0-0 (*ebook*)

www.healingearththerapy.com

To my nieces when you grow up, know that there is love to be found in every dark corner.

I hope you are able to see the magic, and rediscover that unicorns are not make-believe.

Healing does not mean you must endure suffering
It is intentionally controlling what is in your means
And lovingly surrendering everything else to the Universe

Table of Contents

INTRODUCTION

Are you ready to dissolve your suffering? It's time to blast your radiance at 1,000 lumens. Time to experience bottomless joy, to love fearlessly, and to have peace of mind as attainable as oxygen. Healing is accessible to everyone. From curing an illness, moving from pain to freedom, anger to acceptance, or sadness to joy, your healing recipe is waiting to be created. Your healing journey will be as original as your fingerprints.

Nearly half (approximately 45%, or 133 million[1]) of all Americans suffer from at least one chronic disease in their life. One in five Americans struggle with a mental health condition, and 14.5% of Americans have a substance use disorder[2]. With the increasing likelihood of facing a health concern, it's time to rethink our approach to wellness and healing.

I was gently kicked by the universe to write this book on healing with intuition. I know that after a kick comes a concussive slap. I listen to the gentle kicks now. I'm not a medical doctor, mental health professional, or naturopath. I'm just a regular person who's been through a lot of health and life struggles. My struggles pushed me to develop my intuition so that I could navigate back to a state of wellness. This journey of self healing has led me to partake in a buffet of spiritual and energetic courses, leading me to become a professional intuitive, and energy healing therapist. I help everyday people understand the intricacies of the physical body and what our energy body is communicating through it. I have taught intuition

---

[1] Raghupathi, Wullianallur, and Viju Raghupathi. "An Empirical Study of Chronic Diseases in the United States: A Visual Analytics Approach to Public Health." *National Library Of Medicine: A Visual Analytics Approach*, vol. 1, no. 15, 2018, p. 431, https://www.ncbi.nlm.nih.gov/pmc/articles/PMC5876976/.
[2] "NIMH » Mental Illness." *National Institute of Mental Health*, https://www.nimh.nih.gov/health/statistics/mental-illness. Accessed 2 July 2022.

building, the law of attraction, and energy healing to tens of thousands of students.

This text will quench your parched lips in their quest for healing. Let's kickstart your health and the health of your loved ones. You are going to learn the imperative systems of the energy body and how to translate its instruction manual for happiness and health. No more snailing it to the finish line. Waft the burnt rubber as you drift to health with a channeled encyclopedia of major conditions, illnesses, and experiences that you and your loved ones may encounter in your life.

To be prepared for deep healing, you must begin with the act of belief. Believe you can heal and live free of suffering. Belief is a tool used to empower your thoughts positively, and a necessary first step. As you cannonball into the ocean of energy, you will have a deeper understanding of just how powerful your thoughts and beliefs are in creating your reality. We tend to hold belief systems that tell us we are not whole, we cannot heal, and are not loved or worthy of love. These chosen beliefs are quicksand on your path to being happy and healthy. You must realize the beliefs that hold you back from health so that you can discard them, and choose beliefs that upgrade you to first class seats on a direct flight to health.

The next paver for the bumpy healing road is hope. Hope is a practice of releasing what you think you know, and jumping hard-nipped naked into the sea of the unknown, trusting that you won't be an appetizer to a great white shark. It is trusting that there is a loving force that is always there to catch you. When you work on healing your life, if you graze the mindset of positivity and optimism, you're sprinkled with hope. If you are in the mindset of doubt and negativity, you are suffocated by fear. You can easily be pulled onto the path of fear and doubt in your life. This book instills confidence to keep coming back to hope and rainbow sprinkles.

The final awareness in healing is knowing. Knowing means you hold certainty, like metal plates absorbing seismic quakes that will never crack. Knowing something cannot be taught, you must experience it for yourself. It then becomes an incontestable truth.

Within your fleshy physique is a concrete space that is happy, healthy, and free of suffering. This concrete space is accessed through the heart consciousness and is always employable. I can't wait for you to know the potency of the love that's within you!

Engage in a childlike curiosity as you venture through this wonderland and the exercises throughout. The chapters provide doorways to new lands, encounters to caress your energy body, and opportunities for spontaneous healing. The practices bring you closer to living a life of wholeness. Your whole self loves every piece of you as you are. Are you excited to sponge up this scrumptious awareness?

You will see your suffering and the suffering of others through the eyes of love as you diminish its power. You will connect to your third eye, your inner seeing, to discover the truth of your reality. This truth exposes the root cause to the suffering you have encountered, and helps you find purpose and gratitude for all of life.

Suffering caused by trauma, pain, illness, and accidents are chunky curdles in your streaming energy flow. The cause and cure of cancer, diabetes, anxiety, and depression is inscribed into your energy body. The disturbance first appears in the aura (energy body) before you experience it in your physical body. Your unpasteurized energy body atomically mirrors your soul, which is your highest potential. The soul is whole, healthy, and thriving. So what is it that curdles the energy field?

In this book, we investigate what disturbs the energy field, which in turn causes disease and disharmony in your life. You will clearly understand how your thoughts and emotions directly impact your health and happiness. With some slight adjustments we can move from the pain body, to a healthier and happier body.

Like a toddler rolling off their tippy toes taking their first pounce in a jumper, you are about to take flight, swooping through the clouds as you unmask your answers. Soaring into healing, and swooshing into a swirly synchronicity with your soul.

Before you proceed, I need to inform you that I am not the one to deliver these gifts. YOU are going to assimilate answers, healing, and integration of your higher self. I will be facilitating this connection for you. YOU will be the healer of your life. You were guided to pick up this book because something within you has heard the call and is ready to uncloak the suffering suit, and shake it in your birthday suit.

Let's dig to the heart of your suffering, heal its roots, and flip our hair side to side as we skip into wellness. Are you ready to begin?

Chapter 1

THE SEDUCTIVE PAIN BODY

Underneath the wounded ego lies the whole soul
Blissfully resting in peace.

A strawberry hue washes over Corrin's cheeks as she twirls her hair around her finger, licking her lips while the butterflies in her stomach whisper *this could be the one.* "Ffpt, ffpt, ffpt," ice cubes whip by her at lightspeed. "Clunk", slapping her collarbone, "clunk", smacking her face. Her ego is piping red and dripping with embarrassment.

I've been stirring in my seat anticipating this evening all week. My party animal high school bros are meeting my dainty college gals from esthetic school. I sanctimoniously orchestrated young lovers to conjoin on Saint Valentine's Day! There is heat and attraction between the two groups. I am befuddled at how this tail shaking night would end in the emergency room.

I look around the hotel room to soak up my presumptuous matchmaking capabilities. There are goosebumps, blushing cheeks, fiery undercarriages and ... tears? I see pools welling up in Corrin's eyes. My high school bro is whipping ice cubes at his suitress in an act of delinquent flirting. Her face is swelling from the blows. She's frozen in her heels. Her acrylic magenta nails swoop to shield her face, as her eyebrows unite in a furrow of confusion.

I screech, "Enough!", as I whip my neck towards the gentlemen in the room. "We are leaving, NOW", as I stomp my feet out the door. I beeline it to my bona fide seat as designated driver. Tapping my nails on the steering wheel, I furiously wait in the truck for my befuddled friends to fill the car. Their regret-drenched shoes slow them down as they begin arguing amongst themselves.

The driver door flings open. My friend strong arms me out of the driver's seat. His eyes widen as his ink black pupils laser beam to the steering wheel. His fragile arm hairs stand erect, like a flaccid private firmly saluting his sergeant.

"Get out", he commands. *What is happening?!* He's always been my role model for kicking your feet up and chillaxing. My stomach rises to my throat as I shuffle my feet around the truck to the passenger seat.

Jim, the gentle giant opens the back door and collapses in the back seat as he gasps for air. Is he having a heart attack? Organ failure? Inexplicable death? Pumped with adrenaline, laser beam's thigh stiffens and the gas pedal collides into the floor.

Rushing to the hospital, I jiggle the button to unclasp my seat belt. I turn to Jim, he's hovered in a shell, wheezing in the back seat. I yell at my friend driving to slow down as I recall the sharp turn and high metal guard rail at the end of the bridge. A low tuba note intensifies as the engine picks up speed. My screaming is suffocated by deaf ears and Jim's shrill breath.

Blank. Black. I lose a piece of my memory that will never be returned. Flashing red lights wake me from my lifeless slumber. My chariot has arrived.

A punch of earthy iron floods my taste buds as a bloody reflection meets my gaze in the window. My left brow is cracked open like a coconut. Blood spews down my face. A gorilla of weight has anchored its bony pelvis on my chest. My eyes venture in front of me, passing the defeated airbag, and find the passenger side of the car is mashed by the metal guard rail.

In the hospital, I yell in agony from the spinal board. The weight of my head on my hair clips feels like rusty nails stabbing my cranium. My friends appear unscathed from the accident. Jim has no words as he sits slouched in the corner. I found out an attack of panic was his culprit. They glue my flappy brow closed and clear me to go. The glue did a fine job sticking me back together but didn't repair the nefarious neck pain that ensued. Chronic pain is a slow torture, like a bruise being poked 24/7 for the rest of your life, mentally breaking down the strongest of minds. This night broke me.

My neck pain serenaded me like a yelping car alarm that never turned off. This bulldozed me on my healing path. I desperately searched for a way to escape my pain: chiropractic, yoga, osteopathy, visceral manipulation, brain therapy, acupuncture, injections, talk therapy, massage, bowen, and spiritual healing. The treatments temporarily softened the blow horn of pain, but never relieved it for more than a few days. I was looking in the wrong places to discover health. I was focusing all of my efforts on decontamination of this malignant pain. I was not in the right vibration for healing. My desire for healing became obsessive, and I feared I would never be pain-free. This took me off course from finding the root cause of my pain and made healing unattainable. The aftermath of the accident shined a new purpose into my life. It sent me on a quest to heal myself. I couldn't shake the feeling that if I can heal myself, I can help light the path of healing for others.

To reach the root cause of your pain, you must go through all of the levels where imbalance occurs and disturbs your energy field. Each soggy layer of disturbed energy you air out results in growth and joy. Your energy body is a boy scout wiggling his toes as he sews on his next accomplished badge. It is striving to match your reality to the wholeness of your soul. When you reflect the wholeness of your soul, you are rewarded with good feelings, health, and vibrancy.

There are deterrents keeping the energy body from reflecting perfect health. Imbalance has been created to bring awareness to you that something is not in alignment with your soul. If the energy body

7

is healthy, then the physical, mental, and emotional body are also healthy and thriving. If there is struggle in your body, then there is struggle in your energy body.

When you heal the physical body, the energy body heals. When you heal the energy body, your physical body heals.

The mind influences the energy body, like a glob of butter, melting into toasted bread. The mind leaves an arterial grease, clogging your body of energy. The soul, unlike the mind, treats your energy with extra virgin coconut oil, moisturizing your energy flow into a sparkling waterfall. When your mind aligns with the consciousness of your soul, homeostasis permeates your energy body and wellness cascades into your being.

After a meditation retreat there is an aura of loving awareness that is emitted from me, until my old judgmental habits kick back in a week or two later. If someone were to slander my name with crusty hostility, I would shower them with compassion and kindness post-retreat. Pre-retreat I would likely respond by going into defense mode and protecting my ego. Going inward daily changes your perception of the world to reflect the level and quality of soul work you have exercised.

Control is the way of the mind; surrender, the way of the spirit. When we relinquish control of the mind and surrender, healing flows like a barreling avalanche. Once you heal, or heal your relationship to your pain, eye droplets clear your foggy vision. Colors become crisp, presence moves to milliseconds, and gratitude engrosses you. The cycle of pain and illness disturbs your birthright of experiencing joy and gratitude. Let's shatter that cycle and be free to twirl in the joy of each moment by taking back your health.

Have you remained calm in a chaotic situation, like getting cut off by an aggressive driver? Or if someone is trying to bring you down, yelling and cursing at you, do you continue to stay in your joy?

Your mind is having an eternal affair with your ego and the reptilian (survival) self. These dark vibrations inject toxic thoughts.

Your ego's flirtatious ammunition is laced with fear — fear of not being good enough, fear of not having enough money, fear of not being accepted, etc. The existential battle wages love against fear. Your soul is love, with an attentive support staff named Joy and Peace. Your mind is fear, with the goons, Judgment and Pain, watching your back. Love creates a passageway for your soul to integrate with your physical body. When you can operate from love, your wounds inexplicably heal. Your mind cauterizes worries and your joy is freed into your being. Fear is the moldy womb, birthing the pain and suffering that holds you back from living a joyful, healthy life. Fear is a terrorizing energy opposing your soul's natural state of balance. The mind does not always operate from fear, it can operate from a space of wisdom when the emotional and rational mind are balanced.

Fearful thoughts spark fearful actions. Say you have been wanting to get into shape and be healthier, but you haven't taken the actions. You haven't been staying motivated and going to the gym like you desired. You can't keep your greasy fingers out of the chip bag, while the green beans are wrinkling in the fridge. Fear has gotten in the way. This fear could be a feeling of not being worthy of health, or of self-love practices. This could be a fear of not being strong enough (mentally) to go after what brings you joy and allows you to feel good. Or a fear that once you are healthier, happiness will not await you on the other side. Can you trace some of your imbalances back to a fear? Why do we continually feed ourselves an unhealthy vibration and stay in this system of fear?

You are worthy, just as everyone is worthy of health and happiness in this lifetime. There is no precursor or quota to meet to have these experiences. This joyful life is only blocked by the villainous shadow living within you, crawling its twisted fingers up your spine, muttering through charcoal teeth: "you my dear, are meant to suffer." Your saboteur archetype thrives on explosive drama, fear, and rejection. You have all the archetypes within you,

9

positive and negative. The ones that run your life are the ones you choose to feed.

How can you recycle your inner villain to live a healthy and happy life?

Chapter 2

INTENTION LEADS THE WAY

The quality of your life depends on the quality of your thoughts.

A man wearing baggy layers of spoiled clothing sits on a cold corner. Dirt and oil fill the harsh crevasses around his eyes. My breathing shallows as my gaze stiffens to oppose his direction. Deeply critical thoughts slither to my mind: *He needs to stop doing drugs and see a therapist. Then he could get a job, be healthy, happy, and have a home.* Turmoil brews inside of me, my vitality evacuates through my shoes. Intentionally ignoring this fellow human while having these fear-based and negative thoughts drains my very essence. A whimper from within illuminates the dark thoughts blocking the love within my deepest self.

I shake off my fearful thoughts and center into my core of love. My gaze softens and I make eye contact with this loving soul. We exchange a joyful smile. His eyes sparkle as I offer him garden peas from my backpack. I feel my vitality return and deep joy emanates from my being! Joy from being in alignment with my vibration of love, with my truth.

When you are feeding fearful, doubtful, and painful thoughts, there is an instant response in the energy field — one of a stand still. Nothing flows or moves, and energy gets trapped. This causes disease and disharmony in all systems of your body.

Your brain does not know the difference between something that is imagined or something that is physically happening. Tor Wager, director of the Cognitive and Affective Neuroscience Laboratory at The University of Colorado Boulder, found through their study "that imagination is a neurological reality that can impact our brains and bodies in ways that matter for our wellbeing" (Wager et al.[3]). The study confirmed with new brain imaging research that imagining a threat lights up similar regions as experiencing it does. It suggests imagination can be a powerful tool in overcoming phobias or post-traumatic stress.

If your body responds to a threat from something that is imagined, how will it respond to happiness and health when imagined? Choosing positive thoughts results in positive feelings. If a seagull drops a bomb of slimy poop on your head, instead of having a poopy day, you can choose to laugh it off. Continually feeding negative thoughts causes you to live in a constant state of negativity and fear. Fear peels your skin away from the loving infrastructure of your soul. You have creative control in how you perceive the world. When you take back your conscious control, you get to decide how you want to feel.

When you operate from your base of love, you bring your deepest self forward. Love is a crucial ingredient to your true nature. This love that you carry is no different from person to person. Because we share the same makeup of universal love, it interconnects us into a field of oneness. The only thing that changes is how each of us perceives it, tries to suffocate it, or lets it flow. It is a part of your infrastructure, and is not a limited resource. This steady state of love can not be exhausted. You can share it and become energized by its contagious nature.

---

[3] Wager, Tor Dessart, et al. "Attenuating neural threat expression with imagination." *Neuron*, vol. 100, no. 4, 2018, p. 17. *The Cell*,
https://www.cell.com/neuron/fulltext/S0896-6273(18)30955-3.

Your thoughts are a God-like force that can create platinum palaces, or 9.0 quakes on the Richter scale. Do not underestimate the power of thought. Not only do thoughts invoke corresponding emotions, but each thought you have carries an energetic vibration.

What happens when your thoughts align with the love vibration? Suffering becomes a dehydrated marshmallow that squanders from the flick of a finger. The love vibration is the DNA of a loving thought, a loving feeling, or loving action. You can live in a fear-based vibration and experience constant suffering, or live in a loving vibration and cease trivial suffering. You can become this love vibration by virtue of raw authenticity. Not by creating a mock reality to model someone you are not but by harnessing an inherent truth that has been suppressed from misfortunes and missteps. This ubiquitous love vibration is masked with fears: societal, formed from your experiences to protect you, inherited or learned through your lineage, from your direct community, and from your disparaged ego. When you surrender and release these fear-based conditions and beliefs, what remains is the pure vibration of love.

To ignore your fearful thoughts is like drinking toilet water while convincing yourself it's spring water. It is human to have fearful thoughts. To ignore them would be to ignore your humanness. What you can do is work on not feeding those thoughts.

Sometimes I catch an unflattering angle of my tummy in the mirror on a bloated day. My mind deploys its missile: *Ewww.* I then feed this disgusted thought with a toxic follow up: *Ewww. I can't believe how fat I am. Why can't I be more beautiful? I would like me more. I need to stop eating junk food.* I create word vomit and thought missiles. It is a continuation of the initial thought and it is me creating a story to support that thought.

If you want to force any process, why not force and feed positive thoughts? At least it might help combat the lifetime of critical thoughts, right? What happens if I leave my next critical thought at that door? Accept it, be strong, and move on? My love vibration steps in and I innately say: *Wow, that was a critical thought, but I am a human and that's okay.* Thankfully, this pattern of loving acceptance is becoming increasingly common for me due to my awareness of the initial thought. Where does your mind wander when you have a negative thought? Do you feed the hell out of the fear, do you flow into love, or do you let it go and be present with what is?

These three paths of after thought are: throw gasoline on it and continue to suffer in a negative thought, be present with what is, or tune in to the love vibration. Being present is a beautiful space of neutrality, nestled gently between the fear and the love vibration. It is not charged with love or fear, it is remaining untethered to your experiences. This can, however, be difficult when your fear-based patterns are engrained with a chisel from a lifetime of critical, shameful, and productivity-focused thinking. It is a Zen Buddhist approach of seeing your true nature without intellect. Zen Buddhism is a powerful path to enlightenment, and if you feel called to this path, I suggest reading *You Are Here* by Thich Nhat Hanh (Hanh[4]). Finding this central space of non-judgement is used not only for negative thoughts, but all thoughts and all experiences.

This makes the third option, choosing love, easier and more palatable for dealing with negative thinking or overthinking, and gives you a supportive technique where you can involve your conscious mind. It is useful to create balance and find the middle ground of non-judgement. By stepping out of the fear vibration, and into love, it is like jumping from ego to soul. Eventually, you will find the perfect harmony between the two. You will embrace suffering with arms of love and maintain a heavenly state in this human experience.

This loving, content voice of the soul comes thundering through your intuition. Intuition is your inner wisdom. Wisdom is not to be confused with intelligence. It is not learned from programs or books. Rather, it is the soul's truth, an inner knowing. From this inner knowing, you connect to the truths of the Universe. Universal divine wisdom is always accessible, and it is all knowing. It is not based on

---

[4] Hanh, Thich Nhat. *You are Here: Discovering the Magic of the Present Moment*. Edited by Melvin McLeod, Shambhala, 2009.

what science has or has not proven, it is not formed from judgment or fear, it simply is the truth. When you access this truth, you find what you've been searching for. You align with happiness in your life, with a way to detach from your stress and suffering and to finally start living your dreams. When you are aligned with this truth, it just feels good.

The bones in your body have always been a foundational structure to your existence, but they hide beneath the skin and go unseen. Your intuition is like your bones. It is present from birth but goes unnoticed as it is masked by your thoughts. It gets drowned out by the perpetual focus and feeding of your mental chatter and fears. We give full authority to our logical mind when processing information and making decisions, so much so that we block out our wisdom and intuition. When you create space in the mind through meditation and present living awareness, your wisdom becomes louder. It's not actually increasing the volume. It is simply that through meditation you are quieting the other voices and creating silence to finally hear your intuition. When you can hear your intuition, you make smarter decisions that cause less struggle and create more joy. Your intuitive consciousness has been streaming through your thoughts, emotions and body for your entire lifetime. The more prejudice you direct towards your mental chatter, the greater oppression you force upon your intuition.

An added bonus of softening the chatter of the mind is that it allows you to see the beauty in this moment. You can be present, instead of living in the sad stagnancy from your past or the worrisome possibilities of your future. If you ever ponder, "What is my purpose? Where is my joy?", the answer is not behind or in front of you, but within you. And it's only accessible in the now.

Soul alignment exercises are found throughout this book at the end of each chapter. They are practices to go inwards, connect with your intuition, and align yourself with your deepest truth. You can journal your answers, speak them aloud, or reflect quietly in your mind. Use your intuition and paint, draw, sing, and express yourself in whichever way flows with ease and is the most enjoyable.

◇ **Soul Alignment Exercise:**

Step Into Joy

- What thoughts do you continue to feed that are creating struggle or suffering for you?

- Can you discontinue these negative thinking patterns? And if you are not able to stop them, can you negate the continual thoughts or stories associated with them?

Chapter 3

TREKKING THE HEALER'S PATH

Wounds sew fear into the fabric of your scars
The healer draws the scalpel to dissect their fear
And plant seeds of love in its place.

With puffy eyes and an explosion of snotty tissues on the floor, I kick on my runners and slam the door behind me. Depression often runs my life but when I go running, depression runs for the hills.

Emotions can leave you feeling paralyzed and stripped of your willpower. Your benign and malignant thoughts trigger powerful feelings. The thoughts are something like: *I'm so lonely, nobody wants me* - sadness and grief are triggered. Your feelings breed incessant thoughts. You make your friends laugh and feel deep joy and thoughts naturally spark: *I love my friends, I feel so appreciated, I'm grateful to have these people in my life.* Feelings affect the energy body at a higher potency than thoughts as their energetic vibration is denser. Let's take your power back in the realm of feeling through actions (outer world), and feelingization (inner world).

Do you ever overwork and drown your exhaustion in the TV? Or stress over the future so much that it causes worry, sadness, exhaustion, and loneliness? Why? Why do we feed these patterns?

You have the power to decide what you are doing with your life. It is your life. You get to decide which activities and experiences you wish to have each day, which directly impact how you feel. Yes, you decide how you feel. Stop feeling like a victim to the world and create what you desire. Create your optimal life by being a conscious creator.

Some days, I wake up on the wrong side of the bed, with my sheets smelling of trepidation. I roll out of bed with just enough energy to brush my teeth. I choose activities to support my negative mood, like watching television until my eyeballs tap out, and eating chocolate until it tastes dull. I feed my funk with thoughts of scarcity: *I'm not enough, why is life so hard,* perpetuating my feelings of sadness. Why do I do this? Is it because I feel like I have no control? To a degree this is true. Hormones, health conditions, and feelings cannot directly be told how to behave — with an exception for those who can move from embodying their emotions to observing them. When you observe your emotions, they are no longer a "negative" or "positive" thing. Your soul truth gives you the superpower to move from embodiment to witnessing. This truth becomes accessible through mindfulness and meditation. It is difficult to arrive at this peaceful awareness when your emotions are being hurled at you like an angry bird. But your soul truth is bursting at the seams, ready to be unzipped.

Indirectly, you can choose activities that bring you joy. You can choose not to feed the fear-based thoughts. You can significantly and often completely impact your emotions by using your power of choice to create an environment of awesomesauce. Instead of feeding and fueling undesirable actions, feed those you do desire.

By doing this, you feel happier more often because you are living and doing activities that spark joy. Your energy responds by flowing freely, breaking through blockages, and refueling your depleted reserves. The body responds in health and the universe sends you an abundance of positive vibrations — things like loving relationships, financial freedom, and joyful experiences. This is the universal law of attraction at work. You are a beacon of energy. Your energy body transmits an outward signal that magnetizes that exact quality of energy back towards you that you have been sending out. Your thoughts, feelings, and actions attract the same frequency towards you into your experiences. You are a conscious creator, but also a co-creator with the universe. Whatever you feel inside, transmits from you. It stretches far past the physical body and into the world, into the sphere of universal qi (energy) which is connected to all things. Like attracts like. So, as you feel good and you think good thoughts, you are pulling a bus load of good things towards you. Isn't that neat?

The physical actions you take create joy derived from your exterior world (things outside of you). You do something joyful and are rewarded with a positive feeling. What about creating interior joy, seeing as external joy isn't always accessible? Internal joy isn't based on your actions or your environment, it is found within you. This is done through the process of feelingization!

Feelingization: instead of visualizing an image in your mind (visualization), you feel a feeling in your heart without needing an outward experience to bring about that feeling. In this way, healing is a creative act as you consciously direct feelings (energy) towards release and wholeness.

Feelingization is a form of meditation that can become a way of life. It allows light to peak into your darkest days. Each time depression strolls into my life, I know it has arrived because joy immediately vacates the premise. Once I started practicing feelingization, depression continued to produce sadness and negativity, but joy was strapped in for the ride. My best year (2020) was a year of depression! I became more active than ever, and I was grateful for every juicy moment. Although there was a lot of pain, there was an abundance of fun and happiness! I realized that just because I was in an inexhaustible funk, it didn't mean I couldn't access joy at the same time. I began sitting every morning for ten minutes and saying the words: love, peace, joy, and freedom. I would spend 2-3 minutes with each word. First, love: What does love feel like? Can I feel it right now, with no thoughts involved? I was shocked at first to find that yes, I can! Then peace, then joy, then freedom. The practice expanded and I used words like health and abundance. What happened after two weeks is ten minutes turned into thirty seconds. I would say the word joy and feel it instantaneously. It wasn't hiding, or waiting for a joyful experience, it was right here within me.

When my thoughts move into hyperdrive, and a panic attack is activated, I say the word peace. Boom! Peace is here, in the midst of a panic attack! Panic and peace can exist in the body in the very same moment. This is how feelingization blindsides powerful thoughts with even more powerful feelings.

If you are working to heal yourself, you are a healer. Healing is hard if that's what you choose to perceive it as. Why not replace the word hard with fun? It may be the same path of peaks and valleys, why not make it an adventure instead of a slog? As a healer, all layers of your health need attention and care. We will venture into the energy body, but the mental, physical, and emotional also need tender love and care. Are you ready to heal all the layers of self?

◇ Soul Alignment Exercise:

- What relationships and activities bring you joy and which bring you stress? These relationships and activities impact your emotional state. They are all choices, chosen by you consciously and subconsciously. Are the joyful activities from your list (*that allow you to feel peace, joy, and love*) being prioritized? If not, what can you do to bring them to the top of your list?

- Let's feel through feelingization. This is something built with persistence and hope. Take 30 seconds (or longer) to sit with each of these feelings: happiness, peace, freedom, and health. Yes, health has a feeling. Be curious and explorative as to how it feels in your body. No need to focus on happy thoughts, simply bring your awareness out of your mind and into your body. Let your body feel these emotions and sensations associated with these words.

Chapter 4

DIAMOND MINING

Like a seed needing darkness to grow
The seismic pressure and scalding heat
Crystalize carbon into sparkling diamonds.

If you are stuck in a cycle of precipitation in your mind and emotions, you are attracting muddy health. Overcast thoughts create a gale force of suffering. Negative emotions feel torturous. The physical body endures typhoons of pain. These murky smears of discomfort are stirred into the crystal-clear waters of your energy body. When you connect with your energy body directly, it shares the answer as to why you are experiencing pain and what you can do to step out of the cycle of suffering.

My emotions remind me to check in with my intuition, and ask: Why are you struggling right now? What do you really need? Recently, I asked and received from my intuition while experiencing a tornado of emotions in the shower:

Hands clench around my throat, like a boa constrictor scaling the trachea's walls to complete collapse. A balloon of air inflates my chest as the villain becomes cognizant. Fear. I am afraid. It's been 12 years of soul growth and expansion post car accident. The trauma and scar tissue weaved into my neck, all around the plexus of my throat chakra (my truth center). I have always been shy, afraid to show up and be seen because being seen means I can be disapproved of like a rotten meat slab being thrown to the street dogs for sustenance. Each time I show up and bear my essence to the world, I trim another strand of scar tissue preventing my truth from being set free.

I face a new chance to speak my truth. A voice within bellows: *you need to write a book*. Barbwire flosses over my throat. I slump into a ball as my inner child quivers. From my negative reaction, I know that writing a book is something I have to do to overcome my old beliefs of unworthiness. As my body fosters these unsupportive beliefs, they break my healthy energy flow and disturb my physical body. The spiders of thoughts creep out of my brain: *I'm not intelligent, not worthy and have nothing to share; no one is going to want to hear what I have to say*. I feel the hands twisting my windpipe, the neck tension becomes deafening.

Luckily, I have gained confidence through diligently practicing to trust my intuition. My higher self speaks through my pain: *Clearly you are still holding on to this trauma, this fear of not being valued and heard. It's time to prove through action that this is not your truth.* I know through past experiences that ignoring intuition brings a locker full of pain. I know that the throat chakra restriction is an opportunity for soul growth, for self love through worthiness by speaking my truth. Intuition is a tool you will be sharpening throughout the book so that you can communicate with your energy body and understand what actions and paths it is suggesting to you for your deepest expansion and soul growth.

Not only did the accident teach me to speak my truth and value myself, but over the 12 years of healing I learned to stop giving into the pain. I stopped feeding it with fear and negativity by focusing on it. I was blessed with discovering acceptance of my suffering, loving all parts of myself, even the "shadow" parts. I was slapped with the understanding that forgiveness lightens my load and hate burdens it. It taught me that physical pain will release, only to return until we have learned the lessons it holds for us. And finally, it revealed to me that health was within me all along. I simply needed to surrender the fight and allow my soul's truth to rise into my physical body.

This book was conceptualized as a resource for students of my energy healing massage course on their journey of mastering intuitive healing. Energy Healing Massage is for massage therapists and healers to learn the cause of physical pain, tension, and connective tissue adhesions in the body through the energy system. After the course, the therapist discovers and shares with their client the root cause of their pain whether it be mental, emotional, or energetic, allowing them a pathway to true healing and recovery. I got sick of whack-a-moling the knots out of my clients' backs, only for them to re-appear a week or two later. Because we focus on our booming physical experience, the subtle energetic roots get missed. We need to remove the cause of imbalance so the body can truly heal.

I discovered as I began writing that these intuitive skills are applicable for everyone on their healing journey, not just therapists. This book is an instruction manual for you to connect to the beautiful lessons your pain or imbalances are wanting you to receive, and to learn what your body needs to heal.

The day before I was "gently nudged" to write a book, I watched Simon Sinek's Ted Talk, "Start with why." I contemplated this question all day: why do I do what I do? The answer became as translucent as clear quartz: I am here to bring my truth (love) to my physical and conscious reality and to help others connect to their own truth. I want to help you connect to the truth within you: that you are a being of pure love, health, and happiness. That you can live your life in this state of awareness of love, of experiencing happiness and feeling healthy. And writing this book is intended to do just that, to connect you to your deepest truth — to listen to it, to experience it, to allow it to flow through you into your life. So, I could not NOT write this book. It is a vessel to access this truth. If I didn't write it, I would not be living my purpose, my why, and I would not have helped you to take a step towards becoming the master of your own health and well-being. And as a consequence, I would have kept experiencing continual pain within my neck. So yet another gift and teaching had come forth from this neck trauma: time to release all fear and speak my truth with more power than ever before!

What creates pain is the energy we infuse into it. Soul coach Claudia-Sam Cataford-Sauvé says: "We cling to the pain thinking negative thoughts, speaking words that make the pain ours and taking actions as victims of the pain." By clinging to it, you drill the matrix of the pain closer to your core. It interrupts your process of health as you empower your pain by resisting it. It then blocks your natural state of love and freedom. Once you consciously let go of attachment to your pain, the soul (your energy of pure health and happiness) rises to your reality. You feel whole and balanced. You become aware of a deeper level of your being — energy.

Light is within you, like a star glistening through the cosmos. Outside this radiance is an occlusive shadow. The shadow coagulates with your beliefs, traumas, thoughts, emotions, and fears (which we will address in depth in Chapter 10: Healing & Ascension). Acceptance is the kryptonite of your shadows. Once true acceptance is offered, the shadow discombobulates because it has been touched by a higher power of love. Your light is free to shine brightly when the cloud of darkness is surrendered to love. The shell of your ego's false identity crumbles into ashes.

Your authentic self takes on a new beginning as you converge with your soul. All layers of the aura, the mind, body, emotions, and energy thrive as your light shines into them. You become aware of your light being, rooted in love and acceptance. The joy rushes in as you begin living your highest potential. Rather than feeling helpless in your pain or the pain of others, you can shine your light, your new awareness, and intuitive clarity onto the lives of those you love so that they, too, can thrive with you.

I do not want you to believe the words you are reading. I want you to directly experience your own truth, whatever that truth may be. I began learning how to directly experience the truth at my first enlightenment intensive workshop which gave me a reflective process to experience the universal truths firsthand. Not thinking them. Not remembering what I've learned, read, or experienced in the past. But to go after the truth, untainted and raw in the now. When you directly experience the truth, it can not be taken away from you. It will never be questioned or doubted once it has been realized. This book is about my encounters with the truth as I have directly experienced it. It is not what I believe or have conceptualized or learned. It has been actualized and lived. It is known. It is the truth of my cells and of existence. These are universal truths. Meaning it is the same truth for all of us to experience, it is accessible to all. It can be a deep process to surrender all you have come to know, to experience what is. If you are not committed fully to it, it will not happen because you will be clinging to what you choose to believe and be unable to experience the truth as it is, for yourself.

In the meantime, if you are drawn to a new concept through intuition, reading or personal experience, follow it. Because a part of you, your soul, knows all truths. And it recognizes these truths by sparking joy and excitement within you. As you read, if something feels out of alignment for you, do one of two things: if it feels good then absorb these truths. If it feels wrong and misguided, then put it to the side and move on to the next chapter or experience.

◇ Soul Alignment Exercise

Finding Gratitude In Your Pain

- Our traumas and the suffering we have experienced will always have a gift, but it can be difficult while in the middle of a difficult experience to see its gifts. Let's reflect on the wounded healer within you. We are constantly carrying unhealed wounds from our past that we have not completed our healing with yet, and they carry that vibration of fear as opposed to love. What experiences have you had that were difficult in your life?

- How have these experiences connected you to a deeper truth (i.e. finding strength or acceptance within you)?

- What gratitude can you discover from your suffering?

Chapter 5

THE TRUTH IS HERE

And so, we go to the source
Instead of trimming the leaves to cut out the disease
We tend to the roots to foster healing.

His slinky black hair coils like a serpent as he purses his lips around his rosewood pipe. Small bits of graphite flake under the pressure as Einstein's pencil skates on a sheet of paper: $E=mc^2$. Energy (E) equals mass (m) times the speed of light squared (c^2). Energy and mass are interchangeable in the equation as they are different forms of the same thing. Energy can become mass, and mass can become energy.

Your happy and negative thoughts are energy, your emotions are energy. The chair or bed you are sitting on is energy. The empty space between you and your neighbor is energy. Everything is energy. So, when you tune into your energy body, you are tuned in to the connecting force between the mind, emotions, spirit, and body. Energy is the string between two tin cans, telephoning vital information. When the cord is connected between your intuition and your consciousness, messages are received that tell your body how to match the vibrancy of your soul.

Your energy body came into form the moment of conception. At birth, your energy field was at its purest state. Within your mother's womb, your energy began to respond and react to her energy field. Do you know what your mother's energy was like during pregnancy and delivery? Was her life easy-breezy, or a stormy mess? It may help you understand undesired beliefs and reactions you hold that are idiopathic.

All imbalances begin in the energy field, they are detected here first. Cancer, diabetes, even an abrupt trauma. Your energy field is emitting disharmony before it manifests in your physical body. Like submarine sonar, you can see it coming before your mind registers its arrival. My client Cynthia (throughout this book I use pseudonyms to protect people's privacy when requested) struggled with a deep cave of self-love issues. She was thirsty to find love from others, feeling broken and drenched in sadness on a fruitless quest to find external love. Cynthia struggled with her weight and tending to her physical body because of her dehydrated self-care. When we lack self-love, self-care is not present to take care of our body and mind. Cynthia's quest was misdirected, like fishing in a mud pit. This created a major imbalance in her heart center, the energy center of love. It was working overtime with no payday, constantly in seeking mode, when all she needed was to be open to receiving love from within. High blood pressure began bullying Cynthia at the age of 28. In her early 30s, she was hit with a heart attack. As Cynthia reflected on this experience, she saw the interconnectedness of her health and her mindset, and knew it was time to change course.

You can tune in to the frequency of your energy as a pre-emptive check up and prevent the physical body from failing. Find out what is going on before you have a near fatal incident like Cynthia.

Why do we attract illness? The reason your energy becomes imbalanced is because it is telling you that you are not in alignment with your soul. You have the power to understand your energy using your intuition. This tool is going to be emphasized strongly throughout the book so that you can receive those signals of disharmony and disease before they form in your physical body. Using only your rational mind to solve your health issues is like scratching a butterknife on a steel wall. Pick up the laser cutter by using your intuition. "ZRRMMM", burn right through the metal wall using your intuition to find ease on your healing journey.

Say you have trouble expressing yourself and your useful ideas to your boss. You hesitate because they could take it as a harsh criticism in their ability to do their job. You fear their ego will scratch you up like a street cat getting a bath. You choke back your truth like a hairball. Then a gentle pressure begins to loom over your throat. Every time you are with your boss you feel distress. Your neck crackles and pops as you roll it in circles trying to get the kinks out. You find swollen glands in your throat welcoming a cold.

Over time, there are more important things you are holding back from expressing, like not going after your dream job or the person you love because you are so afraid of failure and rejection. The energy blockage slops inside your being, cascading into hyperthyroidism and eventually throat cancer. This proves our suffering has an intention. If you choose to live in the vibration of love and not of fear, you will, in your own time, become aware that your struggles are a gift!

Your body is constantly communicating to you, trying to keep you on track to live your best life as your best self. You have a master consciousness that is all knowing within you. You have the ability to understand it and take the path of least resistance to get you to the intersection of where your soul (highest consciousness) and your physical reality meet.

My client Jan is a wonderful example of using her intuition to connect her body and higher self. She had been working all of her life to preserve the natural state of the environment for future generations. Jan began to experience destructive patterns. She was enthralled and passionate about developing her dream career in resource conservation, which led to a suppression of much needed self-care. She began to feel hollow inside and was struggling with a right shoulder injury (inflamed supraspinatus) and chronic pain due to an overdeveloped left trapezius muscle. During this frustrating time, asana movement and yoga practice ignited moments of joy and clarity for her. Jan was bursting to free herself of this constant state of unhappiness. She knew in her mind, body, and spirit that a shift was required. She decided to end her work contract early and fly to India for 6 weeks to complete Hatha Yoga training.

It was here that she learned about Yogic philosophy and practiced the asanas (poses) and pranayama (breath exercises to calm the mind) three times a day. There were weeks of tears, joy, anxiety, and calmness. It was here that Jan finally found balance in her mind and in her body. Both trapezii were of equal size and the fiery pain of the inflamed supraspinatus was gone when she left. Her body followed her mind, which followed her heart. It was the first time she did not suppress her heart's callings with rational thoughts. Once she listened to her inner compass, Jan finally experienced the physical health and balance that she sought. She took a prance of faith traveling to India to follow her heart. Not everyone's inner compass is directing them to another continent. It may be a much smaller step, like doing 10 minutes of meditation a day, or stating stronger personal boundaries.

Your intuition connects you to your deepest truth. Jan was in alignment with her truth when she ended her work contract to go to India. Meditation, presence, and contemplation are a pathway to your truth. The truth is like an 8 layer salad, there are many realizations and layers you must go through to arrive at the deepest level. Once you cut through the truth of the physical, you make your way past the field of energy and arrive at non-existence.

Nothingness. No thing.

Once this truth becomes known, a wave of deep peace is felt in your entire being — a true state of balance. In this void, thought and feeling do not exist. It's like gazing into the night sky where the stars and the moon have faded away and an endless darkness remains. When you are able to connect to the truth that a part of you is non-existent, you gain a calming neutral perspective on life. Without this awareness life can gyrate you, twerking you around when you think life works from the outside in. This allows your environment, relationships, mind and body to procure the driver's seat of your experiences. As a result, this empowers your outer world to dictate your joy and your sadness. While focused on your outer world, judgment and guilt often cloud your mind, like a coastal oil spill. No wonder we suffer.

Imagine living from the inside out. Instead of being affected by your environment, you instill calmness into perceived chaos by accessing this space within you that exists in a non-sensory way that is unaffected by your outer world. This is a difficult self-discovery of nothing (nothingness), because it is not a loud sensation or experience. It's not like your drama queen mind, or flabbergasting emotions. It's not the vivacious physical body that screams at you when you are in pain. To discover the nothingness within you, I find meditation is the path of least resistance. Meditation softens the voices of the mind, body, and heart. It is your best shot at touching in on this space within you.

Occasionally, you get lucky without having to do the precarious work. A moment may manifest where you are suddenly and inexplicably in alignment with your nothingness. I was fortunate enough to contact my non-existence by chance.

The needle jolted out of the hay-stack my first time consciously experiencing this inner truth: "Pitter patter" on the bathtub hollow as the epsom salts rain into the inviting water. "Plop plop" drops the lavender essences. "Haaaaa" a deep sigh escapes as I melt into the soothing water. My neck pain dissipates in the relaxing soak.

Sparklers ignite and time stops. A wave of peace rushes over my being. Swirling in and out of me. I don't know where me, the water, or the tub begin. I am at peace. I am peace itself!

I realize after a few moments in this state of nirvana that I had just experienced no thoughts. The sun and moon had aligned and nothing was blocking me from this truth within, for there it was within me. No borders, no walls, just existence in a non-formative way. After this experience, I began indefatigably seeking to find it again through meditation. I was struggling to recreate this nothingness and the deep peace shimmied into it. I thought it was something I needed to build through practice, or try with persistent intention to find.

You can not create what you already are. It was through letting go of the belief that this peace is something I need to create, that I found peace once again. We need to let go of everything we believe and have created, to experience the beauty of what is. It's not hiding in Batman's lair. It's more like trying to find a Starbucks in New York City.

Your energy body is trying constantly to align you with this truth, this space of no-thing. But we push our energy into everything outside of us. We drain ourselves because we are operating in overexertion of our natural resources, giving it away to others when we are already feeling depleted. Using it to try and align the physical world with our wants. Instead of allowing ourselves to be what it is we are seeking. Surrendering to find that all we have been fighting for will not be found outside of us because it is and has always been within us. Joy, peace, love, abundance, freedom — it's already here. The fight to find happiness and contentment outside of ourselves has pulled us away from this truth and thrown us on a wild goose chase. Can you stop fighting? What will it take for you to trust and allow that truth to be experienced?

◇ Soul Alignment Exercise

Releasing The Inner Fight To Find A Deeper Truth

Create a space of relaxation:

Allow your mind to find ease and space (physical exercise can help, a bath, meditation, use what works for you). Relax your body and the pain you may feel, creating a softness or detachment from any tension you carry (nap, massage, bathe, yoga... again, use what works for you).

Emotional release:

If you are carrying some emotions that are heavy in your energy field, allow yourself to express these by either singing, dancing, screaming, writing, or however you can allow yourself to process and feel them to do this work.

Discover the truth:

Once you have gently tended to the mind, body, and heart, you can move forward to this practice. Ask your highest self: "What is my truth?" Ask this three times. Hold no expectation, release all judgment. And surrender to experience your truth. If you find it difficult to connect with this space within you, no worries. This can be a constant practice to return to, and each time you will be closer and closer to your truth, experiencing small hints of it until you feel it and know it fully.

Chapter 6

MAY THE FORCE BE WITH YOU

Something deep inside
All logic and science defies
A space of truth, that, once experienced cannot be denied.

We are going to build a steel bridge to your intuition (inner knowing). Your intuition is an 8k fiber optic crystal ball, transmitting all of the answers on how to align you with your health and happiness. You can trust in the process of receiving guidance from your intuition because it operates from the soul. The soul navigates us back home to love and joy. Let's unhinge the happiness within the broken body.

Your energy is speaking to you now, as it does in every moment. You decide whether you see, hear, and feel it, or ignore it. I have been guilty of rubbing plaster around the door frame to my intuition, out of fear of what is on the other side.

I nestle under my fluffy blanket each night, leaving my feet exposed so I don't overheat. A feather like touch tickles my toes and begins to trace patterns on my feet. *Is this really happening? Do I have a spirit visiting?* I ponder. *No, must just be my circulation with some empirical hypothesis I don't care to research.* I smother the electric butterflies in my tummy and fall asleep. Tomorrow passes, and the feather fingers return as I retire, this time caressing my feet and my calves. I feel oddly calmed by this sensation, and something in my gut tells me I am safe. After a few more nights of the kinetic foot caressing, I give in to the idea that these are my spirit guides saying hello.

As I accept this possibility, a doorway is opened. Energetic pulsations then dance around my whole body. Shifting and healing pieces of me that have been broken and long forgotten. Imagery floods in through my third eye, guiding me on navigating the rapids I will soon face in life. This incredible gift was only made possible for me to receive once I surrendered my fears. My guides touched my feet because it was a gentle, and less frightening approach. I still leave my feet naked outside my blanket each night, inviting my guides to a soiree. The moment I close my eyes, the gentle vibrations swirl around my feet. *Hello my friends.* Spirit, energy, and intuition burst into your life when you are ready to receive it.

You can continue plastering cement over your intuition for the rest of your life. It's like plopping your derrière in front of a roller coaster with a smug smile, hearing joyful shrills of laughter and deeming them dangerous. It is whimsically delightful when you open the doorway to a deeper dimension of your existence. Jump on the roller coaster and have some fun exploring the unknown! Or miss out, on the sidelines in the comfort of the known.

Intuition is a sly fox. If you try to block or ignore it, it will sneak freckles of guidance into your life anyways. During my twenties, I was inaugurated into my quarter life crisis. I didn't believe in intuition, but intuition believed in me.

I had recently graduated from fashion school, thinking it would be a fun and creative career. The reality is I would be stuck tailoring garments, which lacked the artistry that my soul craved and was not my strong suit (pun intended). Finding a career is serious business. If we spend one third of our time working, why not enjoy the work we are doing. *I really want to find happiness.* The pressure begins to build as I search for joy. With the 5 metric tons of weight on my skull, there is a fog blocking me from clarity of my career path. Panic attacks grace me daily.

"Crackle creak", the porch of my father's home shifts. Two tentative knocks hit the front door. I slide across the glossy hardwood floor, anxious for a distraction from my misery. A service rep is coming to give me a quote for resealing the blemished bathtub. I open the door and my eyes engorge. It's Donald! Donald is an ex-boyfriend of an old friend of mine. We had never said more than 20 words to each other before this moment. Donald politely does the quote with haste, I ask if he would like a tea before he heads out. He sits beside my dad's sparkling blue electric guitar that contrasts the 1960's dandelion decor. Donald combs his glossy black hair with his fingertips and dives into a philosophical conversation on life. The puffiness in my eyes pokes him to ask me personal questions. We talk for hours, and I express the hardships of deciding a career. He pauses in his thoughts, his voice deepens: "You are never going to figure this out. You have hundreds of paths you are considering. You need to take action. It doesn't matter what action, just take **an** action. Action is the only way you will find out which career sparks joy."

He was right! I didn't have a clue about intuition and higher self at that time in my life. All I had was my mind. It was my only resource for decision making and it was letting me down big time. So I took a chance and allowed myself to begin experiencing different paths. The purpose was to find the best path for me through experiencing what felt right, joyful, and good to me, instead of getting lost in my mind and the thousands of possibilities it presented to me.

That afternoon, August 31st, I called Marvel College to register for a full time hairstyling program starting the next day. The monotonous voice informs me that the hair program is full, but the esthetics program has an opening. I have never been drawn to esthetics, but a friend once suggested it would suit me. I commit to an 8 month $14,000 program starting the next day, in a matter of minutes. Am I being spontaneous? Utterly. But my anxiety attacks and depression force me to make a change. Maybe this was all by chance, or maybe the seedlings planted by Donald are part of a divine plan.

"Click clock", a pencil chiseled European woman in black stilettos enters the classroom. She introduces herself as our ethics teacher for the esthetics program. Her eyebrow elevates as she tells us she is a Reiki Master. My expression flattens as it flies over my head. Later in the year she demonstrates life force energy for us to witness. Her shoulders melt to the floor as she flutters her eyes closed, inhaling the air like a fine wine. She stands a meter behind another instructor and begins making a slow pushing motion with her hands. The instructor whose back is turned to her begins swaying each time the Reiki Master makes the pushing motion. She is being pushed. Pushed by this unseen energy.

There is no way for the woman to see behind her what is happening, yet she sways in synchronicity. *Mind=blown!* I know this isn't a trick because she is an honorable person, as one would expect to find in an ethics teacher. She has us hold out our arm while someone tries pushing it down (strength testing). Then crinkles our ear and again has our arm pushed down. A feather-like touch moves my arm like a bodybuilder lifting a 2 pound weight when my ear is crinkled. She has shown me the power in the reflexology of the body in a matter of seconds. The ear contains all of our reflexology points, and when disturbed, our whole system is immediately affected. When experiencing energy first hand in physical form, I realize science has some catching up to do.

That summer I went on a gal's trip to the mountains. We decide to venture through a crystal store. At the time, I wasn't yet connected to crystals and was oblivious of their energetic force. I thought they were only adorned for their beauty. Near the back of the store is a basket of small matte black onyx spheres (little black balls the size of a malt ball/whopper candy). *Hmm, that's ugly, why would anyone buy it?* I pick it up to see what all the fuss is about, unimpressed, I plop it back in the basket. Three of my fingers that touched it tingle with warmth. *That's weird.* I leave the store and slip it into the back right pocket of my jeans. As I walk down the street, my entire right butt cheek lights on fire. The light pings above my head, *I get it.*

This is my big experience that energy is real. I can physically feel this stone's energy! It is undeniable. The tingly sensation is heightened because it is bulldozing heavy and stagnant energy in my field. The onyx helped me clear the stinky hockey bag of negative energy I was holding onto. This was an epiphanous experience that led me to becoming an energy worker.

In the esthetics program, we learned relaxation massage. I loved the relaxation "high" tattooed on my client's faces after their treatments. That was also the year of my car accident that created so much suffering for me. The pain forced me to receive therapeutic massages, which graced me with drool worthy moments of feeling good and helped me psychologically manage the pain. These salivatious deep tissue treatments had me tapping my toes in line to register for massage school next. Here I discovered a career that brought me deep joy and purpose for years to follow. Massage gave me the security, and platform I needed to begin a spiritual healing practice. I know I would not have found this path if I didn't take that first leap into the esthetic program. All because of a conversation with an almost stranger.

Energy can be experienced, not just read about. You can experience it right now, in your physical reality. The proof is within you. I'm not stating that you must believe in it, but you do need to be open to the possibility of energy. Otherwise you will excuse it as a foolish imagination.

Take my client Heather, for example. She has become so trusting in energy, signs, and messages that she seeks out answers through the field of intuition. Heather was in her thirties when she had her second child. He died when he was only 2 weeks old. Her heart was steamrolled into a fine powder. Heather's despair needed to know that he was okay. She desperately sought out different mediums and psychics. Each visit helped her find greater peace. They confirmed things that they would not have been able to know about Heather and her life. They validated that it really was her child's spirit they were communicating with.

Twelve years after he died, she went to a group mediumship session where her son came through. The medium shares his message, "Tell mommy the lights – it's me!" Heather gasps. For the previous couple of weeks Heather noticed the lights in the living room flickering on and off. She also noticed dimes appearing constantly, so she asked if they were from him, and he said: "They sure are!" Tears of happiness stream down Heather's cheeks.

A few years later, Heather goes on a camping trip. She is deeply missing her son as she hasn't seen any signs from him in a while. She decides to ask him for a sign to let her know that he is nearby. "Thtt, thtt, thtt" a butterfly's wings clap as it angelically flutters around her. The butterfly spreads its golden wings and lands on Heather. It takes comfort resting on her for 5 breathtaking minutes. She knows in her heart it is him. This gives Heather the confidence that her little boy is still here and connecting with her.

When spirit and energy crossover to physical reality they communicate in distinguishable signs. This expands the limited view of life and allows a delectable layer of rich experiences to be accessed. The higher universal consciousness is connecting you with the earth and sharing hidden messages in your external world. You can pause and look around to discover messages at all times. Lift your eyes from the text right now, focus on something in front of you. Find a message through the color, shape, or uniqueness of the item. This is an outer process of intuition accessible to your physical eyes, opposed to the inner one you are harnessing. If you go for a tea leaf reading, your reader will interpret the leaves in the bottom of the cup by connecting the dots and seeing the shapes that form. The leaves are not magically falling into place because your reader has super powers. You can read your own tea leaves every day. Spit your toothpaste out in the sink basin and see what message the bubbly saliva and mint have concocted to share with you.

Signs are everywhere; all you need to do is be open to receiving them. It can be small simple things, like coming across a feather, an eagle in the sky, or a butterfly landing on you. Once Heather ended up parking in a random spot at work that she had never parked in before. She had been thinking about her son on the drive in and when she got out of her car, a dime was laying on the ground! Heather has become masterful at asking for signs and messages to connect to energy and spirit. This is possible for you as well, the signs are already flowing. If you want clarity on a question, or to connect to a specific spirit, all you have to do is ask.

Let's try some exercises for you to directly experience energy.

◇ Soul Alignment Exercise

Experience Your Energy

Open the palm energy centers:

Rub your palms together for 5 seconds (this activates your palms to feel energy). Massage your forehead for a minute or so (this relaxes the mind and activates your intuitive center). Take 3 deep breaths to be present and release any expectations. Now raise your hands in front of you with your elbows slightly bent by your sides, palms facing each other inwards, as if you are holding a basketball between them. You will then close your eyes and simply feel. Pay attention to any sensation in your palms. Move them a little closer and a little further very slowly. Energy can be felt as a vibration, a pressure, a push and a pull, or a temperature change (hot or cold). Simply feel. It is very subtle, especially at first. Take your time. And breathe.

Feel the aura:

What did you feel? You were actually feeling the layers of your aura and energy body. If you did not feel any sensation, keep coming back to this practice. A calm mind really helps you to experience what is there. And

---

you will be able to feel the different layers of your aura, as you will feel different sensations.

Trust your gut:

Your "gut" feeling is your energy body communicating to you. Next time you are in a public place, listen to your gut. Do not allow the mind to get involved. Sit next to or near a complete stranger. You are in their energy field now and it will change and impact your energy. How does your feeling change? This is what their energy is conveying to you. Do you feel heavy, tired? Sad? Energized? Joyful? This is you interpreting another's energy. Now once we build this skill, we can start to help people who are struggling to lighten their energy. But before we can do that, we are going to focus on our own energy.

Chapter 7

THE UNIVERSE HAS A PLAN

The Universe cradles you like a warm blanket
Ensuring your encounters point you towards love.

Everything happens for a reason. This phrase either makes you dry-heave in opposition, or makes your heart smile in agreement. If everything happens for a reason, the big questions arise: Why do some children get sick and die? What about murder? How can you suggest that there is a higher power or force behind these malicious acts and suffering? The windburn from your life experiences leaves you with knotted hair and fissured lips.

My manifesto is "trust the Universe." Trust that everything happening and that has ever happened to you is a gift. It seems out of the question to see death, depression, and trauma as a gift. Yet a gift is always discoverable. The rainbow comes after the rain. Pain precedes pleasure. When you experience hardship, you are pulled into your fear and your pain body. You can get stuck in this space of pain and recirculate it your entire lifetime.

The moment you open yourself to the possibility of purpose, to an inkling of meaning, everything shifts. The clouds part and you can finally begin to see the gifts of these experiences. I equate a purpose with a divine force. It is easy to align with the statement "everything happens for a reason" when good things happen. You get a raise, well you deserve it, "the Universe has my back." You meet your soulmate, "it was destiny." What if your mother dies? Suddenly, it shifts to "God doesn't exist. Why me? This is not fair." Death is a big problem for the living. Those who die are fine, they are back home being cradled in love and ultimate peace. Take the hundreds of millions (1 in 10 people) who have had a near-death experience (NDE). MD Jeffrey Long's study on near-death encounters shares that there is a common thread of experiences observed in NDEs: "These characteristics include a perception of seeing and hearing apart from the physical body, passing into or through a tunnel, encountering a mystical light, intense and generally positive emotions, a review of part or all of their prior life experiences, encountering deceased loved ones, and a choice to return to their earthly life (Long[5])." Dr. Long concludes that near-death experiences are medically inexplicable. These miraculous yet common experiences indicate that there is bliss on the other side of death. Suffering is for the living and their physical loss of a loved one. Through death we can receive gifts such as:

✧ Gratitude for life and living life with greater fullness, as we realize we have an expiration on our time here

✧ Connecting to spirituality, trusting in life after death

✧ Allowing yourself to grieve

✧ Letting others support you

These are all remarkable gifts received through this heart-wrenching pain.

Even the small things we struggle with hold meaning. "Beep, boop, boop", your computer stubbornly rejects your commands when you have a deadline to meet. Your fingertip strikes the enter key like a punching bag. You think: *what a waste of time. I'm not good at this stuff* (at least that's what I think when I have technological difficulties). But when you connect to purpose, you can see the gifts of patience, of asking for help, of being kinder to yourself.

---

[5] Long, Jeffrey. "Near-Death Experiences Evidence for Their Reality." *Missouri Medicine*, vol. 111, no. 5, 2014, p. 372. *National Library Of Medicine*, https://www.ncbi.nlm.nih.gov/pmc/articles/PMC6172100/.

For what we cannot prove, we must choose a path of belief. Why not choose the belief system that brings you the most joy? What if you believed there is good in every situation? Gratitude washes over the boulders of each day. Challenging obstacles become opportunities for growth. Everything, action, and person has a beautiful gift for you waiting to be revealed. Even in the darkest times you will see there is always a glimmer of light. If you focus on the darkness, you won't see the light. Shake off that tunnel vision to find the rainbow in the storm.

Everyone here on planet Earth is trying their best with what they know. Everyone is trying to find joy and be happy. For some, that comes through downward dogs, for others through sniffing a white line. For many, it is hard work and a vault full of money. For a special few they have discovered that joy is within, not outside of us. It doesn't matter where everyone is on their journey to joy. But it helps to understand that the actions we take are motivated by pleasure and joy. When someone causes harm to you, it's not because their root motivation is to make you suffer. It is because they think it is going to result in more joy for themselves (by subtracting your joy). I'm not condoning harming a fellow human. But when we can begin to understand that others' deepest motivations stem from love, we access compassionate forgiveness. Resentment and holding on to the pain is rooted in fear. You have the power to choose your path of love or fear, anger or acceptance.

Every experience is an opportunity to step into love or fear. Love expands your vital life force energy, allowing you to live an energized and healthy life. Peace prevails as love balances the heart. Love allows you to be grateful for all things, loving them as they are. This gratitude cascades into joy, and happiness is unearthed.

Fear is a vampire, sucking your vital life force. It creates imbalances in your health. It disturbs your thoughts and impacts your decision making. You lose trust in humanity and close yourself off from the world. Fear creates grudges, shame, and sickness. The energy of fear causes us to feel heavy and fatigued.

It seems like a no-brainer. Choose love. Always choose love.

What if your purpose is to discover your true nature of love? That would mean that everything has a driving force of positivity pointing you towards loving more deeply. That means that every experience holds a gift. Acceptance is one of the largest gifts one can receive. Accepting illness, depression, death — accepting everything. Acceptance means loving unconditionally. It opens you to what love truly is. It's not a commodity you give and take, it's not an emotion you have only under joyful circumstances. True love has no conditions. That means if you really love yourself, you love yourself when you fail, and when you are at your worst. It means you love your neighbor who votes for the other side. It means you love that kid who bullied you in elementary school. These challenges are opportunities to be the love that you are. What a gift! When you are not love, you are resisting your truth. And your body, mind, and spirit will reflect that you are imbalanced with illness and dysfunction. When you are in the vibration of fear, your body becomes a bucking bull. Your nervous system is on high, creating irregular bowel movements, shakiness, feeling nervous, getting sick, and feeling fatigued.

Acceptance does not mean you are against change or ignoring something painful that causes you suffering. It means you are honoring the truth of your experience in its entirety. It is an expression of love different from our traditional views of love. You can love and have compassion for your painful experiences, and still be angry and sad about them at the same time. You then need to go a step further and accept the angry and sad emotions by also loving them. The final puzzle piece is rubbing acceptance on the part of you that may feel guilt about wanting to change your situation in life. Love that you desire change and that there is a part of you that is not okay with how life is going. In this way you are coming from love 360 degrees.

Let's stop sipping spirits to numb our pain. Let's start living life in alignment with love. There is nothing supportive that can be lost and everything good to gain.

◇ Soul Alignment Exercise

Living Through Love

Choose love:

> When conflicted with a decision, ask yourself, what would love do? If love were a person (where fear did not exist), what decision would love make?

Infuse love into the past:

> Reflecting on your past, allow a memory to arise that still inflicts pain to you. Now, if you could view this memory through the eyes of unconditional love, how would your connection to this memory change? Notice how you feel when you step from fear into love during this painful time.

Chapter 8

YOUR SUPERPOWER SENSES

A whole world awaits your discovery
Open your mind to let your senses explore it.

The air thickens and my throat congests when I massage George. I naively shrug off the weekly pattern emerging in his treatments: he requests we work on his upper thighs, and a stiffening banana rises under the sheets. Although I learned in massage school that increased blood flow to the penis can happen during a treatment, there is an awkward energy that churns my tummy in discomfort. His twisted nose, lanky body, and greasy thin hair is how I imagine a preying pedophile would be cast for a role. This time he asks me for a hug as he leaves. I feel obligated to say yes, as many of my clients offer me a hug to show gratitude after their treatments. George places his hands down on my hips and sensually strokes my body. The violation freezes me, like the cold floor of my basement suite. I hold my breath out of fear for my safety, until he leaves through the front door.

How could I be such a fool?! I think. The week prior I saw a vivid image of a black snake swirling around George's hands. I felt evil for the first time in someone's aura. I shook off what my intuition and energy told me about George, because I wanted to believe I was misinterpreting it as one of his past lives coming forward. I texted George after the assaulting hug informing him that I will no longer treat him. He asked no questions which confirmed my suspicions of his guilt. I open all the windows and sage my home like a BBQ smokehouse.

After this experience, I pushed myself to honor my energy and create firm boundaries from ill-willed individuals. I have cut ties with clients and "friends" based on intuition alone. I tell them the honest truth, "I can't have you in my life, because something doesn't feel right." They shake their heads in disbelief, but I see it in their eyes that they have been caught before committing the crime. The proceeding weeks after I cut ties I begin to realize how many lines have been crossed and boundaries broken by them.

Your energy is speaking to you, guiding you away from darkness by feeling discomfort while guiding you towards bliss by feeling ease and excitement.

Energy is spoken in a whisper. In the beginning, it feels hard to connect with and understand. This is because we are on the wrong radio station. We need to turn the dial to hear the right frequency. Energy is always being broadcast. The dial is usually stuck on the messages of the logical and ego mind. We trust the logical mind to calculate and make informed decisions based on our experiences. We use the ego mind to protect us from feeling small or looking stupid. You also listen to the beautiful frequency of your heart. Although the heart starts with pure intention and love, it gets stepped on by others and even yourself. It holds the pain of not being accepted, and fear oozes in with a message of not being worthy of love. You have listened to your body. The body lets you know when things feel good and healthy. But it also craves unhealthy activities, foods, and desires because it seeks short-term benefit for the ego and emotional self.

Energy is a consciousness of its own. It does not stem from ego, desire, or emotion. It does communicate what is going on in the body, mind, and heart. It is integrated with the soul. Its goal is to align the mind, body, and emotions with the truth of the soul, your deepest self. And you connect with it through your intuition. Let's turn the dial and see what message your energy body is emitting.

Your intuition does not strengthen through force. It is something you allow by softening the focus you give to your mind, body, and heart. Through quieting the other voices, the voice of intuition can be distinguished. Messages from your intuition have already been communicating with you, but often go unnoticed. Intuition is mistaken as thoughts, imagination, or even a symptom. When you have something undesirable, you believe it to be the root cause: "I'm sick. It's because someone got me sick." Intuition is knowing the sickness is a symptom of a deeper root.

The sprained ankle, the heart attack, the seizure — all symptoms. Intuition connects you with the purpose and cause. You will discern the meanings of these symptoms with great depth as you attune yourself with your intuition throughout this book.

You do not build your intuition, you build your connection to your intuition. Intuition is the language of truth. It is the wise and all-knowing part of you that is always tapped into the stream of universal truth. It is all knowing. You are all knowing. The other voices of the mind and body you've empowered and focused on, block the all-knowing part of you. To tap into this all-knowing space within you, you have to first trust that it's there, so that you can move forward into connecting with it. I'm sure you have experienced it before. A cringing nail on chalkboard gut feeling, or deep belly giggling bringing an unexpected smile. A powerful dream. An inner knowing of which way to go, which path to take. An omen or oracle (a physical sign like an eagle flying above you in the sky that has a symbolic meaning to you). That is your intuition connecting with you.

My client Heather's story of her grandmother reminds me of the importance of trusting our intuition. Her grandma had an innate ability to foresee things that were going to happen. One night, Heather's grandfather was supposed to be attending a formal function and Heather's grandmother told him that he couldn't go. He digs his heels in the ground, shakes his head at her silly suggestion, and prepares for his jolly night out. With mysterious omniscience, she tells him something is going to happen and that he can't go. After some resistance, he heeds her warning and doesn't go. Thunderous crackles zoom through the evening air as gunshots fire at the formal event. *POP POP POP* like the sound of popcorn kernels exploding into form. He turns stark white as his friend relays what happened at the party. After that evening's close shave, he took his wife's warnings to heart.

Intuition can be as simple as a feeling we cannot explain. When we don't listen to these feelings, there can be fatal or serious consequences. Has there been a time you have ignored a gut instinct telling you something isn't right? What happened when you ignored that feeling?

Heather followed in her grandma's footsteps, trusting her intuition. As Heather grew older, she began trusting her sense of inner knowing. One evening, her mother was hosting a jewelry party with a dazzling necklace being gifted as a prize. To win the necklace, you needed to purchase an item. Heather used some of her savings to buy a piece because she knew intuitively she was going to win the necklace. After Heather bought the piece of jewelry, she won the draw for the necklace as she had foreseen. Her sixth sense also benefits her friends. Heather's stomach contracts when a speed radar trap is ahead on the road. She tells whoever is driving to slow down unless they want a hefty ticket. Thankfully they listen, as they always discover a radar trap just ahead.

You have this powerful intuition that travels across time and space. The all-knowing force within you is not limited by the relativity of time or distance. The CIA disclosed documents in 2008 releasing an experiment from 1973 , where they took two psychics (Harold Sherman and Ingo Swann) to test how far they could psychically probe their skills (Sherman and Swann[6]). Jupiter by-pass NASA Space Module Pioneer 10 was on its way to relay information on the unknown planet. Sherman and Swann recorded their psychic findings at the same time (while in separate cities) before the Pioneer 10 had made its journey to Jupiter. Both men reported a tornado and active volcanoes/large peaks, that the planet is very flat (very large), has

---

[6] Sherman, Harold, and Ingo Swann. "An Experimental Psychic Probe Of The Planet Jupiter." *Central Intelligence Agency*, vol. NSA-RDP96X00790R000100040010, no. 3, 2008, p. 14.

crystals that glitter, powerful magnetic forces and gases that give off an orange color with stripes around the planet. Jupiter is reported by NASA as having a massive spinning storm (the tornado), that Jupiter is the largest planet in our solar system (1,300 times greater than the size of Earth), and the strongest magnetic field of any of our planets. The white clouds in the light zones are made of crystals of frozen ammonia, and with many active volcanoes it forms the gaseous orange swirling stripes around the planet. Gifted psychics like this are used for remote viewing, to help locate missing people, and discover secret locations of potentially hazardous weapons.

Your intuition speaks to you through your extrasensory perceptions (ESP), which are all utilized in different ways and at different times. People tend to connect more strongly with one over another. Here I am listing your primary extrasensory perceptions for you to go through with an open mind and open heart as you invite these senses to awaken within you. Allow yourself to find a transcendental state; this can be done through meditation, breath work, or yoga. It will assist you in connecting to your own psychic gifts more clearly. Remember that the more you calm your mind, the easier it is to receive the messages of your intuition and energy body. Using your extra sensory perceptions makes the cardboard-dry events of everyday life pop like an eye-straining neon waterfall. Take some time with each perception to see if it connects you to a sensory experience, or message from your intuition. There is no need to do them all at once. Come back to them when you have energy, focus, and an openness to receive. There is no person that cannot access their psychic abilities. They are a conscious tool within everyone. If you trust that you have these gifts, you remove the doubt that blocks your connection to your truth. You are psychic, you have intuition, just as you can speak, see, and feel. You can connect to your inner sight, your inner knowing, and extrasensory perceptions. It may feel a little foreign to you because you haven't flexed these muscles before, or in a while. Below, we'll explore different ways that your intuition can choose to speak to and through you. Let's give it a go:

1. **Sensation:**
    Wind sweeps across your face in an airtight room. Sensation is feeling physical sensation in your body. You can feel energy and its movement or stagnation. Energy often feels like a subtle vibration, a pressure or a temperature change. Areas of pain are another way that sensation speaks to you through your intuition. Take some time to scan your body head to toe with your eyes closed and feel into any sensation of energy in your body that wants to bring something to your awareness.

2. **Clairaudience:**
    The fine hairs stand on the back of your neck as your name is whispered into your ear when you are all alone. Clairaudience is inner hearing or celestial hearing. You can hear the sound of energy moving, you can also hear spoken words of guidance from your higher self or spirit helpers. It can sound like a ringing noise, a vibration, hum, or words. Many channelers (and mediums) work with clairaudience and clairvoyance. If you are in a quiet space, tune in to your inner hearing and see if there are subtle sounds that you connect with.

3. **Clairsentience:**
    Your massage therapist deliciously kneads your left forearm, and a stream of unexpected tears run down your face. Clairsentience is your emotional body speaking to you intuitively. Your emotional body speaks to you through feeling. Some days you may feel sad, heavy, or joyful and not have a specific reason as to why. It may feel idiopathic, however, this is not the case. Your energy body is speaking through your emotions. It is trying to communicate, release, or heal a part of you. Ask your heart center if there is an emotion that wishes to express itself that may have been going unchecked for some time and allow it to arise.

4. Clairgustance:

The taste of tinfoil fills your mouth, you are taken back to a time in your childhood that was long forgotten. Clairgustance is the intuitive tool of taste. Taste can speak to you through flavors that connect you to memories or meanings. Through taste, you can perceive the essence of a substance from the spiritual or ethereal realms. Ask your higher self to connect you with a taste that has meaning for you. And wait to see if a flavor arises in your palate.

5. Clairscent:

You are meditating peacefully on your cushion, and a gust of incense from foreign lands sweeps through your nostrils. Clairscent is the sense of smell. Spirit and energy also move in the frequency of smell. It is smelling a fragrance, odor of a substance or food, which is not in your surroundings. Ask your higher self to communicate an important memory or message with you through scent. Sit and see if something arises for you.

6. Clairvoyance:

You see an image in your mind of your mother filling tissues with her tears, you pick up the phone to call her and check in. Clairvoyance is your inner vision, a more commonly known psychic sense. Clairvoyance allows you to reach a higher frequency of vibration where you can visually perceive deeper realms of truth through your third eye. These images work beyond the limitations of time and space, meaning you can connect to imagery from the past, present, and future. As you quiet your mind, see if any images or memories come up that hold meaning or a message for you.

7. **Words:**

   Standing with your arms crossed at the grocery store, you just can't decide between the ambrosia red and the granny smith green. The letters *G R E E N* flutter like a flag in your mind's eye. You can see or feel words. Words can be literal or symbolic. Take a moment to see what word your higher self wants to share with you.

8. **Clairtangency:**

   Your eyes drag you towards a rose quartz ring in the thrift store. You place it on your middle finger and feel lustful young love with a sour ending. Clairtangency, also known as psychometry, means that through touching an object or area you are able to perceive through your hands information about the article. To feel into its history, previous owners and where it has been. Try this with a piece of jewelry or item near you now. Pick it up and feel into its life. See if there is a message or energy here.

9. **Clairempathy:**

   You sit next to a young man on the bus, and fireworks of joy explode within you. Someone who is known as an empath is one who can feel within themselves another's emotional experience. This is felt for people, places, or animals. This helps us truly understand what their body is going through or holding onto. Bring to mind a loved one. See them in your mind's eye. Now invite yourself to feel what they are feeling. See what emotions arise.

10. **Channeling and mediumship:**

    Your heart aches after your dear friend who recently passed. You feel your friend within you saying, "I'm okay." Someone who channels allows their body and mind to be used as a mechanism for a higher intelligence to bring psychic information or healing across through them. Channeling can be done while still fully conscious, and it can also be done while not conscious where one allows full control of an entity or higher power to come through their being. I love channeling, but I am always specific as to who I am connecting with as I do not want to leave an open invitation to just any spirit. I am always fully conscious and have control of my own mind (this makes me more of a medium, or in between, where you are able to see and connect with the spirit or information but it is not integrated fully into your being and consciousness). This is done by choice and setting an intention. Let's try channeling through writing as it is a fun and easy exercise. I like to hold a specific intention such as, "I invite my higher self to share a message through writing." Without thinking, just write whatever is coming to you with no filter.

These are just some of my favorites and the most common ways of connecting to your intuition and source. If you are interested in trying other methods that you feel drawn to, explore this list:

- ✧ **Telepathy:** The ability to receive or send thoughts. You have probably unknowingly been doing this and had those shocking moments where you or someone else speaks what the other is thinking. This is a fun one to practice with pets, as it can be helpful to read their thoughts. If you don't have a pet, you may try with a person. But check in with them first and ask their permission.

- ✧ **Remote Viewing:** The ability to see a target. This is used for finding people, objects, and places. Tune in to where an item or person is through your intuition. See what you connect with.

- ✧ **Levitation:** The ability to float or fly as we tune into the power of our energy body. It helps to surrender to the field of energy and its existence. Energy alone can lift you, if you allow it to.

✧ **Scrying:** Using a medium (crystal ball, fire, water, etc.) to see messages and images.

✧ **Claircognizance:** Inner knowing, where you just know. You can't describe why or how you know, you simply know.

✧ **Astral projection:** Projecting yourself (astral body) to another place, dimension or time outside of your physical body. This can naturally happen while you are sleeping, and some people become aware of it through dreams or as they awaken. It is a feeling that you are physically here but your spirit and awareness is somewhere else. If you are projecting with intention in a conscious state, ask that you are protected by the field of love as you travel.

✧ **Oracles and omens:** Receiving messages through your physical environment (animals, nature, etc.). Go for a walk and ask for a sign. Be aware of everything around you.

These are all tools for accessing and understanding the energy body and the world of energy. You can tap into every single one, but some will take more practice than others. Just as some people have better eye vision or sense of smell than others, this is true for our psychic abilities. The greatest tool in connecting to these methods is to have a clear and calm mind so you can notice the subtleties of the messages and how they arrive.

◇ Soul Alignment Exercise

Strengthen Your Senses

Find your intuitive gift:

Reflect on ways you have connected through these methods in the past. Have you had dreams relaying messages? A vision? An inner knowing? However a message or sensing has arisen may be a clue as to which tool is naturally instinctive for your connection with your intuition.

Build your senses:

Create a fun practice to begin strengthening and expanding your tools to connect with your higher self. Try each evening or morning to pose a question and perceive an answer through any of the senses listed. At first, it may be hard to connect or know for sure. But with time, it will strengthen and become very clear.

Chapter 9

THE GIFT OF SUFFERING

*The silky pearl is created only after the irritant
invades the clam.*

Why is suffering a part of our human experience? Why can't life just be fun, easy, and full of good things? I want to pose a hypothetical situation to you. First, take a moment to reflect on the activities that genuinely make you smile.

Now, let's say that life is only these experiences that bring you joy. What would that look like to live in pure bliss for the rest of your life? Envision it, feel it.

When living a life only filled with joyful activities and peacefulness, would you be challenged to grow as an individual? What is your favorite treat (chocolate, wine, latte, etc.)? Imagine unlimited access to that treat. Would you appreciate it as much? Or would it lose its specialness? If every day was an amazing day would you be able to recognize what a gift that day is?

For a lot of people, this visualization of a happy-go-lucky life is boring and predictable. Darkness can be a jostling water slide to the light. If you feel pain, you feel gratitude when the pain disappears. Being happy is sawdusty and dry if you never feel sad. Having experienced a lack of something allows you to appreciate having it. You become aware that the unpleasantries are a precursor to greatness and joy. This awareness makes the hard times easier to swallow. With that said, you can have a life of pure bliss, that is still an option. Why not? Who says our life has to be packed with pain? The path however of pure bliss requires indefatigable belief that it is possible. With pure belief you can harness bliss through the laws of attraction. You can attract positive experiences towards you. You do not have full control of what everyone else is doing unfortunately. This means negative experiences will still occur, but with a positive mindset engrained it will be perceived as a positive experience as you find the gift in the situation. The blissful life also requires a mindset of gratitude, this gives you the ability to appreciate and soak up all of the goodness surrounding you currently and from your past. There will always be things within your control, and things outside of your control. Both are influenced and directed by universal wisdom. If you trust this guidance of the loving universe that all experiences outside of your control have a gift to offer you, then your perspective will become a buttery paver for the pothole filled gravel road of life. The question is, what does your soul crave? Is it craving a blissful zenned-out life? Or, is craving a bit of contrast to have a broader experience? To ascend suffering, we need to understand suffering's purpose.

Life is extremely difficult when you see it as a torture device, stretching your bones until you give up or toughen up. When you see gifts in the good and hard times, this thing called life becomes pretty darn fun. A great way to find gratitude in the undesired experiences is by tuning in to your deeper self, the part of you that is witnessing life unfold, unattached, and neutral. When you are aware that you are observing your body, mind, heart, and energy from this space of non-form, everything changes. Suddenly, you see all of life as a gift. This world is a breathtaking gift, knowing you come from non-form (nothingness). Could you dream of such a beautiful planet? The sky, the ocean, the mountains. Sometimes I look up at the sky and think *this must be heaven, this beauty is miraculous. I couldn't have dreamed of a more beautiful place.* Each and every one of your experiences is a tremendous gift. They are the gift of life. Without life, you are non-existent. You do not get to experience anything. Nada. No blue sky, no white fluffy clouds, rain, cheese. God… no aged cashew cheddar! The thought of a cheese-less life is not a life I want to live. Back on topic, the hard days are a gift! Difficult emotions, depressing thoughts, and hard experiences are a gift. Who am I, or you, to label them as bad? They are just an experience, a gift of life, a creation. And get this, you are the creator!

You create your life, but not every single aspect, because it's fun and spontaneous to have some mystery. But you choose your perception. You choose your reactions. You choose what work you do, where you live, and the people who surround you. You are a creator! When you can see the gifts in your suffering, you are now living from the space of awareness, your deepest consciousness. Because from that space there is zero judgment, just acceptance, and simple awareness. How beautiful.

With all of these sprinklings of knowledge about the beauty in suffering, that does not mean it has to be present in your life. As you are the creator of your life and have conscious control over how you feel and what you do. You can create a life of non-suffering by changing your attitude to gratitude. You can live in joy and happiness all of the time, even through challenging times. This is an option for you, if you believe in it. If you so choose it. What a beautiful life it can be! We would assume that everyone desires a life of non-suffering, of pure and blissful joy in every moment. But we already get to automatically experience that in non-life, when we return to our soul form. Life gives you the contrast to feel the diverse charcuterie board of all emotions and experiences. This is why we consciously (and unconsciously) create experiences that may not be so blissful. You have the power to create a life of non-suffering. Suffering within is created, chosen, and perceived. It is 100% in your power. When a bus clips you into a 360 degree faceplant and two broken legs, the physical pain is real, but the mental suffering is chosen. Bliss can penetrate every dark corner of your life.

A few years ago, during a long winded bout of depression, I see a four day event being advertised called Enlightenment Intensive. My eyebrow raises as the title punches my curiosity. To pre-register, I have to do an interview with the instructor to see if I'm a good fit.

"Hello," an assured gentleman answers the phone. I ask if doing a retreat with the word "intensive" in it is a good idea for someone battling a hellhole of depression. I bluntly say, "I don't have the emotional capacity to go through an intense experience." In a benevolent voice he responds, "It is whatever you decide for it to be." Those words sang to my heart.

I decide the day before going that this experience will be life-changing for me. As the four days unfold, Niagara Falls gushes out of my eye sockets. I break the veins in them from excessive crying. My eyes are blood red, like a demon has bewitched me. The only demons that presented themself throughout the retreat were my own demons. The tears cried are of euphoria and soul trembling epiphanies. The truth hits me so hard that my legs collapse under me. I squat, crying uncontrollably, I chuckle like a madwoman because I am exploding with excessive happiness. It was the most profound four days of my life. If I had gone in without an intention, I would have been shattered by the intensive work. My depression would have encompassed my being and I would have not connected to my deeper truths. Instead, I welcomed the universal and individual truths, and allowed them to flow like an orgasm of lava.

Pain is part of the human experience. It is indicative of life, as is joy and love. Suffering is the aftermath of clinging to the pain by choice. We label our experiences as good and bad. But when we can view them from the eyes of the soul, we will see, there is good in it all.

Having chronic neck pain from my car accident, I have built a very close relationship with suffering. Dealing with constant headaches and spearing pain, it was tough for me not to get caught up in my own suffering. I went through years of being a victim. *Why me?* I thought. Sadness, anger, and general unhappiness fumigated my life. I literally felt like I was pain. While in pain, it was all I felt, all I thought about, and I reflected it through my being. That was brutally unfair to the parts of me that are healthy. I never vocalized and appreciated my health, and all the areas of non-pain. Only 5% of my body was in pain and I raised it to 100%. As soon as I stepped out of the fear and the darkness, the pain shifted. Stepping out of the cycle of fear is hard, but the benefit is instant. I stopped associating with the pain, and persuaded my stubbornness to accept it. It taught me to stop identifying with my experiences. After 12 years of fighting with my body, once I accepted it and received its lessons, it healed. If I don't fall asleep in a pretzel position, I awake blissfully pain free.

Why do we give all our power and our focus to our suffering? This was one of the many gifts I've learned through suffering: to have perspective and not get caught up in identifying with our pain. Our pain is just an experience. It is not who we are.

♢ Soul Alignment Exercise

Painting A New Picture

Finding the treasure:

Reflect on a hardship from your past. Visit this time in your awareness, noticing how you felt, the emotions that arose, how your body responded. If this situation or circumstance were to occur again but now, how would you respond? Has this experience empowered you in some way, or given you a new awareness/belief?

Softening its hold:

Can you reflect on this hardship, but view it in a new light? A nice visual is to picture your energy body as a flowing stream of atoms and picture your pieces that feel painful, or even broken as an opposing current. Can you accept the straight flow and contrasting flow from a neutral state, seeing them together as a whole picture? Not the contrasting flow as unwanted, but just present and surrounded by the straight flow? Together they make your wholeness in this moment. In time, the contrasting flow will align with the straight flow, but right now, can you be okay with all of your pieces as they are?

Chapter 10

HEALING INGREDIENTS

*You are the artist brushing your dreams into life
Pick your colors to paint your life's work.*

Soggy eyelids and hot crusty nostrils graze the tissues. Suffocating anxiety pins me to the floor, as I curl into an embryonic position. A ray of sunshine touches my forehead through the windowpane. I follow the sunshine into the forest behind my house, equipped with the tunes of *Owl City* in my headphones. Bubbly joyful music cuts through my poisonous thoughts, and flows down from my ears into my heart. The joy radiates through my being as I dance like a faery amongst the elk and evergreens.

Optimal health is encoded within every cell of your being. We have talked about how fear and getting pulled by the mind and outside forces imprints your healthy whole self. With intentional steps, we can charter your course back to this place of health within you that is thriving and balanced. Healing is always accessible.

Belief is the first step to abundant health. Believe that you can heal, and that everything is unfolding for your highest good. Trust that health and happiness are possible for you. You are not creating them with outside forces, see their existence already within you. Stop begging the universe for a miracle, and empower what is already here within you. This inner radiance can break down the barriers and blockages, the sickness, the pain, and shine through until it is the only thing that exists. Dream, and see your greatest potential: a healthy mind, a healthy body, and a balanced heart. It is achievable, but first, it needs to be realized as your potential. Your mind must be unequivocally clear in the direction you want to go. Give it a vision and have a desired end point.

Take a moment now to see yourself in your optimal health. What do you look like? How do you feel? What is your mental health like? Dream big, as big as you can dream. This is the outline you are sketching on your blank canvas before taking your first brush strokes in your life's work.

After trust and belief are established, we will find the roots of what is holding you back from this space of health. We do this through listening to your energy body using your intuition. This second step can be achieved by outside supportive mediums like psychic surgery, healers, reiki practitioners and those who have built up their intuitive muscles through years of practice. Healing can occur the moment you ask for help. Receiving support from outside sources may be the soul growth lesson that your imbalances have been trying to deliver. Or, your deep soul growth may be guiding you to take the lead in being your own healer. This is you dabbing your paintbrush in the paint pot. Choose the colors you feel inspired to use in creating your masterpiece. You will procure the intuitive tools to discover this healing pathway for yourself over the next few chapters.

It can be hard to defy a world with a collective belief that suffering is normal and a part of life. It can be scary to step into your power and be your own creator, to listen to your deeper truth over the conforming tidal wave of societal belief systems. But man, is it worth it! Take back your own power of belief, seek the deepest truth, and don't keep falling into the "easier" path of going with the grain. It takes courage to grapple the grain and weave your own path. When you do, everything flows. You begin to access your desires, because you are on the path you created. The path that makes sense to you, that feels good to you, not the path that others desire for you. Others may raise their brows when they see your path isn't in alignment with their limited views. Sometimes you just need to be the trailblazer. Paint a Picasso, not a Stickman.

Take for example my client Deveeda. She had sensed something was wrong for years with her reproductive organs. Deveeda was struggling with heavy menstrual cycles that were long and painful in a disconcerting way. In 2003, she was denied testing and told that just because her mother's irregular periods were a sign of a larger problem didn't mean that hers were.

She became a trailblazer and advocated for her body. Feeling something was off, she continued seeking expert advice, until she connected with a general practitioner who investigated her worries. Her GP sent her for testing in August 2014 where a gynecologist diagnosed Deveeda with endometriosis. Endometriosis is a painful disorder in which tissue that normally lines the inside of your uterus grows outside of your uterus. She was given a couple of options: potent drugs that would push her into menopause early with side effects that sounded worse than her current symptoms, or surgery. All communication cornered her to feel like surgery was the only option. The doctor's eyes widened as she described how excited she was to get in there and yank everything out.

Deveeda's trust in this scalpel-jonesing doctor was little to none, so she asked for a second referral. The second opinion was less eager to lacerate her uterus, but again confirmed surgery was the only option.

Deveeda asked the doctors if there were any natural approaches to remedy her condition. Both retorted with a "no" without a second of consideration or research. If they had paused to ponder a less invasive option, she may have trusted they were there for her best interest and gone forward with the surgery. It was their inability to offer any information about natural remedies or admit that they were not familiar with them that broke her trust in their relationship. She felt an air of arrogance waft about, as they preached that nothing beyond surgery could help, which motivated her to seek out other avenues. She followed her sense of inner knowing and went against the grain.

She contacts her TCM (Traditional Chinese Medicine) doctor to share her fear of the fibroids that are on both sides of her ovaries surrounded by cysts. The measurement of one of the fibroids is the size of a grapefruit. The TCM Doctor advised Deveeda she will treat her on two conditions: first she must send all her results to her as she was not only going to take Deveeda's word of progress at face value and second, if she felt treatments were not working she would tell her the surgery is necessary and she would assist in replacing the pharmaceutical post-care drugs with natural therapy.

Deveeda began drinking Chinese herbs and having weekly acupuncture treatments. She changed the food she was eating and began ingesting turmeric pills and a daily probiotic to help decrease the inflammation of the body. When the acupuncture needles are inserted into the focus area, "Oye!", she yelps with a full body twinge as a jolt of pain radiates momentarily. She had never experienced such discomfort in years of treatments.

Her TCM doctor referred Deveeda to me to address emotional and energetic roots to her physical problem. We did two sessions of energy extraction work. This extraction practice entails me merging with a spirit helper to pull the energetic blockages from the body and transmute the energy in our local glacial river. I place the unhealthy energy in the river because the water element is wonderful at neutralizing negatively flowing qi. When I scan her energy body, I feel the thick hot energy trapped in her pelvic region. I work to pull the root of these energetic blocks as I channel my spirit guide to assist me in removing the imbalanced energy out of Deveeda's body. I am sweating and working for what feels like hours to clear her energy field. The stagnant energy is clinging to her body and resisting letting go yet I know we are making progress because I can feel it shifting and starting to lighten. I know we can heal her body. Deveeda connected to her own intuition and felt her partner and best friend holding each of her hands, as well as two previous spiritual healers holding my hands. She could see a circle of healing, holding the space for the release of what she was holding onto. Deveeda felt love, support, and security throughout the clearing process.

I knew we would need a second extraction session as I could still feel a bit of residual negative energy and my physical body needed a break from the work, as I am sure hers did too. During the second session, we were able to pull the full blockage out of the body. By the end of the session, the energy in her pelvis felt clear and healthy. I told Deveeda to be cautious of her thoughts from this time forward. To only hold thoughts of health and healing, as this is what will dissolve the physical masses within.

After our session, Deveeda had a follow up with her TCM Doctor. The needles were placed in the focus areas as usual, except this time there was no shooting pain. Deveeda and her TCM doctor were shocked by this response. The cysts and fibroids did not disintegrate, but the symptoms had stopped, the length and heaviness of her periods altered dramatically and the pain associated with pre-menstruation had ceased.

In May 2016, the doctor received Deveeda's results and her fibroids were no longer growing and suggested she not be tested for a year unless symptoms returned. Deveeda rejoiced in her inner knowing, in her ability to listen to her body and her instincts, and that there were physical results to prove it. Deveeda was able to begin the maintenance portion of her healing journey.

Deveeda is a trailblazer, going against the typical treatment protocol. She listened to her intuition and took back her control to heal in a way that feels good to her. This is not an example to prove that Eastern medicine works better than Western medicine. It is an example of what can happen when we listen to our own inner compass, even when we are being advised by others that we are wrong. Only you know what is right for you.

When healing your energy body, I have used the visualization of pulling in pure energy from nature, Mother Earth, and the universe. The truth is, we are not introducing a new energy within you, some pure magical potion of healthy frequency. Your frequency changes based on your thoughts, actions, and feelings. Your thoughts launch energetic thrusts into your aura. Your feelings propel energy rockets into hyperdrive. When you visualize calling in powerful energy from outside of you, it's easy to connect with the purity of a positive force. This is because when we go outside in nature we can feel the beautiful flowing energy and its positive impact on our body. In nature we relax with ease, and find gratitude for life. It pulls us away from our everyday distractions and forces us to take a breath and arrive in the moment. This positive frequency found in nature is already within you. Your soul's only struggle is exhausted cheeks from joyful giggling. Before you took on beliefs, traumas, and hardships, you maintained this pure potent frequency naturally. You have the ability to transform heaviness, shadows, and energetic blockages into flowing loving light in the snap of a finger. I want you to feel empowered on your journey, and know that it is possible to radiate a healthy frequency instantaneously, with the power of thought, belief, and action. Your intuition is always guiding you towards this truth, that you are an ultimate creator in your reality, when you step into ultimate presence. This is where magic happens.

I am going to share two potent methods in addressing your own path to health. You can use one method or both. Listen to your inner knowing and what feels best. In Deveeda's healing journey we used both of the methods to create the most effective and powerful healing.

The first technique is to become aware of the health and positive energy within you and to expand it. We do this by feeling this healthy and whole self. It can seem difficult to be aware of this self, but it is always within you and accessible. To feel it, you must let go of all attachments to the parts of you that don't feel healthy. Let go of your thoughts, your body, even your emotions, as these have been imprinted and tainted by your experiences. To experience this balanced self within, we must let go of the parts of us that carry old belief systems. Once you become aware of this space, the healing has already begun. Over time, it becomes very easy to connect with this healthy self because you are giving it power by placing your attention here. We are allowing it to shine and to be brought to the conscious level. Eventually it will grow and transcend from your energy body into your physical body, bringing you health and contentment.

◇ **Soul Alignment Exercise**

Healing And Accepting

Connecting within:

Let's try connecting to this space within you now. Take some deep breaths and see if you can feel the part of you that is whole, healthy, and happy.

Visualize:

If you struggle to feel it, we can do a healing visualization. This is not to create some false sense of your wholeness, but to give you a visual aid (training wheels) until you build your connection and feel it on your own. See a light within you, any color — maybe white, gold, silver, rainbow, however it appears. This is your enlightened self, also known as your soul. It is unaffected by ups or downs, it is a consistent light. Allow this light to shine brighter and bigger, permeating your physical body, filling your aura (energy field), and shining through any darkness you perceive. Notice how you feel after you've raised your vibration through this visualization.

Expansion:

Now whether you are experiencing this space or have visualized it, let's expand it. Allow a sensation of this whole, healthy, and happy space to move through your whole body. Let it shine into all parts of you, expanding and strengthening. Notice how you feel.

The second technique we will do is to remove the blockages. The first technique is the most powerful as it is easy to stay in the love vibration while we expand the energy of love. Things will shift easier for our conscious mind. The second technique can pull us into the fear vibration if we are not in an optimistic space. As you work on removing imbalances, it helps you understand if there is something you need to learn, or an action you need to take to step into your truth. Often, both of these methods are needed.

To remove your blockages and negative energy directly, you must understand why they are here. This isn't a Houdini show where you can make things magically disappear. Your blockages and negative energy have a message from your soul. They are trying to align you with love, but there is something you are clinging to that will not let you move forward. This is why you do energy work. This is why you have intuition, so that you can decipher the messages that lead you to living your life in your highest potential.

Holding space for the undesired:

Let's connect to your blockages and imbalances. Right now, as we connect, we are not intending to heal these wounds, we will get to that later. I want you to simply be aware of your blockages and negative energy and to come to accept them. This is an important step in healing. If we can say, *I am aware of you* (my pain/suffering), *I honor you for the gifts and teaching you have given me, I accept you* as opposed to, *I see you pain/suffering, why have you been hurting me? Go away! I hate you.* That is the fear vibration. Nothing will shift from that mentality. You will only make it worse by empowering it with more fear. So let's just take a deep breath and hold our pain in love and acceptance, as it really is only trying to help us. You may not understand how it is trying to help you yet, but you will. Have a little trust.

Feeling your pain body:

To become aware of the pain, close your eyes. Notice if there are areas of pain, heaviness, or perceived darkness in and around your body. Once aware, don't get pulled into the fear vibration it holds. Be aware with love and compassion. For this moment of awareness, have acceptance of this pain.

The gift of acceptance:

Sometimes acceptance is the message the body has wanted you to learn. And by accepting your suffering instead of resisting and fighting it, it shifts!

Dreaming of health:

What would it look like if your pain/negative energy were not present in your body? This is your soul truth shining through.

Chapter 11

ANATOMY OF ENERGY

Hidden systems come to light
We become aware of our energy and our path takes flight.

Energy moves through channels, like a river watering the plains. It is designed to flow. If the river dries up, the land shrivels into dust. This is the same for your body and how energy weaves through your organs, nerves, and tissues. There are endless channels of energy coursing through your body. I will simplify my favorite energy systems of the body that directly impact your health and wellbeing. Understanding this allows you to decipher why certain areas of your body and life are imbalanced or struggling. There is a functional and symbolic correlation to your body's anatomy. Take for example the knee. It bends in a mono direction. The knee represents your flexibility in life. Are you too flexible for others? Putting aside your wants and happiness to ensure others accept you, and that they are happy? Or are you too stubborn in your flexibility? Are you unwilling to try new things and go with the flow? If your knee feels healthy then your flexibility is balanced. If it feels painful or injury prone, then your flexibility can be shifted to greater reflect balance.

The vast systems of energy are worthy of independent research to help you better understand your body's energetic channels. Some areas you may feel called to understanding in greater depth are: Reiki, the Chinese meridian system, acupoints, the Hindu 7 chakras and Kundalini, the 7 layers of the auric field, the dantians, your constitution and doshas in Ayurveda, yin and yang, and nadis.

There is always an in-depth synopsis of information your energy is openly communicating to you. That is where intuition comes in, to assist you in deciphering your energy with accuracy and specificity to you. You can learn about all of these systems, including the energetics of the organs that I am about to share with you through research, channeling, and years of practicing energy healing. You can choose to bypass all texts and shared information on energy, and listen directly to your intuition that will channel universal knowledge to help you interpret the energy blockage and how to fix it. I chose to first research and take courses on understanding the energy body before I had developed my intuition enough to experience it firsthand. I did this because I hadn't learned to trust my intuition, and did not know that it could share all of the answers with me that I was seeking.

Every organ or area that we will discuss will leave an interpretation to be dissected. It will be asking yourself or whomever you are working with: is this an overabundance of energy or a scarcity? You can intuitively ask the body and receive your yes or no (dousing is a good tool for this which we will talk about in the next chapter).

Determining if it is a shortage or an overage is not rocket science and can be discerned using logic. Let's say your throat has a blockage of qi. You know because your throat feels like a marshmallow trapped under a car. An overage of throat energy would present itself by getting into lots of arguments, trying to preach your opinion to the world, and not allowing others to speak because you just can't stop yourself. A shortage would show up by never expressing your truth or you cross your arms and sit quietly in the corner at a party. Understanding if you have an over-abundance or scarcity of energy helps gauge what your next steps will be in creating balance.

I enjoy the ease of saying energy moves in an over abundance or shortage, and I love the imagery of sending in white light for healing the energy channels. However, energy does not actually contain a color or have a lack of abundance. These are ways that our intuition interprets it for our conscious mind, and allows us to utilize our intention to direct the flow of energy. Energy flows constantly and it is not charged with negativity or positivity. What changes is the rate at which it flows, and the pattern it flows through. Healthy energy flows in a different pattern and at a different speed than unhealthy energy. Joyful energy, for example, flows quickly and in a vertical pattern through your body. Sad energy moves much slower, and the energy will be more sparse as compared to joyful energy. When working with shifting your energy, you can tune in to see how it is moving within your body. You can hear it, see it, and feel it, when you are able to soften the noise of the material world. You may see it as a color or feel it as an abundance or shortage, this is your intuition interpreting your energy body for you. Similar to how our eyes and different species have a variety of rods and cones that see different colors and ranges in their sight, your intuition has a specific lens in which it perceives energy. If you begin to see energy with your eyes closed or open, it does not matter how it appears to you, what matters is how you interpret it (flowing, not flowing, good, bad, etc) as you will then know what to do with it.

Energy work is a supportive tool that allows you to understand your physical and emotional imbalances. It shows you which areas in your life are weak and need to be empowered and improved. In the weaker areas of your life, energy will not flow as smoothly. It may be tangled, moving too fast (anxiety), or too slow (lack of vitality). Energy healing uses your ability to sense your energy field using your hands or see it with your inner sight. We can do this with a body scan. A body scan is scanning over the body to assess where the blockages are found. You can feel them through a sensation in your hands as you move over the body: hot, cold, push, pull, vibration, heaviness, or waves. Any sensation is an indicator that your qi is telling you that the area is imbalanced and blocked.

Once you discover your blockages, you call upon flowing universal energy to assist you in redirecting the blocked flow of energy that is creating struggle for you. You can direct it through your hands to align the channel of energy to move in harmony, so that your struggles can be released. Because energy responds to your thoughts, whatever you intend is how the energy will flow, which is why intention is everything in energy work.

The Body

Your body is a treasure chest of wisdom. Every limb and organ in your body holds an attached meaning. Here is a list of your major body parts and their symbolic meaning. If you are drawn to a different interpretation, go with what your intuition is guiding you towards as that will be the most specific truth. If you have pain or imbalance in a part of your body at this time, read the symbolism corresponding to that part of the body and see how it applies to you now. Reflect on the meaning of each body part. Pull up past experiences, health concerns, or injuries you have had and what you were going through mentally and emotionally at that time you experienced the initial insult.

For medial and lateral specificity, especially for ankles, wrists, knees, hands, and feet refer here:

Medial Near the midline (MCL): Corresponding to your inner world, your relationship to yourself and individual growth.

Lateral Near the outside of the body (LCL): Corresponding to your outer world, your relationship to others and your experiences.

Adrenal glands: Are you in your power and full of courage to take on the world? Or are you feeling exhausted and unable to withstand small stressors? Your adrenal glands house your spark that powers you to persevere.

Ankles: Are you resisting the flow of the universe? Are you fighting the current of life instead of moving with it? Your ankles struggle if you are constantly feeling pressured and stressed by your environment. This means it may be time to surrender and go with the flow instead of against it. You will be surprised at where you end up, as it will be even greater than you dreamed.

Appendix: The small things matter. What potentially small things have been overlooked by you? Is it possible that they are more important than you give them credit for?

Bladder: Are you afraid of conflict with others? Is there fear in socializing and communicating externally? Are you feeling threatened in your own space? Bladder houses fears in how you relate to others.

Brain: When there is an imbalance here, there is a paper jam of too much energy — too much thinking, processing, and not enough surrendering. Not enough allowing for life and experiences to flow. You can get caught in wanting to control all aspects of life, which creates endless unpaid overtime work for the brain. It needs rest and to be used only when necessary. Have you been giving your brain the rest that it deserves? How can you surrender to a greater truth outside of thought?

> ✧ *Brain stem*: If issues are found here, there is way too much control happening in your life. You need to disengage, surrender and receive. Go with the flow and loosen up.

> ✧ *Cerebrum:* This area represents open mindedness. Are you able to take on new challenges with ease? Are you open to adventure and change? Or are you restricting yourself to potential possibilities?

> ✧ *Cerebellum:* How can you move through life with greater balance? There is a tendency towards black and white, back and forth. How can you find the middle path, and incorporate a bit of everything?

Buttocks/glutes: Are you sitting on your butt (figuratively speaking, possibly literally too)? Time to strengthen that tooshie and make some big moves in your life. No more procrastinating, or lazying around what is really important to you. Go for it!

Bones: What are you certain about in life? Are you solid in knowing what is unchangeable? Can you accept what can not be changed?

Breasts/chest: Gratitude is here in the breasts and chest. Are you grateful for all you have done, for all that you are? Or are you always seeking more, more, more?

Chin: Are you taking the advice of your intuition and putting it into use? Solid and firm action is needed when listening to your wisdom.

Circulatory system: Everything works together. There is no contrast, or black and white. Have you been separating parts of your life? How can you see the greater picture and interconnectedness of all?

Diaphragm: Are you making space for newness to enter your life? Are you allowing death and old stories to be vacated from your life?

Ears: You need to listen and receive from others. Receive from friends, families, strangers and spirit. There is medicine and teachings in all.

Endocrine system: There is a force at play in your life that is not in your complete control. It is influenced by your actions and thoughts, but has a mind of its own. Can you allow control and surrender to a greater power to take place simultaneously?

Eyes: You are looking directly at the physical world and missing the layers in between. The deeper truths (mental, emotional, energetic, and spiritual) are ready to be seen.

Face: Energetic portal that expresses your thoughts, emotions and soul to the world. Your face reveals your deeper levels and superficial levels of self. If there is an imbalance here, what are you showing others that is not a true reflection of you? Can you remove obstacles and lies that block others from seeing the true you?

Fascia/connective tissues: Everything is connected. Your toe is connected to your scalp through fascia. Just as your thoughts are connected to your reality. Your soul is connected to your body. You are connected to everyone. What connection are you not seeing or ignoring?

Feet: Blockages in the feet show that you are cut off from the earth. That the energy you need to release is being pent up and held onto. It can also show that you are ungrounded and not feeling at home in your life. You need to be more present.

Fingers & Toes: If they twist outward away from your midline: You are giving too greatly to others and not showing yourself enough love. If they twist inwards towards your midline: You are too closed off from others, and stuck in your own world. It is time to open up. If they are centered: You are balanced in your relationship to the world of giving and receiving.

If you have injured your fingers, have pain or numbness: You are reaching into the wrong places to find what you desire. Let your heart and not your ego drive your momentum.

If you have injured your toes, have pain or numbness: Your connection to the material world needs to be reassessed. What is rooting you, holding you into the moment? Is it something you really care about? Or is it something you believe in that is actually causing harm?

Gallbladder: Are you making life decisions that are in alignment with your highest self? Are you feeling weak or strong in making important life decisions? A weak gallbladder can result in feeling discouraged about yourself and your ability to make clear decisions. It is a pivot point that can also be seen as a hesitation between courage and fear.

Head/forehead: When you are over thinking, over-worrying and over-processing life, you will have major imbalances in the mind. It creates pressure and does not allow things to flow. This blocks the ability to surrender and receive from the universe. Control needs to be softened to allow for greatness to unfold. The forehead is an intuitive center opening you to your intuition. Are you able to connect with clarity to your inner knowing and extra sensory perceptions?

Heart: Your heart is your emotional center, and when imbalanced the place where you hold despair and anxiety. Have you been feeling overly emotional and heavy? Is there a lack of enthusiasm for life? You hold grief in the heart when you experience loss. Can you go deeper than your emotional pain to find the space of love? Love all of your emotions and hold space for them. The heart houses your loving capacity. The love you hold for yourself, for life, and all others is located here.

Hips: Your parental energetic attachments are here. Your mother's energy in your left hip and fathers in your right. If there is an imbalance in one or both of the hips, what negative belief, energy or experience has been passed down to you by your parents?

Kidneys: The kidneys house your own fear. Is there an overabundance of fear that is holding you back from living your soul truth, from being your authentic self?

Knees: Your flexibility arises at the knees. Are you being a pushover and people-pleasing constantly, not following your own path? Or are you too rigid in your own ways, not open to the flow of others and the Universe, but being stubborn in thinking you always know best. Another flexibility issue may be that you are too trusting of the universe, constantly surrendering and never consciously creating.

Large intestine (colon) and rectum: Are you holding on to things that are ready to go? It's time to let go of what is no longer serving you, create a clear path and let it flow.

Left elbow: Surrender and trust. Find balance and openness in who you are receiving from. Love, energy, and abundance comes from many sources. Do not just receive from one source.

Receive equally from yourself, from the universe, family, friends, coworkers, and strangers.

Left hand and arm: Receiving side of the body and heart. Are you constantly trying to do everything on your own and not receiving the help and gifts of loved ones? Are you closing yourself to receiving love? Or are you taking too much from everyone and exhausting them in hopes that they can fill an emptiness within you?

Left side of body: Have you been resting and going inwards? Are you tending to your inner world? Imbalanced left side of the body means you are imbalanced in your connection to your inner world, higher self, and soul desires.

Left wrist: Live with greater direction and intent in your actions. Be specific in the actions you are taking and how you interact with the world.

Legs: Your action in moving forward comes from your legs. If there is a blockage in the legs, ask yourself: Am I getting too far ahead of myself? Or am I stagnant and procrastinating? Are your legs tight and engaged even if you are not running a marathon? This means the nervous system is in a constant state of fight or flight. Mental stress is being interpreted as survival stress. It's time to take a breath and relax.

Liver: The liver holds your anger and your potency. Are you holding on to any anger that you have not expressed and processed? Are you overly angry and stuck in a mode of anger and irritation? If your anger feels healthy, are you strong in expressing who you are?

Lower back: Are you stuck in the fear vibration? You are not allowing yourself to move forward beyond your past experiences and create a new path for yourself. Has the fear vibration led you into heavy judgment? Is there shame/guilt for being your authentic self? Is there a fear of others judging you for being your true self?

Lungs: The lungs hold sadness in your body. If there is sadness you are holding and not expressing, it will manifest in imbalance in the lungs and your breathing.

Lymphatic system: Take a look at the secondary systems in your life. Have you been ignoring aspects of yourself or lifestyle because you are prioritizing something else? What else is in need of your attention right now?

Middle back: You are doubting your worthiness of being happy and not going after what you desire. You are not taking care of your self-needs because you nourish others and their desires before your own. Do you care too much how others perceive you? How can you step into your power and be more authentic in who you are?

Mouth: You are aware of your truth that you need to speak and express through your actions, but you are still holding back at the last moment. Or, you are pushing out more than you need to. You're over-expressing your thoughts and judgements while not allowing silence and space to be expressed.

Neck/thyroid/parathyroids/throat: Do you have a fear of expressing yourself as you have been rejected by others in the past? Do you struggle with worthiness and not feeling good enough to show up and make a splash? Or, are you over expressing yourself, in hopes to find acceptance from others as you try to prove your worth?

Nervous system: How are you connecting with the world? Are you over stimulated, or understimulated? What would it feel like to have a balanced connection with your inner world and outer world?

Nose: Are you connected to spirit and to your higher self? Or are you disconnected and listening to the ego mind? It's time to put the fears aside and listen to your inner guidance.

Ovaries and Testes: The birthplace of your ideas and dreams. Are you holding yourself back from becoming aware of your dreams? Or are you constantly dreaming and getting overwhelmed with your energy being scattered and not nourishing any growth?

Pancreas: Have you found a sense of balance in your creations? Or, are you overworking your mind and body to try and force things to happen?

Pelvis: Birthing canal for men and women. Are you allowing your creations out into the world? Or are you holding back, and not letting your creations be seen?

Pineal gland: The pineal gland connects you to higher dimensions of self and the universe. This gland has retinal tissue composed of rods and cones (photoreceptors), similar to your physical eyes. This light sensing organ can see light (qi) moving from within. It connects us to the field of energy, and this gland helps us to sense it. When it is open we feel divine support and a flow to life, instead of fighting the current of a river.

Pituitary gland: The pituitary gland is where we find our intuition center. Are you listening to your wisdom and inner knowing? Or are you following only your rational and emotional brain?

Ribs: Are you open and sharing your heart and authentic self with others? Or are you shielding and protecting yourself out of fear of being harmed by others?

Right elbow: You are giving too much in one area of your life. How can you give your energy and time in a more balanced way? Giving to yourself, friends, family, strangers and the planet with an even distribution.

Right hand and arm: Giving side of your body and heart. Are you giving too much to everyone else, and not enough to yourself? Are you not giving enough, holding back your love and affection, out of fear of being used by others?

Right side of the body: Are you tending to your outer world? Are you creating and going after what you want? The right side of the body represents your connection to your outside world and how you interact with it. Are you expressing yourself, and taking action for your desires in the world around you?

Right wrist: Slow down and pace yourself. There is no rush to leave a legacy behind. How can you make your mark in a more balanced and successive incremental way?

Sinuses: Your safety reservoirs. Are you carrying old baggage? How can you clear your channel and make space so that if an emergency happens, you are able to stay afloat?

Skin: Do you have a balance in your protective energetic layer between you and your outside world? Are you open and receiving to positivity and love? Are you able to block out negativity and fear?

Small intestine: Are you absorbing the nutrients of life? Are you receiving healthy energies in your experiences? Or are you moving too quickly to take it all in? Are your experiences in alignment with your health? Do you live a healthy lifestyle that nourishes you?

Spine: Are you connected to the greater forces outside of you — to spirit and to the earth? If not, and you are battling this life in isolation, your spine will reflect imbalance.

Spleen: You house your worry here. Are you often thinking ahead and creating mini-panic vibrations in the body unnecessarily? Are you able to find calmness within and release your worry?

Stomach: How are you stomaching life? Are you able to digest everything as it is unfolding or is it difficult to process?

Teeth: Do you feel stable in your life circumstances and strong? Or is there weakness and uncertainty?

Thymus: Your thymus degenerates as you age. As a child it is a housing for your spiritual energy. Often, this is why children are more intuitive. Are you being playful in your intuitive practices or serious and stern? It's time to bring the fun back.

Tongue: How are you interacting with the world? Are you tense or relaxed? Are you connecting or disengaging?

Tops of shoulders: Here, you carry your responsibilities. Are you feeling weighed down by your mental and physical responsibilities? This can affect your breathing to be apical (upper body breathing) creating tension in the neck and shoulders. It is time to shift your perspective of responsibilities and lighten the load. Responsibilities range from family and self to planetary ones. Tune into the areas that you are feeling weighed down and set them free.

Upper abdomen: This is an area of self empowerment and confidence. Do you believe in yourself? Or are you constantly doubting your worthiness?

Upper back: Are you feeling weighed down by the world? This weight causes you to hold back your love and hold back your truth. You are feeling disconnected, or as if you have stepped back from living passionately and purposefully.

Uterus and Prostate: Are you allowing your dreams to come to reality? Are you putting them into action and watering the seeds of your desires and your calling? Or are you resisting and procrastinating?

Vagina and Penis: The final stage of birthing your dreams. Are you resisting out of fear to unleash them into reality? Let go of the fears of the potential greatness that is awaiting you.

When reflecting on the health of your physical body, which areas and organs have been affected negatively? Does the energetic meaning resonate with a struggle you are facing?

David E. McManus, PhD, published a study in October 2017 reviewing clinical studies done on Reiki (traditional Japanese energy healing) to discover if Reiki provides more than a placebo effect

(McManus[7]). Within the Reiki treatment, arm controlling for a placebo effect, only 13 studies were found suitable. Eight of the studies showed Reiki being more effective than placebo, while four found there was no difference. These four studies had questionable statistical power. One of the studies provided evidence for Reiki not providing any benefit. When viewed collectively, the studies showed a strong reason that Reiki is more effective than placebo.

McManus stated, "From the information currently available, Reiki is a safe and gentle complementary therapy that activates the parasympathetic nervous system to heal the body and mind. It has potential for broader use in management of chronic health conditions, and possibly in postoperative recovery. Research is needed to optimize the delivery of Reiki."

One of my favorite studies out of the 13 researched is by Baldwin and Schwartz. This study investigated if Reiki could reduce the effects of noise-induced stress in rats. A loud noise causes damage to the tiny blood vessels of the mesentery (a fold of the peritoneum which attaches the stomach, small intestine, pancreas, spleen, and other organs to the posterior wall of the abdomen). This damage can be quantitatively measured by the level of stress the rats experience.

There were three treatment experiments. The first was exposing the rats to noise and Reiki. The second exposed the rats to noise and fake, or sham Reiki. The third experiment exposed the rats to noise only — this was the control group. The group that experienced Reiki and the noise exposure had significantly lower micro vascular damage than the group receiving sham reiki and the control group.

An extended study was done to measure if Reiki can reduce the heart rate and blood pressure of the noise-stressed rats. It was found through telemetric transmitters that measure physiological data, that Reiki drastically reduced the average resting heart rate, and reduced

---

[7] McManus, David E. "Reiki Is Better Than Placebo and Has Broad Potential as a Complementary Health Therapy." *National Center For Biotechnology Information*, vol. 22, no. 4, 2017, pp. 1051-1057. *National Library Of Medicine*, https://www.ncbi.nlm.nih.gov/pmc/articles/PMC5871310/.

the rise in heart rate produced by exposure of rats to loud noise. Again the sham Reiki and control group had no significant decrease in affected mean arterial pressure. Let's explore the immediate benefit of energy healing right now:

> ◇ **Soul Alignment Exercise:**
>
> Energy Healing & Scanning
>
> **Scan your energy body:**
>
> Activate the energy centers in your palms which help you to feel energy. Do this by tapping each palm a few times, then rubbing your hands together as if you are warming them up. Now with your hands facing your body and fingers touching each other side by side (like the Queen's hand when she waves), palms facing toward you, do a body scan. Move slowly, hovering a foot above the body (in front of the body). Feel for any sensation. Move all the way from your feet to the top of your head. Once you feel a sensation, spend time there with your hands above that area. Call in a positive energy flow to help realign the negative pattern, and expand your loving soul truth to your energy field and body.
>
> **Healing:**
>
> You can use intuitive visualization to empower the energy healing. Picture a constant stream of energy flowing through the area of misaligned energy. You will feel a shift in the sensation of your palms; this is when you know your body is reacting and shifting from the universal energy.

Chapter 12

INTUITIVE TRAINING WHEELS

It has always been within
Coming home is where we begin.

After the miniature yellow people in my lego soap opera are done falling in and out of love, I flop on my creaky brown sofa. I gaze at the popcorn ceiling watching the blue, purple, and white orbs floating in the air. The room begins slowly spinning, like a painting beginning to melt. *My eyes do strange things,* I think as I shake it off. This was a typical experience in my childhood. Eventually, I stopped seeing the energy orbs and the shapeshifting of the room because I related it to poor sight (even though I have 20/20 vision). As children, our intuition is at its peak because it's still encouraged. We are allowed to have imaginary friends (who are often our spirit guides and helpers). We have a spontaneous thought of what will be fun and we do it fearlessly. We are free to be creative through our art and our personality. Our imagination has no limits. At some point, we start being stripped of these experiences. We are told to live in the "real" world, a world where only the analytical mind is valued, and intuition is for airy fairy people with big imaginations who can't get a real job. Yet it is your intuition that keeps you on the path of the greatest joy and least suffering. To connect with your intuition, you need to sharpen your tools that were misplaced in your childhood.

Intuition is a birthright. Trust me when I say **you have intuition**. Just as your logical brain is inherent, so too is your intuition. Your two eyes help you to understand your physical world.

Your third eye helps you see through the veil of the physical into the depths of the soul, of the deepest truths. It speaks to you often but gets blocked by your conscious mind. If you are an over-thinker or worry wart, your thoughts are smoke screening your soul consciousness. We can reinstate this connection and build it through use and practice.

Your intuition is what will communicate the root cause of your suffering. We have gone through the extra-sensory perceptions in Chapter 8: Your Superpower Senses. These are the most valuable tools to build upon. The red tape you need to cut through is building the confidence to trust your answers. The answers are easily accessible but a foundation of trust is necessary to take the messages seriously. You may doubt what your intuition has shown you because you cannot decipher if it is intuition or imagination. Trusting your intuition comes with time. We don't accept that the messages our intuition has given us are true until after things have been proven. Messages are either predicting something that is coming and preparing us for it, or they are informing us of what we are currently going through and giving us guidance about it. Only after these moments have unfolded do we get the "aha" moment, where we realize that our intuition was bang on.

The extra sensory tools (like inner knowing, clairvoyance (seeing), clairsentience (feeling), and celestial hearing) are the best tools, because they are always accessible. They are within you! We are also going to open you up to a world of physical tools you can touch and feel. These tools give you a visual that your two human eyes can see, which will help you trust your intuition as you take your imagination out of the picture. The universal all knowing life force is woven into everything, including these tools you will be using. This means that your messages are not only going to be internal through your third eye, but also external in your physical world. Let's begin exploring these physical intuitive forms now:

Dousing

Dousing is using a pendulum to create clarity with a yes or no question. It looks like a small chain often with a pointed crystal on the bottom. Dousing is an easy intuitive practice because it gives you a visual response that your physical eyes can see. Give it a try. If you don't have a pendulum, you can use a necklace or a string with something hanging on the bottom. The base or piece on the necklace needs to be bigger and weighted evenly for it to work best.

First, clear any energies your pendulum may be holding onto (from gemstone miners, shopkeepers, or previous owners). You can do this by lighting a dried plant or incense (depending on your tradition or preference), with the intention of the smoke clearing the piece so that it can hold a neutral energy. Then hold the pendulum above the smoke. Use your intuition to know when it feels clear. You should feel a slight shift within yourself, or a good feeling in your stomach where you can breathe more deeply. Listen to your body as it will give you a sign.

Now ask your pendulum to show you its yes. There are two ways to do this: the first is dangling it straight in front of you, holding it at the top so the weighted portion is at the bottom. Hold it still so it is not moving, and it will begin to move. The second way is to begin with a straight movement back and forth and wait to see which direction it moves in. Choose the method that feels best to you. However it moves, this is your yes. It may be clockwise, counter clockwise, a straight line or a zigzag. Now that it is determined, ask for it to show you its no. And whichever way it moves (it will move in a different direction from your yes), this is your no. Now you can use it for yes and no questions.

A word of caution:

Don't ask future questions: Will I find a wealthy lover? Will I get the job? Should I become a lawyer? Nothing is predetermined in life and choice is what makes living fun. Knowing these answers can debilitate you from going after the job, looking for the lover, moving to another country, etc. You are at least living if you get up and try, rather than sitting on the couch and doing nothing at all. Taking away choice takes away what it means to be human. And it also can sabotage your shot at expansion and soul growth.

Ask about the present moment, as the only thing that matters is right now. For myself, I never use my pendulum for anything other than clarity. If I have a question, it is immensely powerful to receive the answer from my intuition. I then get to receive a short story of information on a subject. A simple yes or no is very basic and hard to get the full story. I use my pendulum when I have received an intuitive message and need clarity. For example, if I ask: "What can I do to heal my relationship with my mother?" And if I see an image of a little girl picking flowers and making a flower crown for herself, I may want clarity. Now I can ask my intuition: "Am I this little girl?" or "Is this little girl my mother?" and receive a yes or no from my mind's eye. Or, I can pick up the pendulum and ask. Both ways will warrant the same response.

As you are building your intuitive tool belt, try asking your intuition first. And then ask with the pendulum to confirm your accuracy in reading your intuition. It is a great tool to support you in finding certainty. And if you are just not connecting with your intuition at all, then pull out the pendulum. It will be your best friend for some time, until you are able to receive your intuitive messages on your own.

Omens and Oracles

Omens and oracles are a spontaneous physical sign that you see in your environment. Like an eagle flying above you in the sky, a lightning storm, a boat-shaped cloud, or stubbing your toe. All of these are omens, and they all hold meaning. Omens are fun because you get to flex your creative muscles and interpret their symbolism. The physical signs speak in a symbolic language unique to you. A black bear to you may represent a nurturing motherly energy. Whereas someone who was bluff-charged by a black bear connects them to facing their greatest fear.

Whenever you receive an omen, like an animal crosses your path or a feather falls before you, or a train makes you late for work, take a moment to ask yourself what this might mean to you symbolically. You can look up meanings online or in a book, but always ask yourself first. Your knowledge and wisdom is the most powerful truth and interpreter you can access. The more often you ask your inner knowing, the quicker you build confidence in your intuition.

Oracle Cards

Oracle cards are one of the easiest ways to connect to your wisdom. There are thousands of decks: angel cards, animal cards, elf cards, ascended masters, shamanic, witch, archangel, etc. Metaphysical stores will often have sample decks for you to use and try. One of my favorite deck creators is Alana Fairchild, she has wonderfully inspired decks full of intuitive and loving messages. It is similar to the pendulum in that it has been handled by other people, so always clear it first. An easy way is to knock three times on the deck of cards, just like when you knock on a door. This "knocks" out anyone else's energy and prepares the deck for you. If someone else's energy is on it, it can give you a response based on their energy.

You then ask a question or hold an intention as you shuffle and mix the cards. By shuffling, mixing and touching the deck, you are infusing your energy into the cards. This helps them give you a more accurate reading. Have the cards face down so you cannot see the pictures, then choose the card you are drawn to. That can be through inner knowing (a gut feeling), or through the card falling out while you shuffle. What I like to do is fan out the cards and scan above them as I feel the energy of the cards. I will feel a pressure or thickness over the card I am meant to pull. It is really fun and an easy way to build trust with your intuition. If you don't have a specific question, you can ask: What does spirit (or my highest self) want me to know at this time? Before reading the description in the booklet that comes with the deck, interpret the card for yourself. Look at the colors, the imagery, and pull a symbolic meaning for yourself. Then receive a second message by reading the description in the booklet that comes with the deck.

To do an oracle reading for a friend, have them knock the deck, then shuffle the deck and choose their card. You can help in interpreting the message of the image and saying on the card.

Tea Leaf Reading

Have a white tea cup (if it has a plate with it, even better). Place 3/4 tsp of black, red, or green loose tea leaves in the bottom. Add hot water. Now as you sip the tea bring your intention or question to mind. Drink as much of the liquid as you can until it is just the leaves remaining. Now turn the cup clockwise three times as you hold it in front of your heart. This is pulling the wisdom from within you into the cup. Then place it upside down on the plate and turn it 3 times counter clockwise. This is spiraling the wisdom out. Then tap the bottom 3 times. This pulls it into the leaves. Now flip your cup over. Once it's flipped over, it's like playing connect the dots. You will notice one, or many images in your leaves. They all are answering your question and intention. It is so much fun! I love doing it for friends. They will do all of the steps and I will offer an interpretation of the messages.

Numerology

St. Augustine of Hippo (A.D. 354-430) wrote: "Numbers are the Universal language offered by the deity to humans as confirmation of the truth." Numerology is connecting to divine messages within numbers. Numbers can be found everywhere! Receipts, invoices, looking at the clock, the date, your house number, bus numbers, the number of freckles on your face, license plates — all around, they are constantly speaking to you. Diving deeper into numerology, we begin to look at the numerology in letters and words. In your own name there is a numerological meaning. Each letter is represented by a number.

I always hear people tell me how they suddenly see the same numbers over and over, everywhere they look. This is a message that is trying to get through to them. Pay attention to the numbers around you as math and numbers is the most universal language and an easy carrier of universal truth.

Here I will share the basic meaning of the numbers 0-9. From the numbers 10 and on you can add the numbers together to create the base number. For example your house number is 2401. 2+4+0+1=7. Seven is the significant number for you to explore. If you see a repetitive number like 1111 or 444 this can hold a very strong vibration and powerful message. But as always, even more powerful than what I am sharing is your connection to the meaning of numbers. If you have always loved the number 8, let's say, and it made you feel safe and peaceful, then this is the meaning of 8 for you when you see it.

1. God, divine, nothingness, infinity
2. New beginning, creation, manifestation, first steps, power, leader
3. Extremes, opposite, duality, lovers
4. Self-expression, creativity, outcomes, awareness
5. Logic, reason, endurance, foundations, balance

6. Pleasure, the body, physical reality, change, challenge

7. Love, romance, sex, loyalty, relationships

8. Spirituality, occult, mystical, contemplation

9. Endless, balance, focus, drive, abundance

10. Wisdom, charity, activism, completion

Take the letters of your first name and find the seed number. Do this by counting through the alphabet, starting with 1 for A, then 9 for I, and back to 1 for J. There will be a number for each letter. Add all of the numbers together, if it is a double digit, add those two together as well. Whatever your final number is, this is a reflection of your essence through your name.

Dreams and Astral Travel

My strongest intuitive weapon has been the dream world. It is a perfect concoction because you are relaxed and your conscious mind slips to the back of your brain, allowing easy access for the intuition to speak. All dreams are important, and there are two types of dreaming.

There are times when we dream and are having out of body experiences. When we astral travel, our soul may leave our body and travel on the Earth plane, inter-dimensionally, or to another time and another life. Another dreaming experience is when we are visited by spirits. The spirits may be helpers, guides, angels or ghosts. Of course there is always free will and we can close those doors to who we want to meet. Meeting our guides through dreams can be very powerful, and they are often delivering direct messages to us, or simply letting us know of their loving presence. Sometimes we leave our dreaming doors open and we meet wonderfully helpful spirits. And sometimes we invite ghosts through our own fear of ghosts (attraction), or there is a piece of our soul that is ready to connect with ghosts and help them.

The second form of dreaming is the most common: receiving messages from your higher self. The messages are always relevant. We will forget our dreams most often if we do not write them down. 50% is forgotten in the first five minutes after waking, and 90% in the next ten minutes. Your dreams can seem insignificant or silly, but there is always a message. It is coming through in your dreams because there is an important message to be heard. It may be coming through in relation to the show or the person you thought of because you have a strong attachment or feeling associated with it at the time. This makes the symbolism easier to understand, as it's fresh in your mind. Have you had a recurring dream? This dream is very important and holds a powerful message for you that is waiting to be interpreted. You can work intentionally with your dreams as well. Try this exercise this evening:

- ✧ Have a journal beside your bed (or in the hall if you have a partner you don't want to wake up by turning on a light to write). But have it close with a pen so that you do not lose the tight timeline you have to write down your dreams. Before going to bed ask a question or have an intention of receiving wisdom on an issue you have been facing. Write it down. State your question in your mind's eye or before you fall asleep, then fall asleep as normal.

- ✧ As soon as you awake (it may be in the morning, or halfway through the night) you must write it down. Then, when you have time in the day to interpret it, you can receive two answers from your dream.

First, write a reflection of what everything means to you symbolically. If you are unsure, then write the first thing that comes to mind. I caution you from looking anything up online. Your dream is speaking to you in your language. You will have the most accurate interpretation if you are the one to interpret.

Don't be afraid of scary dreams where there is death, murder, or rape. Remember it is symbolic. Even the people may be symbolic. So seeing your mother does not mean the dream is about your mom. Usually, the dream is for you and guiding you on your path. If it is for your mother, you will feel a strong yes or no inside when you ask if this is literally your mom or the meaning you attach to your mother. I once had a vivid dream of my brother dying in an electric chair. I woke up panicked and afraid, I was a little heartbroken having feeling I had lost him. I was younger at the time and did not understand the dream. When I reflect back now I know at that time my brother was experiencing a painful death, he was transitioning as a human being and a piece of him was dying. But it was a beautiful transition, allowing him to discover his true nature more closely.

This first reflection is powerful and often gives you all that you need to know. But you can go even deeper; there is a second message to be interpreted from the dream. To dive deeper, you are going to consciously ask your highest self for the meaning of this dream. You ask with intention and wait for the answer from your intuition. You may receive a whole other storyboard (it will appear like a dream in a conscious state) that can feel even more fantastical than the initial dream. Write it all down and, again, interpret it. To do this second method, it is easiest if you are in a calm state so you can receive a clear message and trust what is coming through. Let things unfold on their own, don't force it or try to control the direction of it.

The first interpretation of your dream connects you to the soul's truth. It sheds light on a current issue you may be having or a dilemma you are facing. It brings forth the truth in discovering what you have been missing.

The second interpretation is your soul's greater truth, meaning a truth based on love and the depths of your soul's love. It takes us a step further to see how this message translates into the greater picture of your world, not just as a simple circumstance, but as a reflection of the journey of your soul and its growth in this lifetime.

Even without a question, your dreams are always reaching out to you to connect you to the truth and keep you on track with a life of ease and love. If you have issues remembering your dreams, or think you are one of those people who just don't dream, know that you do dream and you can remember your dreams. What is needed to dream is clear intention. By doing this practice, simply having paper and a pen out is a dedication and an intention that you are prepared to receive and interpret the messages. Give it a try!

Spirit Safety

Ghosts are spirits of people who have passed and haven't made it to the afterlife. There are two ways in which you can connect with ghosts: by attracting them through your fear, or being ready to assist them in their soul's journey back home to love. Even if you are afraid and have attracted a ghost into your life, you can use the method I am about to share with you. This method pulls you from the fear vibration into love. We attract ghosts when we are in a very negative state of fear-based vibration. They can show up in our lives when we are at a rock bottom. Sometimes you can look into a person's eyes who has been through deep trauma, abuse, or neglect and who is greatly suffering and see that it is not only their soul occupying their body. It is a feeling that someone else is in there. This can happen, and it's not a terrible thing, it just means the person was in such a low frequency, it offered a safe space for this spirit to reside in the same frequency it holds. A suffering spirit cannot enter the body of someone who is in the love vibration (someone who is not suffering), because it is like throwing an ice cube in a hot tub; the different temperatures (vibrations) are not compatible. Often, when I do deposession work, it is for people who are going through or have recently gone through a dark time in their lives. They are not doing self-care, or they are giving their consciousness over to drugs and alcohol which makes space for the low frequency spirit to enter. It is actually a blessing, as it is an indicator that they need to make healthier lifestyle choices that express self-love. Once they take those loving actions, the spirit can no longer reside within them or around them. These actions are needed to maintain a healthy and whole energy field.

You are a ghostbuster if: you are not afraid of ghosts, you are feeling moderately healthy, and you are seeing them in dreams or reality. Your soul is connecting you to these spirits for a reason. You have the power to assist this ghost in their journey back to love (home/higher self), and off the Earth plane back to source. This is where most spirits go when they pass. This does not mean we can't connect with them once they return to source, we actually connect with them more strongly when they are in the love plane and not the Earth plane.

I will do a brief description here about encountering a ghost who has not ascended, in case this is happening to you and you feel unsure of what to do. The most important thing is to stay in the vibration of love. What is a ghost? It's the soul of a person that has not merged back with its higher self. So there is nothing to fear, see them and treat them like a person. Talk to them, ask them how they are doing. If they are a ghost, you will feel that they are suffering in some way, by how they show up or what they say to you. They may appear decrepit or washed out and gray, then you'll know that you can help them.

There are spirits of people who have passed and have ascended that can show up for you. Meaning, they followed the natural flow after their death back to "the light", back to their home, the place they came from before birth and they've merged with their higher self. You will know when someone is an ascended spirit because they will not be suffering; they will be in the love vibration and the stream of consciousness of all knowing. There is a big difference and it is easy to feel.

Once you know they are suffering, you can help them by telling them "I see that you are suffering, and you don't deserve to suffer, you deserve to feel loved and supported." You offer your hand to help take them back to God/source/the light/love (whatever term feels best for you they are all the same place). You wait for them to take your hand, never force it. If you try forcing a spirit to ascend, you are using fear and not love, and it doesn't work. Once they are ready, they will come, and you gently guide them to the light. You connect to the light with a simple intention. It is an easy process, it's fun, and makes you really operate from your heart center. There is nothing to fear when you are in alignment with your heart. You are aligned with oneness/all knowing/the divine and are essentially untouchable. Nothing is stronger than love. This method is here only if you are approached by ghosts (suffering spirits is the term I like).

If this is work you want to get into, there are many courses you can take. No one deserves to suffer. But sometimes, as we suffer in life, we may decide to continue suffering in death for one reason or another. They may want to stay behind because they feel they have unfinished business, or need to be there for grieving family members who will not be okay once they pass. A soul may feel that they are a bad person and do not deserve to be loved. A spirit can have a shocking and unexpected death, and not be ready to move on to the next step of their journey. This is what happens to these spirits, they are not ready to be loved, they are not ready to return home, and so they stay. They are alone, they are scared, and they are not receiving love. Love is all they need. Love is all everybody needs, isn't it?

Chapter 13

UNEARTH THE ROOTS

All imbalances stem from love's guidance.
Once your fears are held with love,
They can finally transcend.

Claudia-Sam's untethered curls surprise me with their soft poise. She sits with her arms crossed and a furrowed brow, as I talk about intuition versus ego in a teacher training course for Reiki. A seriousness comes into her voice: "I don't know where I want to live. I can't decide between here (Canmore Alberta), Montreal Quebec, or Nelson New Zealand." I ask her to close her eyes and feel into each location, "Trust your intuition, it knows." She closes her eyes and thinks of Canmore. It is dark, distant, and she feels a repulsion. She brings up Montreal, and again feels the cold blackness. Claudia-Sam tunes into Nelson, and a bright rainbow enters her mind, it is light and airy. She feels an open-ness, as though she is being drawn towards a warm light. Her furrowed brow releases and tears stream down her cheeks. She is so certain that Nelson is where she must be that it scares her to move across the planet away from home. It scares her because she knows with absolute certainty that it is where she is meant to be.

Finding the root cause of your issues comes down to asking and receiving. Your tool belt is pulling your pants down because it is jam packed with intuitive tools you have just picked up. Now it's time to use them! You now have access to universal knowledge. All you have to do is reach within and listen to the whispers of truth.

It does not matter what part of you feels broken or imbalanced, it has a root within your energy. Once the root is addressed, removed, or surrendered, the side effects and symptoms discontinue.

Big things tend to have big messages. Like you break your right arm and your soul is telling you: "That's it... no more overdoing and over thinking, time to slow down. You are on a break." Or you get a cold sore and your soul is telling you, "You've been holding onto some toxic thoughts and it's time to let them go." You develop cervical cancer and your soul shouts, "We need to give birth to your dreams!"

Whatever is going on, it is always stemming from love and your soul wanting you to align with more love.

You can approach your health with logic: I broke my arm because I fell. Fortunately, we unintentionally address the root cause. The broken arm hinders your productivity; you have less responsibilities and receive the deep rest that you need. You may not get the message and resist the universe by continuing to take on more projects and allowing worry to fester in your mind. This results in the injury not healing properly, or new conditions forming.

How amazing would it be if you didn't have to break an arm to get the message? What if you asked your soul: "Dear soul, what can I do to be in alignment with you?" before you broke your arm? And your soul replied "You need to slow down, calm down and rest." If you listen, these physical traumas and imbalances are avoided. It's okay if you ask your intuition after you get sick, hurt, or stressed. You can still find the root and now consciously work on healing the cause. Once the root is addressed, the symptoms heal alarmingly fast, because you rose to find what your soul has been trying to get across to you to see the bigger picture. You didn't claim ignorance and just continue on in the "poor me" mentality.

Your intuition has been communicating with you throughout your lifetime. However, it may have been mistaken as an egoic thought. Or, an egoic thought may have been mistaken as intuitive insight. There is a way to know where a thought or feeling is sourced from. Let's break down the two fibers of ego and higher consciousness further so that you can understand when it's your soul speaking to you, and not your imagination.

The ego mind operates from your reptilian brain which is all about survival and self-preservation. The ego mind formulates answers and decisions based on judgements you have created through the experiences in your life. It makes calculations based on observable and measurable data. The ego mind is often rooted in the vibration of fear — fear of not being good enough, fear of failing, fear of not being accepted, and fear of not having enough money to survive, to name a few. To make it more clear for you, here is an example of an ego minded decision: I make a little road trip to visit friends and family. It's a short weekend trip, and I squeeze in visiting 6 different groups of people. I saved seeing my parents until the last day, but by this time my energy is tanked out and running on fumes. I feel guilty because I just can't muster the strength for one more visit. I tell them I'm not feeling well, and won't be able to visit. *A little lie isn't going to hurt anyone. I'm taking care of my needs which is great and my family won't know any different.* My ego is protected; I'm safe from judgment and rejection. No one gets hurt, it's a win-win.

Let's look at the second system, the higher self-consciousness. This refers to your deepest level of self. This level is connected to source energy. It receives information from the space of all-knowing. No calculations are needed here. It simply is your deepest and most beneficial truth that has your soul's development and wellness at heart. This system is based on the vibration of love, meaning all information that stems from your higher self-consciousness results in you accessing more love, more peace, and more joy in your lifetime. It often benefits the planet and the people you interact with in a selfless and loving way. Let's use the same example but with a decision stemming from your higher self. This time I choose to tell the truth: "I overbooked my weekend and I am needing some self-care as I don't have a lot of energy today. I messed up, I'm sorry I didn't schedule our visit first. I will be sure not to overschedule and exhaust myself on my next visit so that we can have quality time together." This second way is in alignment with your higher consciousness. You are trusting that you will still be accepted and loved by expressing your truth. You are also stepping up for yourself and voicing your needs, honoring them and not being ashamed of them. You are showing others that we all struggle sometimes, it is nothing to be ashamed of and that you are a loving person not only to others but also to yourself. This is the path of love.

This was a small example I shared about the two streams of consciousness. Reflect on the big decisions you have made in your life. Were they fear-based? Love-based? Or a bit of both?

The clicking of the keyboard drills anxiety into my nervous system. The sound of my friend chomping on potato chips drives my fight or flight into hyperdrive. I struggle with Misophonia, a condition where certain sounds and textures create stress and anger. My mind tells me I need to heal this condition because it is impacting my quality of life. On bad days I cannot work, or even go outside as I try and avoid the triggering sounds. My ego says *I am broken.* My intuition tells me to accept and love myself as I am. The condition worsens the more I listen to my fear based thoughts. My heart knows that when I am able to embrace my intuition and love myself as I am my condition will heal.

You can see how it's easy to fall into the reptilian brain of security and logic. It is about protection and preservation. When rooting in the higher-self consciousness, you move into a space of trust and compassion. Neither system is wrong, but we tend to exhaust our dependence on the ego mind. This is why we need to work on injecting your higher consciousness into your thoughts and energy body. By building this resource, you step into the vibration of love more powerfully, and access greater balance in your life.

When a love-based decision is made miracles can occur. During a full blue moon I was ready to sleep early while my husband watched a movie. I wake up to a deep and loud vibration ringing in my ears. A white light so bright forces me to close my eyelids to make it bearable.

I am confused by the intensity of what I am seeing and hearing, but my inner wisdom tells me *something important is happening.* My fearful mind wants me to shake it off and go find my husband. I choose love instead and surrender to the experience. Energy begins to run through my body at mach speed. My jaw clenches and I cannot open my mouth because the force of energy moving through me is so strong. I feel like I weigh a thousand pounds because of the high volume of energy passing through me. If someone were to shout at me from two feet away, I could not hear them because the sound of energy was so loud. The wrinkled sheets brush my backside as my body begins to rise above the bed. It is a peculiar sensation to be floating while feeling heavy. I hover for some time suspended in the air. As my mind tries to control what's happening I glide lower, as I surrender I glide upwards until eventually my body is gently placed on the mattress. My legs then continue the levitating motion moving up and down, being carried by this energy until my husband arrives for bedtime.

The act of surrender and trust was the pathway of love. It was so clear that when my fearful mind intervened, this beautiful experience dissipated. When I continued to let go of my mind, love allowed me to have one of the most magical experiences in my life.

To connect confidently with your higher consciousness, it helps to calm the ego mind first. You can do this with a bath, meditation, exercise, silence, or a nap. Be playful to find what works for you. And if you don't have a "thing" that helps you soften your mind, that's okay. You still receive the answers. You will need to utilize discernment to filter thought from intuition.

Thoughts and imagination have a precursor. They are stimulated by your reality and your experiences. With your active participation, simple thoughts become a pecking pigeon in your mind. Intuition cuts right to the truth without a precursive instigator. There is no run on continuation with the process of thinking involved. Intuition flows like a babbling brook all on its own. Both intuition and thought can feel random. But thought is created by experiences of your past, worries of your future, and what is in front of you right now. Intuition is not based on experiences or a timeline. Time is irrelevant to energy and intuition. It can advise you on your future/past/present, past lifetimes, anytime. It will communicate in the simplest way possible for you to understand the messages needed for your soul growth and human benefit.

Often, your intuition relays messages by showing you unpredictable images. They can appear as thoughts, but they seem illogical and random. For example, you are asking your higher self: "Why am I struggling with saying how I feel?" You start to think, "My boss is rude and if I tell them how I feel, I won't be accepted or listened to. Like that time when I was young..., etc." This is clearly a thought process, as you are creating your story. Eventually, your intuition peaks through: you see an image of a black parrot on a branch. "Hmm, that was random. What does a black parrot mean to me? Parrots are normally vibrantly colored. Parrots represent communication to me. Am I afraid of showing my true colors? Why isn't the bird flying?" Interpretation: When I don't flaunt my vibrant colors and true self, I am dimming my light and not being free (soaring). Intuition is not a created story. A created story comes from the imagination and the mind. Intuition just is. And it's not always images that we need to dissect. It can be a feeling, words, voice, or inner knowing as you've discovered in Chapter 8: Your Superpower Senses.

Now it's time for you to connect with your soul and its wisdom. I will give you three methods for asking and receiving. Try all three of them at different times, and find what works best for you. They are aimed at connecting you through different mental states (calm, feeling triggered/irritated, and high stress). You can use these practices to discover the root of pain, illness, and suffering. Or, use it to gain clarity in any area of your life that you are feeling stuck in.

First, you need to formulate your question. It is easy to focus on the bad stuff like emotional and physical pain. If nothing comes to mind, my go to question is: "What does my soul want me to know at this time?"

I love to add "for my highest good" so when I ask my question it comes through as: "What does my soul want me to know at this time for my highest good?" This allows me to trust that whatever answer I experience, it is coming from love. Even if it feels negative or scary, I know it is here to benefit me. Let's say my question was asking about depression. My question would be: "For my highest good, what is the root cause of my depression?" Put your question together, write it down, or speak it out loud to see how it feels.

◇ **Soul Alignment Exercise**

Finding The Root

Method #1 Clear and Calm

Clear and calm is for when you are feeling good about your question. You feel calm, and you are in a good place. Whether it is a good mood, you had a good day or you are in the love vibration (positive, optimistic, or feeling neutral). Use this method if your question is about something that creates a lot of suffering for you, but you are already holding it in acceptance and compassion.

- Pro tip: Set up a sacred space, light a candle, go to a quiet room, or in nature. Have crystals, essential oils, and items that connect you to peace. If you have loved ones who have passed, place their pictures around as they will support you. If you follow Jesus, Allah/Muhammad, Buddha, Ganesh, any and all Gods/Deities and gurus that bring you joy, have a totem or picture of them nearby as well. This helps you connect to divine love. Pictures and totems are not needed; you can always just invite your helpers and higher power to be present by asking. Do what feels best for you.

♦ You have your question written down, or have a voice recorder ready as you are trusting and preparing to receive your answer. No matter what the answer is, you are calm, open, and ready to receive.

♦ To quiet the mind, meditate! If you suck at silent meditation, use a meditation app (like insight timer, you can find me on there under Carrie Suwal) and listen to a free guided meditation (I have a quickie titled: 5 Minute Slow Down). This helps calm the mind and let it breathe, as you make space for your intuition to come through.

♦ Now let's begin. Your soul truth is woven with the fabric of love. To connect to your soul, let's connect to the love within you. Close your eyes and feel the love in your heart. Maybe it feels like self-love, or love for the planet or a partner, or family. It is all the same. It doesn't have to be directed at anyone, it can be general love. I want you to feel it. What does it feel like? Now expand it. Let it flow into your whole body and into your energy field.

♦ Now ask your question. Say it out loud or in your mind's eye. I choose to say it 3 times. This makes it clear and direct. Each time I say it I feel in alignment with the words of my question more deeply. Try saying it 3 times if you feel called to it.

- After asking, all you have to do is be open to receiving the answer, however it arrives. It is a process of surrender. You are surrendering to the answer that is within you, not seeking something outside of you. It comes through ease and gentleness, not forcefulness and fighting. After some time, journal or record your experience. If it was a feeling, thought, body sensation, or image, whatever it is, record it, without judgment. Then you can go to the next chapter to decipher the message.

Method #2: Triggered and Bull's-Eye:

Write down or record your question as you are going to receive an answer. This method is for when your symptom or pain is strong and triggers the fear vibration within you — anger, sadness, victim-mentality, pain, negativity, etc. You may be feeling tension around your question even by thinking about it. We need to start by diffusing this trigger and softening its power so you can be open to discovering its energetic roots.

- Let's not ignore this trigger. Instead, be aware of the greater picture (which does encompass this moment and how you feel). It's as if you have been focusing just on you and this experience. We are going to pan out, and see everything around you wherever you are. Now we pan out further, see the people and relationships in your life. Even further, see the country you are in. Even further, seeing all of the earth — the beautiful blues and greens, the city lights, and swirly clouds. This helps to shift your perspective and soften the power you give to this issue. As it can feel like it is your whole world, but that's just how you have chosen to perceive it and empower it. When you see the whole world, you can see a balance of love and fear, a sliding scale of suffering and joy. That same balance exists within you. Try and feel this balance within you. You exist within the whole world and universe. The whole world and universe exist within you.

◆ Let's begin. Take three deep breaths, remembering this is one aspect of your life you are asking about. It is not your entire world, it is not everything. It is one small part of a very big picture.

◆ Now ask your question out loud or in your mind's eye and patiently be open to receiving your answer. Surrender the mind to connect to your truth, to your answer.

◆ If you keep getting pulled into the fear of the mind, take another 3 deep breaths and ask again. Breathing reminds you of the gift of life which pulls you into gratitude and the love vibration.

◆ Once you have received your answer, write or record it and move on to the next chapter if you feel you need help interpreting it.

Method #3: Chaos and Communicate

This method is for when you are being crotch-kicked by life and your emotions. You may be super triggered, angry, panicked or in a chaotic environment where you need to figure out an answer now. You need to know which way to go on your path, or are in need of some heavy assistance. Essentially you are deep in the fear vibration and pain body. Now is the time for this method. Take a deep breath in. Smile. And exhale. You got this.

- We are going to jump right in. You ask your question once and receive your answer.

- If you are being too pulled into your environment and your feelings, follow up your question by saying: "What is the truth?" Say it a few times with confidence that the answer will be revealed to you. The truth is always here, always within you. Even when life is on full blast, you can still find your truth. You can feel it, it never leaves you. It's just deeper than all the BS of the mind, the heart, and your experiences. So ask yourself, "What is the truth?" until you feel it. Maybe it's a second of calm, or a deep inner knowing that you are a soul and not this body or this experience. You are a cosmic consciousness. Keep asking until you feel it. You will never be more ready to experience this truth than when you are in chaos. You need the truth now.

I can vouch that the chaos and communicate method works surprisingly well. I was choking to breathe in the middle of a panic attack, enthralled in the depths of darkness and anxiety, surrounded by complete fear. Usually, it takes a long time for me to come down and out of a panic attack, and I end up forcing myself to breathe because I get a huge headache, and feel like puking. But this time, I looked down at my palm, on it I had written the word "truth". I did it earlier in the day as I felt I was emotionally spiraling into a dark place. I saw this word while struggling to breathe. And I asked myself, "What is the truth?" The moment I asked, I felt it. I connected to it. That peace was still right here, inside of me. I could feel that panic was just an emotion, not who I was. My world was not falling apart, it was just a moment of deep emotion for a flicker of time. Suddenly, I could breathe and the panic stopped dead in its tracks. It takes courage to ask this question in a time of struggle, to step out of the process of fear and deep pain to ask a question. But it is usually all that is needed.

These 3 methods are great to come back to depending on where your mental and emotional state are at. It shows that you can discover and connect with your truth at any time. Our next chapter is all about deciphering your message to get the most meaning and clarity you can from what you just received.

Chapter 14

INTERPRETING THE SPIRIT

The language of spirit is expansive
Not singular like our thoughts
It can relay a wealth of wisdom through a single word

Y ou've asked and you've received. Now, what does it all mean?
You have been given the answer, the message from your soul.
Soul answers ignite a fire within, without burning you, even if
you've received nothing. Nothing is a profound "thing" we will
dissect. Maybe your intuitive answer feels dry and insignificant. Every
answer is meaningful and juicy. Extracting the juiciness comes
through the process of interpretation.

If you receive a grain of sand or a continent of information, it
does not matter. The symbolic meaning will reveal a novel of
intelligence. Symbolism speaks your intellectual language. Colors,
numbers, phrases, and smells are all unique to you and your
experiences. Symbolism packs a loaf of information into the small
slice of intel you get. When you have asked your question and written
down your answer, go piece by piece from beginning to end. The
order you received it in is the order for it to be interpreted in.

Here is how symbolism works in my unique language. I ask my
highest self: Why am I struggling with anxiety today? I see: a circus
elephant in a glittery purple and pink dress, sitting on a small wooden
stool. The elephant's eyes glaze over and I feel the emotion of
confusion stir within me.

I ask my intuition: Is there anything else? The colors the elephant is wearing change to red and blue, it now looks revitalized and strong. It stands on one leg, in a statue-like position. The feeling I get is drive, strength, and belief in oneself.

Now the fun part, breaking down the symbolism.

To me, an elephant relates to memories and how we carry our past. To you, an elephant could mean strength, fear, etc. A circus elephant means entrapment — being held against my will or feeling imprisoned and doing something just to please others. Seeing the feminine colors of spirit (purple/crown chakra) and love (pink/heart chakra) show that in these aspects of my past I am worn down and done with trying to impress others. My soul and my heart are no longer in it anymore (the lack of enthusiasm the elephant had). The elephant's clothes changed to wearing red and blue: red is how I am affected by my environment and others (red root energy center). Blue is how I express myself verbally and through my actions (blue throat chakra). I am still acting as I did in the past, responding to my environment in the same way, using my energy to be a show woman (elephant) in the circus.

This makes sense to me. I asked about a physical way I was feeling today and didn't know why. I am becoming aware that spiritually and through my emotional heart that I don't want to keep repeating old patterns of enslaving my authenticity. Yet I still do and speak in ways that reflect those old people-pleasing patterns. So moving forward, this message shows me it's time to break free of the self-imprisonment and be my truth.

Isn't this fun? It's decoding, only it doesn't require much work. The symbolic meaning is the first thing that comes to your mind. You see a pink rose, and your first thought is friendship. But then the logical mind kicks in and says, "I think to most people it is a color of romance and love, so maybe it means a romantic love." Go with your initial instinct. That is your body's natural response and truest meaning. Friendship is the message. Trust what you feel and receive before all else.

If you've asked a question and feel your answer is completely unrelated, connect the dots. Allow the connection to take place and trust that the message does make sense. Maybe you need to go through your interpretation again. Clarify and refine it until you have your "aha" moment and the puzzle piece fits. Another possibility is that it makes perfect sense, you just don't see it yet because your mind already has a story or an expected answer you have been telling yourself. This is where trust enters the room. You build your intuition through trusting it. It's okay to not fully agree right away, some of the information you are receiving is new and your conscious mind needs time to process and absorb it. In the meantime, just surrender and trust what shows up for you.

The grim reaper hacks off your foot with a rusty blade, blood pours out as you hobble away. What if something dark, scary, or negative arises from your intuition? Remember your intuition is rooted in love. That means the message you are receiving is coming from a place of love. Do not fear what arises for you; remember, it is symbolic. Death is an intuitive image I see often, as well as child birth. To me death signifies a death of unsupportive habits, or death of the ego. Birth may be a new job, relationship, or awareness. It is symbolic.

At times it can be literal, but that is rare and usually comes through a well-practiced intuitive. I ask my intuition: *What do I need to heal?* I see the word "acceptance" and it melts into a deeper word, "love", softening further into the word "peace", and finally evaporating into a field of calm emptiness. Your message can be experienced as if you are reading the words in a book, or seeing actual events like a movie. You can connect to your intuition with this same acuteness. Symbolic answers bring greater depth than a literal word or sentence. There is a feeling being conveyed, and feelings give us greater insight than words.

What if you are trying to connect to your intuition but keep getting stuck in your thoughts? The mental chatter: *Is this really going to work? I need to do so many things today, etc.* Even this is a message and it is up to you to interpret. For me, if I have these thoughts while asking my question, it means my life is too full. My mind is so busy, I can't even have a moment of silence when I am alone. It is a message that I need to slow down, practice self-care, meditate, create space, and be present. That is a pretty powerful message.

What if nothing comes through? If absolutely nothing is felt, seen, or experienced... Well, first this means you are a master meditator. Did a thought not even arise? A well-practiced meditator can arrive in this space of no thought after years of practice. Most likely, mental chatter did happen. Look at that chatter. What were your thoughts? There is a message here. Let's say you asked your intuition why your partner doesn't communicate well and you want guidance on this. You have a thought: *This is silly, my partner doesn't believe this intuitive stuff, nothing is happening.* There is your message to interpret. No, you did not get a message from your intuition, but your blocks that create a wall between you and the answer arose. Dissect it: *This is silly*: You don't value your intuition as you value your logic. *My partner doesn't believe in this intuitive stuff:* You are allowing your partner's beliefs to outshine your own beliefs. *Nothing is happening:* You are affirming that an answer will not come through; there is a feeling of this topic being a lost cause. This is an example, but an important awareness. Your thoughts can sabotage your wisdom from coming through. Listen to your thoughts so you can tackle these obstacles. Once that is done, you can take the next step to connect to the truth and go deeper in clarifying your answer.

Gliding through the galaxy as the stars disappear, the planets vanish, and the asteroids dematerialize. What is left in this endless void? Nothingness is discernible. If you ask a question or ask for healing and no thoughts or feelings arrive, nothing is a perceivable sensation. It can be a quiet place of peace, of disconnect from the world of experience. A profound message is waiting for you to interpret.

A magical encounter on your intuitive journey is a spirit guide revealing themselves to you. A guide is a reflection of you, but appears as a separate entity from you. You can confirm it is in fact a guide by asking: *Are you my guide?* And perceiving a yes or no. You could see a whimsical faerie and think *Wow, what a beautiful message for me to be playful and bring out my inner child!* But the faerie doesn't disappear from your inner sight. It's waiting for you to receive the message that it is in fact a guide and here to help you.

Once you meet a guide, they are always accessible to you. All you have to do is call on them when you need help. Whether that's physical help, healing, or guidance. They can appear as animals, plants, angels, ascended masters, Ganesh, Buddha, Jesus, aliens, unicorns, any and everything. They are messengers, bringing you guidance from your higher consciousness. The core of their message comes to you in how they appear. Any guide can show up for you no matter what your beliefs are. They are all a part of you as we are all collective consciousness. Jesus and Buddha have very different vibes and meanings. When I see Jesus, I know gentle healing from his sacred heart is about to burst on the scene. When Buddha appears, inner peace and surrender are crashing the party. Your guides can spontaneously show up when the mood is set and the time is right. You can also ask them to come forth and make themselves known to you. They can appear in real life (an animal, scrying), in your dreams, in an oracle (someone sends you a birthday card with an angel on the front), or through meditation and one of your extrasensory perceptions.

You have many guides. Many spirits and energies are supporting you and teaching you at all times in your life. In my energy healing sessions, I use my guides for all of the divination work I do. Divination is connecting with spirit and higher realms to access their gifts in our 3D reality. When I want to know the root cause of my pain or someone else's pain, I journey (a form of meditation) to my power animal and ask them to show me. They show me a scenario, and guide me through a carousel of events. It gives me a crystal clear idea of the cause and takes out any confusion or preconceived judgment my ego may have. Divination creates a distinction between thought and intuition. This is why I enjoy working with guides, because if my power animal shows me something, then I know 100% it is my intuition speaking. Guides are not necessary to use or connect to, but it is a fun avenue to venture down. Why not give it a go and see if you are ready to connect with one of your guides!

◇ Soul Alignment Exercise

Connect With A Guide

Create a sacred space:

Make sure you are in a quiet room, if it is dark that is better as it makes it easier to see with your third eye. Light a candle or incense. Create a small ceremony that has meaning for you.

Calm the mind:

Do a short meditation practice that you enjoy to help clear the mind of its chatter. Maybe a silent practice, or guided meditation.

Invite your guide:

It can be easy to meet one of your guides. Use a clear intention, and ask for which guide you would like to meet. It can be a power animal, healer guide, a teacher guide, an archangel, or ascended master. Choose whichever you feel called to meet at this time. State your intention to meet them, and close your eyes. Trust whatever appears! It may feel like your imagination, it may be a feeling, a knowing, or a visual.

Ask and receive:

Ask your guide a question. You can ask for your guide to show you the answer to your question (wanting to know the root cause of_____). Or simply ask for what they wish to share with you at this time.

Take all of your answers and experiences you've received from your question(s) in the previous chapter, as well as from the spirit guide exercise and interpret them now. I like to journal my response, as it is useful advice to read at a later time. You can record it as well. Go with your gut of what feels best to you symbolically and piece it all together. Once it is together, trust and accept that this is your truth.

Once you have your answer, there is often action that is needed to heal, to release, to strengthen or surrender. Whatever guidance comes through, if you follow it and see it through the eyes of love, it will create the quickest transition you are looking for. Trust, trust, trust. This is the root, and you have received the wisdom. Now you can take the action or non-action in the direction of your highest good.

Chapter 15

WEAVE THE TRUTH INTO EXISTENCE

To know holds no power
To be is evolutionary.

When I was just a cub, a trinity of giggling girls united. We would fill our days with secret passwords cryptanalysts couldn't dimple, tooth chipping uncooked pasta snacks, and code names of peace, love, and joy. Peace's buttery blonde hair highlighted her unruffled cyan blue eyes. Joy's chipper smile was unceasingly set to high beams. They called me love. My sparkling obsidian eyes reflected a wall-less world. Love shined like a carebear stare blasting from my fuzzy heart. Someday, my benighted beliefs would rival the cold winds of the world.

The practices you have been doing are funneling you to a deeper truth, your soul truth, within. Your intuition is feeding you information from your soul. As you receive this information through spirit, energy, and intuition, the next step is to create action based on these new discoveries. You can be told 20 times a day by your intuition that you need to stop smoking. Your intuition tells you it is a reflection of poor self-love and that you are sabotaging yourself. It tells you that you are deserving of love and health, that you deserve self-care in a gentle and compassionate way. Yet you don't do the self-work. You know the truth, but you continue to act outside of the truth. Lung cancer chars your lungs and great suffering is experienced. This is an extreme example, but a common one nonetheless.

You must be the truth. To be your truth takes action and action takes courage. It takes courage to say: *Okay, I am deserving of happiness and thriving. I know what I have to do. And I'm going to do it, no matter the difficulty.* It takes courage to change a lifetime of habits and a family lineage of suffering. It takes courage to take back your power as the conscious creator of your life. To own that responsibility can feel heavy and painful. It forces us to step out of the fear vibration of being a victim: *Why me? Poor me. There is nothing I can do.* And step into ownership: *Yes, my past was hard. But I'm here in this moment and I am going to do things differently. I am going to see things differently. I am going to be my truth and live my highest potential.*

Your intuition is not guiding you to becoming a "brand new" person that you create. The creation is actually a disassembly of the old you, the you that you have become through experiences and choice. The you that you are becoming is the you that you have always been, the purest you. You are not sculpting a Barbie with the dreamy mansion and pink convertible. You are allowing your true and authentic self to rise from the ashes of the lies you've burned away. No longer will your highest potential be a hope or a concept. Your intuition tells you it is your truth and you can live from it. You could question it until the day of your death, having never given it a shot and never allowing yourself to live from this untapped potential. But why not just take the action? You will know that if it brings you joy, it is aligning you with your truth.

Once aligned, your words can come from your soul, from pure love. Your actions come from your soul, from pure love. Your thoughts come from your soul, from pure love. You can be that with which you are, pure love. You can share who you are with the planet, this pure love. Why do we sabotage this truth and revert to fear? We hold on to pain and suffering and continue to feed it, even though our intuition is saying: *Let go, stop feeding the fear, stop stroking the ego.*

It comes down to choice. We get to integrate our consciousness in a decision. We have all of the information we need. And it breaks down into this question: Do I choose love or do I choose fear?

When we choose love, everything aligns — everything heals, and everything becomes balanced within. We can never control our external environment. But if we can live from love within, the external world does not matter. We are at peace, always. This question of love and fear seems so easy, but it's not. There is a natural pull towards fear, to staying in our darkness and pain. We can find comfort in it. We find connection to others through our pain. We identify and believe we are pain. Our family lineage can cling to trauma and fear, and these beliefs wrap into our way of being.

I'm telling you, and your intuition is telling you: You are not fear. You are love. When you identify with fear, you suffer. When you identify with love, you flourish, because you are finally allowing your truth to flow through your body and into the world. Fear pulls you out of alignment and blocks the natural flow of bliss.

In the past, I have been very intimidated by strong people who speak their ego and fear vibration loudly. The people who feel like they own the world, are entitled and always right, and I was a soggy dish cloth standing next to them. I would curl up in a ball and feel myself being compressed. This was me giving into my own fear vibration. Fear of not being accepted, fear of not being heard, and fear of being told I was wrong and unworthy of my opinion. I would avoid these people, or cringe when I knew I was going to have to interact with them.

I was not being the love vibration; it was not my soul's truth. I knew this within. I knew they were in my life for a reason and I was continually giving in to the same fear-based patterns. One day I chose to stand in my truth, in the vibration of love. I was not afraid to speak my truth, even when it opposed their views. I loved them even when they did not show me compassion. Since making this decision to stand in my love vibration and not give in to the fear, I have noticed our conversations change. I am showing up, I get to be a part of the discussion, and what a wonderful thing to introduce some light to a dark room. It required courage on my part. I know these relationships were essential in my life, for me to be able to step into love where love was missing.

The fear and darkness is here to help you discover your truth. It is essential to your soul growth. Whatever you discover through your intuition, if you listen and do the work, you are aligning with your soul and highest potential. When you don't listen and don't do the work, you will struggle, suffer, and feel lost. You become derailed, and your soul is going to do everything it can to try and pull you back. Be strong, you have it in you. Decide, believe, trust, and be. It is you, and you deserve to feel whole, happy, and healthy. When you choose your loving truth, you are unshakeable like rail wheels on the train tracks.

It took Natalie, a fellow energy healer, time and injuries to accept her highest potential. In her early 20s, she began questioning her go-go-go party life, and asking herself if she was ready to trade it in for a more centered and healthier life. She asks her intuition: *What is my next step to reach my highest potential?* A magnetic force directs her to the rugged mountains of Banff, Canada. She begins working long hours and continues to party her blues away. Her meditation cushion starts collecting dust bunnies, and making its way further and further into the back of her closet. Natalie's long blonde hair flies in the wind as she snowboards the slopes, and she takes a terrible tumble. Tangled and concussed, she became dizzy and exhausted. She pushes down her post concussion symptoms, and carries on with her quick highs of the party life.

Skateboarding down the gyrused paved road, she gazes up at the mountains in awe. "Fppt", her toe catches on a rock and she stumbles face first into the pavement. The pavement left her with a purple eye, a cramping jaw and headaches for months. Natalie pushes herself back to work in only two weeks, and grants her racing mind passive permission to block her intuitive messages telling her to slow down. This second concussion forces Natalie into a chronic state of stress.

This gale force of stress triggers an autoimmune disease in her body. Her itchy skin and face rash from her autoimmune disease strips her ego of its prideful beauty. The imminent decomposition of her body is suffocating.

A gut-wrenching cry from within gasps, *No more!* Natalie begins to connect with her intuition, and listen. She is guided to quit her job, and move to a quieter workspace. She shifts her focus to her health, and feels it returning to her.

At her new job, a gigantic steel pot falls from on top of the fridge and clunks Natalie in the head. A third concussion! She takes off 4 months from work. Her inner knowing tells her that this is the last straw, it is time to really listen. She becomes vegan, gluten-free, and rocks a powerful solar plexus after claiming her body back. She clears her brain fog, and begins connecting with her higher self. Natalie knows her angels are with her and she can finally hear them. She accesses a new sense of inner peace during these four months of slowing down. After this healing journey, she steps into her own shoes as a healer, and lets her concussive journey be a warning to others who are dismissive of their own intuition.

Healing is not a bland journey. It can be difficult and wrenching, or it can be pillowy and gentle. It will manifest how it needs to for you to align with your true self and listen to the messages of your intuition.

◇ **Soul Alignment Exercise**

Choosing Love Or Fear

Giving in to fear:

> Reflect on a time in the past you gave in to the vibration of fear or ego. What decision was made and how did you feel after?

Giving in to love:

> Reflect on a time in the past you gave in to the vibration of love and your higher self. What decision was made and how did you feel after?

Choosing between love and fear:

> With a current issue, reflect on the love and the fear vibration. Does the fear vibration or fearful action feel in alignment with your soul or is it stemming from your ego and your shadow self? Is it in your best interest to act from fear? What about love, what would the decision and actions from love look like? Is that from your soul, or ego? And is it in your best interest to act from love?

Chapter 16

EXTERNAL FORCES IMPEDING THE FLOW

In the end, we are all seeking love.

The lotus flower radiantly blooms each morning, rising from a slew of mud. The mud does not deter the lotus' radiance. The lotus holds true in its beauty and stands strong in its essence.

With exhausted eyes from too much sleep, I toss in my bed loathing to get up. *I want to live a more joyful life, but it's not possible. I think suffering is the purpose of life.* Many salty tears later I stepped out of this torturing belief system. A side effect of living through the pain body is that we tend to think people and the universe are working against us and want us to fail.

You have the power to feel how you desire, that is within you, not external.

Consider a scenario where you and a co-worker are competing for a promotion within the same company. Your co-worker receives the promotion. Begrudgingly sour unworthiness swirls in the pit of your stomach. You feel undercut by the company and not good enough, this is your chosen perception. The other candidate may have been better suited for the position, and this occurrence is freeing you to receive a grander opportunity that is in greater alignment with you. It can be difficult to open yourself up to a better opportunity when you are stuck in the "poor me" mentality instead of an optimistic grateful mentality.

When the "poor me" mentality is activated, you begin to feed the belief system that "I am not good enough, I always get the short hand, life just sucks, I'm over it." You then attract experiences that are in alignment with your beliefs. You attract a job that you are not happy about, you attract relationships where you feel under-appreciated, and your confidence flattens. When in an optimistic and grateful state, you become hopeful that there is something greater for you. You not getting this promotion does not mean you are unworthy, it means this opportunity was not meant to be for you. It means you are preparing for a greater opportunity to arrive. Can you see how the choice of how you perceive things affects your enjoyment of life?

In middle school my pubescent pimples and flat chest give me a deflated tire of confidence. I walk behind the new student Reagan with my head held high as I throw pieces of muffin in her hair. I actually like Reagan as a person, but my friends began making fun of her, so I think I will gain popularity by being a bully. People who are stuck in their pain bodies (suffering) can intentionally try to bring you down. The truth is that they have been inflicting self-pain for so long that now they do not know the path of compassion, much less how to share it with others. Instead, they push the domino of pain onto the next person because that is their reality. That is the truth they have chosen to accept and the energy they put out to the world. We have all done this, operated from this place and might be doing it now. It is not you against the world, it is you against yourself. When you are fighting yourself, you deflect your hardships onto others. This is why hurt people hurt people.

You can affect another's energy. This means they, too, can affect yours. When someone thinks negatively about you, that energy is directed towards you. A gloomy naysayer vacuums up your energy with their suckiness. They can be so strong in their negativity that they easily pull you into their mucky vibrational state. Through belief, you are allowing this person to affect your energy. You have given them the power to manipulate your energy field. The same goes for curses, voodoo, and bullying. Maybe you, too, have wished ill will on a fellow human: *I hope her big head throws her off balance and she falls down the stairs!* It is clear that to wish harm or suffering on someone is operating out of the fear vibration, right? Whether it's you or another sending bad intentions, hurtful words, or actions, it is not in alignment with love and your soul's truth.

Can these actions, words, and energies thrown at you from others actually create negative energy in your life? Can it be the root cause of your pain and suffering?

You are a conscious creator and you choose your life. You choose how you charge your energy. You choose how you react. You also choose if you want to be affected by others or not. If you believe others can shift your energy and mood negatively, you will grow a thick skin of protection. Protecting yourself means you are living in fear of being hurt by others at all times, when in fact, you are the one imposing your own suffering, not someone else. Suffering is self-created. It is your choice in how things affect you. When you are in the vibration of fear, you are susceptible to being affected by others. You are in fact attracting and perpetuating it, because your thoughts and emotions are focused on the worst case scenario.

Energy responds to intention and thought. You can heal others by being your highest self. You teach those who are struggling by showing them the way. They need to see that it is within them, and that they, too, can live from this space of pure potential. Your energy supports them in making this choice. Just as a negative person has rubbed off their muck on you, you can rub off your effervescence onto them. All you have to do is access the vibration of joy within yourself and stand strong in it. Others will raise their vibration to meet you in your peaceful frequency. Instead of you lowering your vibration to someone who is in their fear and suffering, you can lift them up, or give them the option to raise their vibration simply by holding space for your own energy to shine.

When you are in the space of love, there is no need for protection because you know you are love. You know joy, peace, freedom, and health are within you. It is your truth and it is a state available to you at all times. You become unaffected by others' energies, thoughts, and actions. When you look at others through the eyes of love, all you see is compassion for their pain and suffering. You can see the bad vibes they are flicking onto others as an extension of their pain body. Your truth knows those bad vibes are not yours and you will not pick up the negative energy that has been sent to you. Your energy can be as strong as a cinder block that remains still on a windy day.

The only responsibility you have is to accept those who wish you harm. Acceptance is in the slipstream of unconditional love. It is miles closer to your soul truth than hatred. Imagine accepting your enemy, and saying: *It's okay. I see you are hurting. I wish nothing but love for you. I accept you.* This is the path of love.

Usually, we fight fear with fear. We feel unloved and not accepted when someone wishes us harm. We get angry, sad, and flustered. We hurtle arrows of ill wishes back to them, thinking negative thoughts about the person or group. When you can stand back and look at this process, it is so easy to see its flaws. You are accepting the fear they have sent to you and you absorb it. You take it on and it feels crushing and icky. It magnifies your insecurities and fears. You pick up their pattern and do exactly what they have done to you. They then absorb it, take it on and send it back, propagating a never-ending cycle.

The person wishing harm to you is one of the deepest blessings in your life. They are giving you an opportunity to live from your heart. The unconditional love of the soul holds no conditions. To fight fire with fire (fear with fear) is useless, it does nothing. It makes the fire burn more strongly, intensifying the fear. To fight fear with love, now that works. The person may not be ready to accept being accepted, or to be loved when they are in a dark place. It can be your way of showing them the way, of showing them they can choose love.

When you choose love, you free yourself from taking on their fear or perpetuating your own fear.

A few years ago, after my psychopomp training (helping suffering spirits transition to the other side who get stuck on the Earth plane), I decided to put my new ghost-busting skills to work. I tiptoe through my father's creaky old home at night time without the lights on. I make my way through the orange shaggy carpet in the drafty basement and see a frightening figure through my third eye. A bead of sweat runs down my forehead, her long brown hair drapes over her face in her torn white nightgown. I am scared shitless (definitely not in the love vibration). I try persuading her to cross over, but she just won't go. She follows me home to the mountains, hours away. Every time I close my eyes to sleep, she is right there beside me. I awake to do my morning meditation, and she is sitting by my side. Boy oh boy, it was a scary and daunting time! The fear keeps building inside of me as she just won't budge. She is just going to be a part of my life now, like a conjoined twin. She was essential in teaching me an invaluable lesson. This work has to be done from love. If fear is involved, then I am just adding gasoline to the fear fire and no spirit is going to shift when I am being a hypocrite. I am preaching that suffering spirits deserve unconditional love, when here I am shaking in my knickers.

I contact an extended family member who also does this work with spirits, she tells me I need to invite God in, to help me do this work. God? My forehead wrinkles. I have never used the word God before. I contemplate the word to discover its meaning and I find pure love in its most potent form. I attempt the ghost-busting work for another round, curious about this new approach. I speak with this spirit, but this time, I give her a big teddy bear hug as she tries to bite me. I connect with the loving force of God and I love her as she is. I love her even though she looks petrifying and is trying to frighten me. Low and behold, she finally crosses over, because I showed her that she is deserving of love, she is worthy, and it's time for her to receive this love in its fullness. Only when I was facing the deepest fear vibration I had ever known, and brought in pure love at its greatest potency (God), instantly the fear (suffering) shifted.

Working with spirits has been such a blessing, because I get to stand in the face of complete fear and darkness of a being who is truly suffering. I stand in front of a soul who is having a really hard time and trying to pull me into their space of darkness with them, and I say *no. No, I will not go there with you. I will hold you in love. I will embrace you. I will show you that you are worthy of love. And then when you are ready, we can go back to your source, back to love.* They always go. Because it feels so good to be loved. It's hard to say no to love.

Another type of draining person is an energy vampire. *Sandra from accounting pulls out her fangs and drains all your blood as she endlessly lags on about her cat's constipation problems.* Energy vampires don't intentionally drain your positivity with their negativity. You believe they have the power to drain you and so they do. You allow your energy to be gobbled up. It's not like your energy is actually feeding them and making them stronger. You are just burning it like it's a limited resource. This is true if you believe it to be true. I know I am super guilty of thinking people are draining and exhausting me, thinking they are unconsciously sucking my healthy qi and draining me to a point of illness and exhaustion. This is the lie I have told myself to accept as a truth, and so it became my truth. I began struggling more and more in large crowds and in social groups, all because of what I told myself was happening.

Energy moves how it is directed to move. When I connect to the greatest truth, all I see is love, love within all beings. Sure, fear is there too, floating like dead logs on a river. But at our core we are all love, we are the river. I had been choosing to ignore that when I was in a group of people. I chose to cling to the fear vibration and let it drag me down, instead of being uplifted by the love that is always present. It's one I'll be working on for a while because I have told myself this story of people exhausting me for so long that I began to believe it. Now I need to un-write the script and go for the truth, the love that is within all, and allow it to flow around me and uplift me.

Right now, I am aligning with this intention and truth: *It brings me joy to be around others. I feel more connected to love when I am with others.* This intention feels good to me, and I am starting to get excited about being around others once again.

Is it impolite to not feel pain when others are struggling? Crutching someone's pain by taking it on lowers your vibrancy. Instead, support them by holding impeccable space for their suffering. If they are ready to desist their suffering, you can show them the way to end it through the action of being. Your vibration spills over onto everyone around you. It does not have to drain your vital life force; do not think of it as giving all your good vibes away. You will lose your good qi at the cost of helping others. If you feed the belief that others can take your energy, it is slapping a band-aid on their burst pipe. Healing flows temporarily because nothing has changed from within them.

Here is the truth: Energy is everywhere and in everything. Energy can feel good or bad. But at its base structure, it is all the same. You have the power to feel full and overflowing with energy at all times — you just need to realize it. When you believe it is limited and you can be exhausted by others then that's exactly what happens. When you believe it is unlimited and always available, it is. Energy moves and forms based on your feelings, intentions, and thoughts. So choose your thoughts, feel your feelings, and speak the intentions that reflect what you desire.

◇ Soul Alignment Exercise

Intention Setting

Try this intention exercise. These intentions are coming from a space of truth, and if they don't feel true for you don't use them, create your own. Say the intention out loud, feel it, and know that you are molding energy into creation. You are attracting and creating.

- I am energy. I am love. All is love.

- My heart is open. I live in love. I love all beings and energies.

- I am constantly abundantly full of all the energy I need to thrive.

Chapter 17

YOU'VE CHANGED AND GROWN
BUT STILL SUFFER

Healing is not always as we envision
It takes many forms and will often break belief systems
For us to truly find our joy.

Depression bombards my life like a nagging aunt extending her visit. I want her to leave, but she's my blood, I have to accept and care for her. Each time she visits I ask my intuition what is the gift? Every "visit" presents a new challenge and gift. So far, the gifts include self-discovery, self-care, acceptance, and self-love. As I overcome each hurdle, the depression evaporates. She keeps returning, each time bringing me a new gift to unwrap. Even though her visits are arduous and long, I am grateful.

You've asked your intuition: *What is the root cause?* You've listened to the wisdom that came through. You have created the changes your energy body has asked of you. What if your symptoms (pain, sickness, mental dysfunction, and suffering) still exist?

Just like pulling a plant from its roots out of the earth, the plant can take time to die. Not all shifts are instantaneous. If you have healed the root of your wound, and the body is still showing signs of dysfunction, there is another lesson to be discovered. The slow consistent effort of the tortoise still pays off as it stretches its neck across the finish line. Patience requires trust, which is a powerful lesson of love. If you stay positive in the process as you wait for your body's links to your imbalance to die, you have truly embraced the process and stepped into that soul truth of love. If you continue feeding it with fear and resentful thoughts, then you are continuing to nurture the plant that is trying to die. The thoughts can sound like: *It isn't working, I'll never get better, why am I not healed yet,* etc. These will delay the healing and plant more seeds of suffering that will manifest in new ways.

Stay in the vibration of love even if you are still struggling; this dilutes the weight of your suffering. When you live with pain or suffering for a long time, you can begin to accept it as "just how it is", or "who I am." It can feel impossible to imagine a life of health and wellness, a life where you are happy and whole. This creates a pessimistic viewpoint where you do not heal because you do not believe you can heal, thus limiting your body's potential to heal through your own beliefs and thoughts. It is the law of attraction: what you think, you attract and become. You are creating more suffering and unhealthy energy because it is what you give power to. Stop standing in your own way of health. Substitute those beliefs with loving ones: "I am healing, I am whole, I am healthy."

You can become attached to your pain body like a clingy tween and their first puppy love. I am guilty of this one myself. My pain has given me permission to do great self-care, by getting massages and energy treatments. This made it easy for me to see my pain as a positive reason to pamper myself. To allow this pain to heal, I had to restructure my beliefs about what being healthy means. It doesn't mean I can't do self-care and get massages and treatments anymore, it just means they will have a different purpose. We all know puppy love includes lots of drama filled with highs and lows. Stop settling for a soap opera life, and go after the fairytale. Unless you like the drama. I prefer blissful ease.

People smiled at Monica as they held the door for her, this kept her limping long after she already healed. People sympathize and connect with you through your pain. You can feel important and cared for. If you connect to your true nature, you know life will be gleeful and effortless when you are healthy. We create excuses to hold on to the comfort of our discomfort. Check in with yourself. Are you ready to heal? Life <u>WILL</u> change. Are you ready for these changes? Have you accepted that you are deserving of thriving? It's time to embrace your darkness in a gravitational hug before it submerges 6 feet underground.

These are some causes as to why the pain or illness has lingered. But the only way to truly know the root cause of why (even though you've addressed the initial reason) is to check in with your intuition once again, to ask your higher self why and what can be done or learned so you can move forward. It is possible that there are layers, and once you have addressed your initial cause, there may be more gifts from this suffering, waiting to be discovered.

The hardest lesson is when your soul wants you to accept your pain body. If your soul is saying you must learn acceptance of your condition, that means you need to be okay with this grueling question: What if I never heal? Can I accept myself as I am? This guides you into a deeper state of love. Unconditional, as you are. When you find that space of deep love for yourself, one of two things will happen. Your condition will heal, or it will stay to consistently keep you in the vibration of love and acceptance. Both are blessings, and however it unfolds is always for your highest good. Trust the process that wherever it takes you, you will be in greater alignment with your truest self and the vibration of love. If you have a mental disability but are a two stepping happy camper, are you broken, or somehow not whole?

I have been blessed with struggling through all of these lessons from my car accident. I have fallen into dark pessimism many times over the years: *I am never going to heal; I am just a person who will always have neck pain.* My pain intensified because I fed it with so much fear. Once I became cognizant of how I was clinging to my pain, I began influencing my thoughts with love: *I accept this pain. This is my life in this moment. Maybe it will be here forever, maybe it will only be here today, however long it stays I accept it.* That statement was a hard pill to swallow, but when I finally believed it, my pain began to soften and release. The final gift I received from my chronic pain was to feel worthy enough to express myself. Once I believed in myself enough to write this book the pain was freed from my body. It gifted my life in so many ways, teaching me forgiveness, love, acceptance, and trust. I healed and became pain free, because I received all I could from it, every last tasty drop.

When you think pessimistic thoughts and get in the mode of *poor me, this sucks,* you are not helping yourself to heal. You are adding ice cubes to your soup, hoping it gets warmer. You are ruining the beauty of life, by creating a story and sabotaging the gratitude of all the good things that are unfolding. You are not allowing yourself to feel the warmth of joy and peace in every moment.

The pain body can be very overwhelming, and at times you may need support. It can be difficult to listen to your own intuition when you are emotionally enthralled in your pain and easily triggered. Don't get discouraged. There are people who can help you, you are not alone. Energy and spiritual therapists do this work for a living. By not knowing you personally, they have an outside perspective that makes it easier to differentiate between intuition and thoughts. When people come to me and I share what their energy tells me, 95% of the time it is not news to them. They are not surprised because deep down they know this truth, their intuition already knows what needs to be done. It just has not been honored through belief and action. When you hear it from another person (especially a stranger), you realize: *Oh, I wasn't imagining it. It is the truth, that was my intuition speaking and not my mind making things up.* Energy workers help heal the body by transitioning unsupportive energies and even root causes out of your system. Rarely is the cause solely energetic. It almost always has a conscious connection, something we need to take ownership of in an active non-passive way. True healing happens within you and from you. A healer simply facilitates that healing and helps to consciously guide you in your own self-healing. They can shift energy, help heal wounds, amplify good energy (your soul's loving essence), and remove blockages. Things shift only when you are ready. You must be ready to make conscious shifts in your beliefs, change your actions, or let things go. If you have made the changes and the energy lingers, it is easy work for a healer to help the stagnant energy shift.

When I go for energetic work, I go when I'm in a really dark place, a fear-based place, and need support. Energy healing offers that loving vibration to help me through. Talk therapy, physical therapy, and medical treatments all help support us on our journey of healing. I have benefited immensely from every single one of these supports. But energy work helps you connect to that root cause, to go directly to the truth and not just address the physical symptoms. This is how you can create lasting change.

♢ Soul Alignment Exercise

Branching Out In Your Healing

Intuitive investigation:

> Ask what your pain body wants you to do or learn in order to heal.

Be a fighter:

> Be strong. Don't just hope, but *know* you can heal. Or accept your struggles with unconditional love as you are. Both paths are a win. Feel into what is in alignment with your soul right now. It is also possible you are needing to walk both paths of acceptance and change at the same time. feel into this possibility.

See yourself healed, full, and whole:

> Feel it in your body. Feel it right now. This is a potential, a reality. Allow it in, allow yourself to heal.

Seek support:

> Try energy healing and seeing an intuitive, or any other therapies you are called to do. If they make you feel good, then they are working.

Ask questions:

> If you are still feeling blocked in your healing and having difficulty shifting your imbalances, ask your blockage: What do you need to heal? And offer it whatever it asks of you. I know what it will say, as it's always the same thing, but I'll let you ask and find out for yourself. If you don't connect with this answer, I will share it at the beginning of the next chapter.

Chapter 18

MEDICATION, MEDITATION, AND MAGIC

What does your blockage need to heal?
Love, it wants to be loved.
That is all.

Indigo Love's patchouli-infused dreadlocks sway in front of her t-shirt like a beaded curtain, covering the words "Meditation Is My Medication." Indigo is harnessing a powerful tool within that sets my smile on full tilt. She is moving from the passenger seat to the driver seat by connecting her inner peace to her conscious mind and body. When you believe in something fully, you are super-charging it with active energy. The stronger your belief, the more potent your outcome. As soon as you sprinkle doubt into the mix, it waters down your results.

If you decide that meditation is the cure to your anxiety and overthinking, then meditation is the remedy. Your belief grows when logic and reason coincide with your chosen antidote. Mindfulness based stress reduction (mindfulness meditation) significantly decreases scores on the Hamilton Anxiety Scale (Hoge[8]). You can access mindfulness 24/7 like your secret ninja warrior on your

---

[8] Hoge, Elizabeth, et al. "Randomized Controlled Trial of Mindfulness Meditation for Generalized Anxiety Disorder: Effects on Anxiety and Stress Reactivity." *The Journal Of Clinical Psychiatry*, vol. 74, no. 8, 2013, pp. 786-792. *National Center for Biotechnology Information.*

shoulder, fighting stress and chaotic situations when the shit hits the fan. Mindfulness is meant to wander off the meditation cushion and into the real world. Your truth is what you empower it to be with your beliefs. Imagine living from a state of constant mindfulness. Bliss!

You can work solely with magic and find surprising results with your healing journey. Say you are feeling witchy and want to create a spell to cast out your headaches. When you get a stinging headache, you softly tap your 3rd eye intuitive center three times. With each tap you say: *Going, going, gone.* You believe whole-heartedly in this playful ritual, and on your third tap, "poof" it disappears. Some would call it witchcraft or magic; others call it the placebo effect. I call this you being a conscious creator and choosing to rid yourself of your headache.

A 2014 study led by Kaptchuk and published in *Science Translational Medicine* explored the placebo effect on migraines. One group took a migraine drug labeled with the drug's name, another took a placebo labeled **PLACEBO**, and the third took nothing. The research found that the placebo accounted for more than 50% of the drug effect when compared to the group receiving no-treatment (Kaptchuk[9]). Which is surprising considering they knew it was a placebo all along. The research speculated that a driving force behind this reaction was the simple act of taking a pill. "People associate the ritual of taking medicine as a positive healing effect. Even if they know it's not medicine, the action itself can stimulate the brain into thinking the body is being healed", said Kaptchuk. This means that ritual and creating a practice that you believe to heal you will assist in healing you, even if there is no science backing it up.

I've always had a bitter taste towards pharmaceuticals. *They are unnecessary, packed with toxic chemicals, riddled with side effects, I can heal myself without them,* I told myself. I was hanging out with depression for a year, like an annoying roommate I couldn't evict. I was accepting it

---

[9] Kaptchuk, Ted. "The power of the placebo effect." *Harvard Health*, 13 December 2021, https://www.health.harvard.edu/mental-health/the-power-of-the-placebo-effect. Accessed 8 May 2022.

fully, and finding contentment in the process. My grandma checks in on me, and in her melodious sweet voice says: "I'm worried about you, you need to take an antidepressant, I don't want you suffering for no good reason." I get deeply triggered, and cry like a toddler having their blankie being ripped away. My reaction is so blown up, I sit with the discomfort and realize my intuition is guiding me towards antidepressants. This is why I was triggered, because I was denying that guidance based on my beliefs around the pharmaceutical industry. I knew that going this route would only work if I believed in it.

I purchase the pills, and place them in a crystal grid. Hovering my hands over them I infuse them with loving thoughts of health and happiness. I color the words JOY, LOVE, PEACE, HEALTH on a placard and place it in front of the pills. I am infusing the pharmaceuticals with healing energy, thoughts, and belief. Each morning I swallow the pills using feelingization. Over time my depression heals and the peace, joy, love and health become my reality. Sometimes intuition takes your healing journey through unwanted terrain because it's what you need for your soul growth.

Pharmaceuticals are created with the intent to heal. They can bring a buffet of side effects, but if it heals and supports you, the benefits may outweigh the risks. What happens when we take a pharmaceutical and tell ourselves: *this is toxic, this is harming me, I'm only taking it because society pressures me to?* You are not helping to empower its healing potential. When you ingest anything in your body, whatever effect you believe it will create, that is the energy you are ingesting. So when taking a pharmaceutical, don't disempower the healing property and empower the side effects. Check yourself, check your thoughts, feelings, and intentions around it. Employ it to heal you with no side effects, only radiant health. Your mind releases endorphins that combat sickness and side effects when you choose to be positive. You are giving yourself a real chance at true recovery when your beliefs are backing the medicine you work with.

No matter which path of healing you choose — medication, meditation, a witch's brew, or all three together — know that it will create healing. Knowing is a combination of belief, trust, and truth. It is trusting that the power of belief works. It is tuning into a deep truth within your body that you can live a healthy and happy life. You are the ultimate creator, and you can create health and happiness simply with intention.

One of my favorite stories is that of my friend Genevieve. Her mother Chantal is a bit of an oddball who colors outside of the lines. Chantal would always tell Gen, "You can create anything you desire as long as you truly believe it and create it in your mind first." Chantal was skillful at creating her reality from finely sculpted thoughts.

At six years old, Gen began scratching her arms and getting the sniffles around cats. Chantal decides to do an experiment and apply her method with her daughter. She cleverly tells Gen that she knows of a medicine that cures cat allergies, but that this medicine only works for children who are seven years and older. Genevieve is excited because her seventh birthday is just a few months away. Months pass by, and Chantal continues convincing Gen that this allergy will disappear on her birthday. Finally the special birthday arrives and Chantal gives her a card with a cat in a party hat on the front. Gen opens the card and finds a pink pill inside. She takes the sugar pill with an eager smile on her face, and Chantal congratulates her for no longer being allergic to cats. From that moment on Gen was burying her face into the fuzziest of cats she could find, allergy-free.

Chantal told Gen about the cat experiment years later. The idea that the power of belief can change the chemistry of your brain and body stuck with Genevieve for the rest of her life. Gen has since created several cellular changes with the power of her thoughts.

At 19 years old, Gen's arms flail as she awkwardly falls and wedges her ankle between a rock and an ice chunk. The fall shatters both malleoli bones on the sides of her ankle. Her doctor informs her that they need to operate and insert a metal plate in her ankle. The healing time after the operation will be 6 weeks minimum, and up to a year for a full recovery. Gen is not satisfied with this treatment plan for her injury as she planned and paid for a trip to China 4 weeks from now. She politely informs the doctor that she will not be moving forward with the operation. The doctor warns her that her foot may never be the same, and that she could suffer greatly in the future. She is convinced of the power of visualization and decides to go home and heal herself. She spends the next 4 weeks in her bed meditating and convincing her mind that she is going to have a perfect recovery and her ankle will heal to be better than new. She sits up in her bed and waves her hands over her ankle, sending it healing energy. She feels a tingling sensation as fragments of bones mend harmoniously back together. She records herself speaking words of affirmation to assist in the healing. Replaying the tape over and over until she falls asleep. Words like: "The bones in my left ankle are mending back together. I feel the accelerated healing that is happening every single moment. My blood cells are working to repair the bones. I am powerful beyond measure. I choose to heal now. Thank you body, I am infinitely grateful to you."

Four weeks later ,she walks into the clinic to have an x-ray taken of her ankle. The doctor drops his jaw in complete shock. He cannot believe it, but the bones have healed perfectly and quickly without the operation. In four weeks she went from having two broken bones on the verge of an operation that would take months to fully recover, to skipping through an airport in Hong Kong. Her mom was right — you can create anything you desire, as long as you truly believe it and create it within your mind first. Genevieve is in sync with the law of attraction. She created a template of recovery in her mind. She asked for and received the healing that she requested.

Gen's story reminds us of the miraculous power of our intentions. Many people heal simply through the power of their mind, visualization, and belief. What is required is true belief. Not to just say to yourself *I am healing*, but to feel it, believe it, and know it. Our bodies are capable of so much more than we give them credit for, and they are bursting with life force energy that wants to be utilized for health.

Healing can only take place when someone is ready to be healed. When a client shows up, I first feel the imbalances in their energy field. I shift them by directing their energy through intention. On rare occasions it will be stuck, like a stubborn horse. This happens when they are clinging to their pain and not ready to let go, or do not believe they can be healed and healthy. We cannot move forward until they decide they are ready, worthy, and that healing is possible.

Shannon has been waking up with an electric headache cutting behind her eyes all week. Each day, she pops a few extra strength Tylenols, and muscles her way through her jam-packed schedule. In contrast, instead of popping a pill when I have neck pain that fizzes into a headache, I sit with the discomfort and ask my body what it needs to heal. It's either stress reduction, emotional healing, or stretching. This is the great debate of holistic versus pharmaceutical medicine. It can be difficult for people who subscribe to the natural way to see a loved one avoid the root cause of their pain and numb it with pharmaceuticals. On the opposite side, it's difficult for loved ones to watch health fanatics deny pharmaceutical medicine and continue struggling in their pain body. They are afraid to lose their wheatgrass friend to a serious illness because of their stubbornness to Western medicine. Judgment is a fear-based vibration that works both ways. We are not supporting our loved ones and their path of healing when we are judging their approach to their health. By doubting the choices of another, we are subtracting the efficacy of their medicine and healing. Even if you disagree, believe. Believe in the power of their belief. This is the greatest way to support someone in their healing. Then you are a part of the solution, and an active healer in their wellness, no matter which side of the fence you are on. We all want each other to do well, be happy and healthy. Who am I to say one medicine works and another does not? All medicine works to support our healing if we believe in them.

If you discover the root and are able to heal it, this does not mean you need medicine. But you may want extra support on your healing passage. Any medicine (be it medication, meditation, or magic) is a support to help align you mentally, physically, and consciously with your whole soul.

♢ **Soul Alignment Exercise**

Healing With Intention

Reflect on this question:

Am I ready to heal?

The power of belief:

You must commit to the power of belief in the medicine you choose for it to fully work. Can you fully commit to believing in your choice of medicine?

The water exercise:

Find your favorite glass or mug and fill it with water. Before drinking this water, hold the cup in your hands and close your eyes. I want you to decide that this water will heal you. Believe it. Envision and feel the health, fullness, and way you want to feel. Feel it in your body. If you want to feel wealthy, happy, or healthy, there is a feeling associated with those desired outcomes. Feel it now. And know that this feeling is transmitting the medicine to allow you to feel this way into the water. Then drink it slowly. As you sip it, feel that good feeling intensely as it enters your body, through the mouth, the throat, and the blood, filling every part of you. Do this every day for 11 days and see what positive shifts it has helped to create in your life.

Chapter 19

THE HIGHER SELF

On your journey,
you are constantly looking forward to the destination
Yet every moment is the destination
You have arrived.

A t age 15, his gold and maroon robe sways warily as he is informed Chinese soldiers are raiding a Tibetan post. The 14th Dalai Lama is given full political authority and left to fight a battle with Tibet's 8,500 soldiers against the Godzilla of China's force. Foreign countries reject Tibet's desperate plea for support, and The Dalai Lama is exiled to India to escape certain death. 1.2 million Tibetans are killed, 6000 monasteries burned, and thousands imprisoned (Baker[10]). This savage invasion did not stop His Holiness from living a fulfilling and joyful life. This grown giggling man shows us that wholeness is accessible to people who have endured unimaginable suffering.

You can be an unconscious creator, a conscious creator, or a conscious being. The unconscious creator gets stuck in old patterns and dwells on the past. *I can't be happy. I am broken. I am not healing.* The conscious creator is day dreaming of a better future. *I will be happy, I will be healthy, I will be rich.* The conscious being is living their dreams now, not waiting for something to arrive in their external world to

---

[10] BAKER, SUE. "Exiled Tibetans say 1.2 million killed during Chinese rule." *UPI*, 17 September 1984, https://www.upi.com/Archives/1984/09/17/Exiled-Tibetans-say-12-million-killed-during-Chinese-rule/9452464241600/. Accessed 17 May 2022.

give them permission to be happy. *I am happy. I am healthy. I am whole. Life is good.*

When I want to feel health, I take a full belly breath with a smile on my face. I feel freedom and gratitude. What is the feeling of health to you? You can feel it even if you are sitting in a full body cast, sipping a chunky smoothie from a straw. It takes a kick-ass warrior to decide to step outside of the rulebook and say: *No more rules, I'm doing what I want.* If you want to feel good, feel good. Be superhuman and just do it. No more procrastinating and feeding beliefs that leave you depleted and broken. Just be and feel whole, if you have the kahunas to live your dreams. Our dreams are not necessarily to be a billionaire with multiple vacation homes and have a butler with a swirly mustache (I will admit this is one of my fantasies). Our dreams are to feel the freedom of a billionaire, the joy of vacationing all the time, and the peace of a butler cleaning up after us. Freedom, joy, peace… These are attainable now, not when your material world gives you permission by reaching an inflated social status. Don't let your dreams tell you that you can't feel good until you've reached them. Keep dreaming because it's fun and it gives your life direction as it unfolds. Be as you dream to feel, because that is in your creative control. Be a conscious being.

I will share two aspects of your being that can help aid you on your healing journey: your higher self and soul. Your higher self is your enlightened self. It is accessible now, no need to throw a search party. There are no imbalances, pain, illness, or conditions affecting it. It is unwaveringly healthy and at peace, no matter what chaos, pain, destruction, anxiety, stress or excitement are occurring.

Your higher self gently rises through the layers of your being until it infiltrates your physical reality. A deterrent from living as your higher self is identifying with the sticky layers between your physical body and your enlightened self. We have addressed all of these layers throughout the book: your ego self that is always wanting to protect you, your heart consciousness, the vibration of pure love and acceptance, and your intuition, which connects your conscious awareness to all layers of your existence. These layers of ego, heart, and intuition are all composed of energy. That energy is converted to love or fear depending on how it has been directed by you. When you choose to perceive everything through the eyes of love and charge every action with love, then you are allowing your higher self to live through you.

Your soul is the one that witnesses these actions and vibrations. When you are watching television, the images on the screen are not your life. Your soul is witnessing the "you" that is watching the television. It is the one that is experiencing the body sitting on the couch, and the images on the screen. It is not charged with love or fear, it is neutral, as it remains a steady witness to your life. Blink open your eyes, like a dewy baby from the womb, see the vibrancy of this glittering unpredictable world. Without life, it has nothing to be aware of, which is why life is truly a gift to your soul. The soul is whole — no voids and no emptiness. The soul is aware of your ego, heart, mind, body, and higher self. There are no feelings of lack of, or not being enough. When you touch this space within you, you realize you are whole, complete and all you desire is already here. When you are connected and aligned with this part of yourself, suddenly a new perspective is available to you, that of constant calm and an objective view from the seat of awareness.

Your higher self is aware that the contrast of the dark and light in you is a gift. It knows that you have the ultimate creative control through the law of attraction. It is aware that your pain body is guiding you to create a life in alignment with your heart, because fear is a segue back to love.

As you journey through life, your pain body will continually bring you new opportunities to strengthen your connection to your higher self and soul truth. As you merge with the love of your higher self and witness through the equanimous eyes of your soul, the perceived intensity of your challenges disintegrates and your challenges disappear. You begin reframing them as opportunities to step into the consciousness of love. You see the gift in each challenge and how it is guiding you to be a reflection of your soul truth, standing in love and light, untethered by whatever darkness may arise. You become more clear in what you are.

At your core, the closest layer to the soul is that of blinding light. It is pure source energy, which is the same frequency as love. This radiant layer can transcend into your physical reality if you choose it. You can vibrate in the frequency of pain when you give precedence to darkness and fear. You can see you are a creator, and have much more power in your life than you give yourself credit. You can decide to be joyful in every moment, and see the gifts that are right in front of you. You can live from this awareness.

Popping my pubescent pimples, I gaze in the mirror with disgust. *Loser, you are such a loser*, I mumble to myself through my tightly wired braces. Transitioning into adulthood with a legacy of low self esteem proved a difficult starting point towards the journey of confidence and self love. The doubtful energy digs its claws into mental and physical imbalances and holds me back from self love and healing. Each time I accept a piece of me I have rejected, something within me heals. When I despise or shun a piece of me, I descend into hopelessness and feeling broken. In this way, we can become trapped in our pain bodies. We accept the belief that we are our suffering, when our pain body is actually a catalyst to connect with our light, like the pressure that creates a diamond from coal. We can fall and fall and fall back into our pain, but our light never stops being an option for us to take. It never disappears, it only dims over time underneath the shadows of our past. But it never leaves us, it is always accessible.

Your higher self does not judge, it loves. You realize love cannot be trampled, taken away, or abused, because it is what you are made of. It loves the parts that are not in alignment with your higher self, and that are not healthy. Living from the vibration of love is genetically adjacent to the higher self. When we allow this energy to be set free, to truly love every part of ourselves, only then will we heal.

If you have not experienced this truth yet, there is no time like the present to jump in. Once you directly experience it, the only thing needed is to begin integrating it into your life. To live your deepest truth, you must surrender your mind to create space for your soul to shine through. For the truth of love to shine through your heart. For the truth of peace to shine into your awareness. For the truth of oneness to be felt. For your health to flow freely and unrestricted. Knowing your soul truth is one thing — living it brings heaven to Earth. It is a potential for every being to live from pure love, joy, gratitude, acceptance, and health. This is the path of non-suffering.

This is a potential for all of humankind. It can be scary to think about how much your life can change when you live from the purity of your soul. We tend to fear the unknown, even fear health, wholeness, and happiness. But if you are ready, it is right here. Right where it has always been — within you. Your intuition and energy body are your tour guide pointing you towards stepping into this endless potential of love.

♢ Soul Alignment Exercise

Connect To Your Soul Truth

Calm the mind:

Begin a meditation practice to calm the mind: Vipassana, a guided meditation, breathing practice or silence practice, until you feel very relaxed and open.

Connect with your higher self:

Now state your intention: My higher self, connect with me. Allow me to directly experience my highest self of pure love. Now surrender to whatever arises. You may connect instantly or you may need to work on calming your mind and releasing expectations to directly experience your truth. Continue this practice as often as needed.

Connect with your soul:

My soul, connect with me now. Allow me to directly experience my soul's truth. Now surrender to whatever arises. You may connect instantly or you may need to work on calming your mind and releasing expectations to directly experience your truth. Continue this practice as often as needed.

Integration:

Once you have experienced your soul truth and higher self, it becomes easy to connect with. Now start the process of integration. When life gets stressful or chaotic, connect. When you are afraid, having a panic attack or in pain: connect. It never leaves you, it is always here.

Continue connecting:

Over time as you build this connection, you begin to live from this space, this truth, naturally. Health and balance become your physical reality as your soul truth rises into the mind, body, heart, and energy body.

Chapter 20

CONTINUOUS HEALING

Healing does not mean you must endure suffering
It is intentionally controlling what is in your means
And lovingly surrendering everything else to the Universe

Healing has become a scribbled prescription write up and a quick diagnosis. Like a firework that fizzles out from a lack of gunpowder. Once you learn about the intuitive and energetic systems of the body, you receive a plethora of knowledge on the who, what and why of your struggles. This allows you to drop the butter knife and resect your health struggles with a precision laser.

This book has prepared you to intuitively discover the root cause of your pain. You have been building your intuition to connect with the wisdom of your soul through your extra sensory perceptions and channeling practices. The guidance you receive from your intuition will be the most accurate discovery in your healing process. As you begin to understand the messages your body has been trying to relay to you through pain and emotional suffering, you are being guided in useful actions to pull the weeds of your discomfort from their roots, instead of trimming the tops and working on symptom relief.

You have learned the energy map throughout the organs and tissues of the body and how to apply energy healing to them. Different intuitive supports like dreamwork, dowsing, and oracles help you discern an energy blockage's mental/emotional roots. These intuitive and knowledge based tools give you a solid foundation on your healing journey.

The channeled encyclopedia of major conditions, experiences and disorders offers the emotional, mental, and spiritual cause of physical ailments you encounter. This reference is here to complement the messages that have been received through your own intuition. Not only is it a powerful resource for your health, but the health of your loved ones or clients.

Moving forward on your journey I hope you feel empowered to be an active participant in your healing journey. Healing is constantly happening for you, and there are enough wounds and blockages to fill your entire lifetime with persistent growth and healing. Don't get caught up in the idea of living your human life as an embodiment of perfection or your higher self. This goal may be tiresome as you are fitted with a human body and mind to accompany you through this lifetime. Anytime we become hyper focused on one thing (such as healing), we are blinded from the greater picture. Healing is a part of life, but so is enjoying, creating, witnessing and connecting. Enjoy what is accessible to you now through gratitude. Create whatever you are inspired to create and achieve. Witness your life and the world from a space of non-judgment. Connect with the other incredible human beings and animals who are just as vast and expansive as you are.

Healing is one piece of your life's work. Now that you have your intuition on board, you can go further and have more fun healing then you knew was possible. Throughout my years of physical pain and mental illness, I have experienced radical healing and never ending insights that inspire me to love more deeply. My conditions have taught me to love myself with the same intensity that I love others, and to reflect what I believe through how I treat myself. I can't wait for you to share your intuitive insights with the world in how you show up each day.

Thank you for having the courage to work on yourself. It can be scary going into these dark spaces within ourselves. But, I know that when we do, we will be pulled deeper to a space of light beneath the darkness, to a space of love. I am excited for you to access more of your loving nature, and share it with yourself and others. Thank you beautiful soul for joining me on this journey!

ENCYCLOPEDIA OF CONDITIONS

*A listing of the mental, emotional, and spiritual causes to
conditions, illness, trauma, and major life events.*

S kiing down the bumpy moguls, I catch some air and tumble down
the mountain in a flailing spin. My knee vocalizes a loud pop. I
didn't know my knee could make noises like this. I take a deep breath
as I lay on the mountain assessing my body. I know I am injured, and
I know it is time to do some soul work.

When there is an injury or illness, there is opportunity for soul
growth and expansion. It is a gateway to greatness and self discovery.
I am sharing a list of common conditions and experiences with a
description of their root causes. I will share the meanings for you that
I have received through the Akashic records and the direct energy of
each condition. Akashic records are the records of the soul, they are
a sacred dimension holding the light of Akasha, which is the primal
source energy. Akasha is composed of pure light, universal wisdom,
ancient teachings, and divine love. These channeled messages are not
a substitute for your intuition and the messages you have received. It
will be complementary to the messages your intuition has already
shared with you. No one is more connected to your truth than you.
If this information is conflicting with your discoveries, follow what
feels in alignment with your heart and feels good to you. Combine
the teachings of Chapter 11: Anatomy of Energy and the channeled
messages to receive a more conclusive action plan in your healing.
For example, if you struggle with arthritis, but it is specific to your
left wrist and left ankle, look up the meaning of these in anatomy of
energy, as well as arthritis in the encyclopedia.

This list is also a powerful resource to look at genetic conditions in your family and understand the emotional and spiritual causes. For ancestral healing, and to heal your lineage, work on the suggested practices described in each condition. If you want to help a friend or your clients have clarity in their condition, refer to this resource to assist those needing support and healing.

What about when children have major health concerns or conditions? When children are afflicted with a chronic condition, it is giving the parents an opportunity for deep spiritual growth. By not taking blame for their child's struggle they access greater self compassion. Once they accept that their child's health is not in their full control, they surrender to find greater internal peace. When the child's developmental years are challenged with hardships this offers the child a greater platform for accessing more compassion, acceptance, and strength in their adulthood. Childhood is meant to be a blissful period free of suffering and bursting with joy. Yet illness can still penetrate their physical, mental and energetic field. What is the spiritual cause? The soul is the one who chooses to have this illness or difficult experience. The desired illness is offering a pathway to greater peace and fulfillment. The soul does not crave suffering, it has a clear directive for us to experience a life filled with love. Whether we struggle in childhood, adulthood, past or future lifetimes, the soul does not see the human timeline in the same way that our limited perception does. There are no restrictions to the experiences it can have, whether difficult or utopian. There is a knowing that all experiences bring an opportunity to connect closer to their true nature of love, and offer an opportunity to uplift those around them to their own loving nature. Although childhood illness is difficult to accept, rejecting it does not help. There really is no greater practice to be present, be with what is, and reach for pockets of joy whenever possible.

There is a common thread of wisdom I found through channeling these 444 conditions and experiences. No matter the condition or challenge you are faced with, it is pushing you towards being your authentic and deep self, towards a layer composed only of love and acceptance. To be healed is when we realize we are complete and whole. Wholeness is realized when we return home to our core nature of love. The fearful thoughts and energies that surround health conditions are offering us opportunities to shine with greater power in our essence of pure love.

List of health conditions, imbalances, & common life experiences:

Abscessed tooth: There is something toxic that you need to say. You need to get it out of your body and communicate where it needs to be communicated. What have you been holding back?

Abortion: Abortion creates a tear in your energy body. It is an open wound that can dishevel your entire life if not properly cared for and allowed to heal. Immense love, time, and energy is needed to allow this tear to re-join and heal. When it is not healed, it causes sadness, panic, fear and hopelessness. This can last your entire life if you never tend to your wound. A practice of deep self-love is what is needed. You must nurture yourself, your needs, and your health. Learn to take care of yourself in a new way with unconditional love. Stop feeding critical or shameful thoughts, know you are worthy of love.

Acne: You are afraid of coming out to the world and showing your true self. This acne is a test: can you define your truth and beauty while not feeling externally beautiful? Allow your innate beauty from within to shine through the veil of acne, unafraid of being seen, and the acne will calm and heal. Acne is also caused by fearing what you are unable to do in life. Fearing that you are not good enough or capable of doing tasks that others can. You have stopped appreciating all that you can do. Don't feel lesser than, or trapped by all that you can't do. See the light and the dark in yourself and accept yourself as a whole. Different types of acne:

- Blackheads are condensed darkness. Are you able to see your shadow self (ego) and hold space for it, accept it, love it, and free it? Allow it to be free and move through expression, rather than being tightly held onto out of shame and guilt (suppressing it, or holding it in).

- Cystic acne is caused by eruptions of anger that have pent up over the years. Release your anger to the stars and free it from your being. You are worthy and deserving to share your voice and stand tall to create space for you and your needs.

- Scarring acne has scarred you, just as your past has scarred you and left an imprint you cannot erase. Heal these old wounds by surrounding your present self and your past self in love and light.

ADD: See predominantly inattentive type ADHD

Addison's disease: When constant excitement floods your mind, breathe. Be still amongst the chaos. Soak up each moment with a peaceful mind. Be the statue in a butterfly garden, and witness the highs and lows of life unfolding around you.

ADHD (Attention deficit hyperactivity disorder): This disorder and dysfunction is pushing you to continually seek and search for answers. ADHD pushes you to look for something better to do, to be, and to see. It causes you to search for the best version of yourself and your life, fueled by a desire to be more. What you are being guided to do through this disorder is to stop. Fight and resist the urge to live in your future, in your hopes and dreams. Stop that momentum, that constant motion, and just be here. Happiness is not in the future. It is right here, right now. But you will never see it as you are always looking ahead and behind. Look here, look now, look at yourself. All you desire is here and can always be found right here, and right now. ADHD is pushing you to move your awareness from the future to now.

AIDS: Your heart center is where your soul communicates through, it is the space of pure love. Every day your heart is being reborn, it is growing and shining outwards more love from within. With AIDS, there is an imbalanced energetic flow in the heart center. Instead of a constant birthing of new life, it is stuck on the phase of death. Death is a part of the process of rebirth, in energetic terms. What are you resisting to let die within you, within your heart? What pain are you holding on to? Why are you not allowing your heart to shine, and soul growth to occur? What action can you take to assist your emotional center in shedding the old to make way for the new? Make space for your vibrancy to shine.

Adrenal fatigue: There is an imbalance of too much negativity and fear in your life. It's time to clear the air and start fresh. Release all old unsupportive habits and thoughts. Habits of not loving yourself enough. Habits of not owning your truth (your authenticity). No more murky waters of uncertainty. Move forward with power and potency in your truth of who you are. It can be gentle or forceful, it is up to you. It can feel difficult making changes at this time of low energy and aspirations, but it will be energizing and fruitful with each small step that you take.

Adultery (cheating): Unhappiness with yourself for the way life is unfolding. You are wanting change, wanting something better, something more, while often blaming the one being cheated on that they weren't enough. But it is always the person who commits the act of cheating that is the focus. There is a hole within that you are trying to fill. You believe it is external, that something in your environment needs to fill this emptiness. But it has always been an internal hole within yourself, not having true self love. You may not even be consciously aware of this emptiness that needed filling. It will not be filled by sex, lovers, money, or things, not work or achievements. Only by the realization that you are a good person, worthy of love, no matter what you have done or not done. You are always worthy, as real love is unconditional, meaning NO conditions. Sometimes you will do harmful things as you crave being rejected by others, to prove you are not worthy. This is self-sabotage as you are reflecting your internal struggles. It is time to love yourself.

Alcoholism: Caused by dormant pain in the body. This pain has been suppressed for a very long time. Left unaddressed, it has festered and grown to an uncontrollable level. Alcohol helps to soften this pain and the awareness of this pain. It is time to go inwards, to clean the cobwebs and do the soul work. It is work, it is not easy. But once you do this work, you will be free of your pain and find fun, joy, peace, and love once again.

Allergies:

♦ Environmental allergies are caused by not being able to accept and adapt to your environment. A feeling of discomfort or not feeling safe when you are in a new social environment, country, or literal outside environment. Feeling like you are separate or disconnected from the world around you. Let down your walls and give in to the truth that we are all one, we are all love. And accept that this life force energy that moves through you is the same energy moving through the veins of mother Earth and all of her creations.

♦ Food allergies and sensitivities: You are too sensitive to your outer world and your inner world. You are extremely empathic, and you are easily shifted and swayed by others' feelings/thoughts and your environment. You are emotionally and mentally weak and give in to negativity and fear easily. Look within and find that there is deep strength. You are powerful. You can use your power to stand in the vibratory field of love no matter what is going on around or within you. Find courage and strength. Be strong in saying no to what is not in alignment with joy and love. Say yes and take action on what is in alignment with joy and love. You are worthy and you are a warrior. Fight for love, fight for positivity and gratitude. Make space for your light to shine. Let go of the fear of being small, not being seen, and giving in to strong energies/people/thoughts. Flex your muscles of choice to create a world that is in alignment with your highest self.

Alopecia: You are firmly planted in your beliefs and ideals. This is not a bad thing. However, your beliefs and ideals are being challenged to shift from your heart. Have you been too stubborn and solid to allow a new awareness to flow through you? A concentration and focus has been placed on your mental/conscious mind, so much so that there is no room for divine to flow, for universal truth to be made aware. Soften the power you give your mind. Let go and discover that there is so much more to this life than you had designated it.

Allergic rhinitis: See hay fever

ALS Amyotrophic lateral sclerosis: See motor neuron disease

Altitude sickness: You are getting ahead of yourself in life, slow down. Go backwards to soak up what you missed. You have been in such a rush to move forward to find the destination that you have missed the destination in each step of the journey. Life is not a race. If it were a race, you would want to be a turtle. A turtle is the true winner because it gets to be present, move slow, and soak up the beauty in every moment.

Alzheimer's disease: It is caused by suffering imposed upon oneself from a lifetime of battling the ego mind, constantly doubting and questioning one's abilities, confidence and value. Over the years, it has created a tension with the body that pulls itself apart (self-annihilation). This is due to not accepting yourself as you are. Truly love and accept yourself as a whole being, light, dark, every part of you. Know that you are enough, and that you are whole. Once this realization is absorbed, the body will remain whole.

Amputation: Losing a limb or body part aligns you with deep soul growth. A deep lesson on your path to wholeness, to worthiness and to acceptance. You are whole. You are not your body, not your mind, not even your emotions. You are a whole, and beautiful soul. Once you know this, it's time to let the world know.

Anaphylaxis: Life is precious. Move slowly with mindfulness and grace. Soak up all of the beauty in each moment. If you move too quickly, you can stumble into a dangerous situation. What happens when you slow down?

Andropause: See male menopause

Anemia (iron deficiency): There is a disconnect with your body. Your body and intuition are trying to communicate with you. There is advice and messages that have been coming through to help align you but you have not been listening, or did not realize it. Journal and reflect on what has been going on in your body and outer world as long as you have had this deficiency. Even your symptoms are speaking to you. There is a symbolic message trying desperately to be heard, and to keep you on your soul path. Reflect and discover what the messages are. For example if you are experiencing chronic fatigue, what in your life is exhausting you (work, overthinking, etc.)?

Aneurysm: The root cause of an aneurysm is a collapse of the mind. Your world has folded inwards. An extreme moment of stoppage is required, sometimes it is fatal. It's like a castle that has been built, but over the years the walls become very porous (from stress, negativity, and things that needed tending to). The walls were not maintained, the upgrades and construction work was not done. Eventually, they can no longer support their own weight and the walls collapse. When you or someone you know experiences an aneurysm, it is an indicator that major changes were meant to happen a very long time ago. Their inner knowing of these changes was ignored and neglected. Eventually, the body cannot support you anymore, and creates this inward collapse. It is time for major and drastic change. Change that supports you. Change that is in alignment with your heart and your truth. There is no more time to put it off. For greater specificity in the area of change that is needed refer to the area of the aneurysm:

- Abdominal aneurysm: Self-love and worthiness
- Thoracic aneurysm: Emotional body
- Cerebral aneurysm: Mental body

Angioedema: What areas of your life can you simplify? Simplifying allows your energy to focus on what is really important to you and not go overboard into unnecessary worry or fear. How have you been contributing to the scarcity mindset? Can you move into an abundance mindset with more gratitude for all that you are and all that you have?

Animal Bites: When being bitten by an insect or animal, the Universe is calling you to pull yourself together. You need to focus and act on your priorities first. Here are more specific meanings:

- Cat bite: Listen to your intuition
- Dog: Open your heart
- Hornet/wasp sting: Have patience, and surrender control
- Jellyfish sting: Spirit is reaching out to you, can you connect with your higher self?
- Monkey: Listen to your inner child
- Mosquito: Work on relaxing
- Snake: Listen to your spirit
- Spider: Stop resisting change
- Squirrel: Slow down, you are moving too quickly in life

Ankylosing spondylitis: You are strong and can create large movements in this life. You have the ability to change the lives of many people. Feel your inner strength and ask yourself, how am I ready to show up in the world in my full power?

Anorexia nervosa: An inability to express, communicate, and accept your truth. A sabotage of yourself in an effort to fight and deny this truth from surfacing, from being known, felt and expressed. The truth is that you are whole and you are perfect just as you are. You are deserving of the deepest and purest love from yourself and others, and you always have been. No matter how you act, react, treat yourself or others, you are special. You are worthy. You are worthy. You are worthy! Know this, accept it, and then you can honor this worthiness. You must stop denying these truths as you are fighting your true nature. You are love.

Antisocial personality disorder: You have barriers and walls all around you to protect what little love is left. You did not receive enough love as a child, or did not accept it as you did not feel deserving. It is a lack of love, receiving love, and now giving love. Open the box of darkness you have been hiding your vulnerability in from the world. It is time to love. Begin with yourself, and then open your heart to others. The world is ready to love you. You just have to open the gates and let it in. You are ready. There is nothing to lose and a world of joy to gain.

Anxiety: Anxiety is caused by overstimulation of the mind. You are not processing what is truly important. Your deep desires, and inner knowing are being masked by an explosive overstimulation of ego based decisions and a sea of thoughts. Stop the tyranny of superfluous thoughts. You need to part the sea. Go deep, to the root, to what is at the sea floor. You will discover inner knowing, your soul's truth. It is always there and it is always accessible, even though it may feel impossible to access. It is always here, within you. You need to drop, or push aside all that is not your soul truth. You need consistent access to the truth that you are love, and that all is love. The truth is that at this moment you are doing the very best you can. And that you have the power to relax the mind and body when you root your consciousness to its depths, its home, where it is only love and acceptance of all.

Anxious personality disorder: See avoidant personality disorder

Appendicitis: You are being slowed down in the actions you are taking. Some things need to be re-assessed. Slow down or come to a complete stop before moving forward. Make sure you are on the path of flow, of ease and of heart desire (not ego). The path towards joy, and the path of love. This path may require some surrendering to the universe. You can't do it all on your own. Loosen the reins and let spirit be the wind beneath your wings.

Arthritis: A space has opened up within your being, a space to grow your connection with hope, faith, and trust in the universe (God). But instead of allowing this life force of support from the universe to flow into these spaces, you have allowed fear in. This fear is represented through pessimism, doubt and an "I'm going at it alone" mentality or hopelessness. Open up to allow trust, support, and hope to occupy these spaces of inflammation and allow doubt, disbelief, and pessimism to be released to the earth.

Asbestosis: Sometimes you need to be in an unhealthy environment so that you can grow as an individual. Sometimes it is unhealthy to be in a difficult environment, and what you need is to get out and get yourself into a healthier space. Asbestosis is a reflection of the latter. It is important to find a home life, work life, and overall outer environment that supports and nourishes you. How can you make your life easier and move into a safer, more comfortable environment?

Asperger syndrome: A break has occurred, a disconnect between your heart (emotional center) and your expression. Look to healthy communicators who voice their hearts around you. Be inspired and plant seeds within yourself to help the world understand your truth. Plant seeds for you to connect with your heart's truth. You are a being of love, light, and power. Use your power wisely and shine it from the space of abundance within. You are such a gift to this planet. Know this and share your gifts by sharing yourself as you are.

Asthma: You have not been living from your truth. You have been expressing solely (mostly) from your ego, from a space of fear and protection within you. You are having difficulty breathing as your body has been housing lots of negative energy, making it hard to breathe (to inhale positivity and life force energy and to exhale negativity and fear based energy). It is as though negative energies are caught within the body and restricting health/breath/positive qi. You can benefit by creating space. Letting go of the fear, pain, and negativity, inviting it out of your body, as you open your channel to love, trust, and positivity. Nourish the seeds of positivity with your thoughts and actions. Release negative thoughts and stop negative actions with intent and power to do so. Let go of the old, it's not a true reflection of you. Let's create space and breathing room for the real you to emerge.

Astigmatism: Do you struggle to see the bigger picture? Astigmatism energetically represents extreme focus and control. How can you step back to see the wider picture and encompass greater depth in your perspective on life?

Autism: Autism has a connection to an abundance of suffering from past lifetimes, from your lineage and from this lifetime. As you begin to unwind the strong connection to your perceived pain and suffering, you allow life to flow with ease and grace. Release what is not supporting you so you can live life adjacent to what does support you including people, thoughts, actions, and inner awareness of your true nature. Let yourself create and just be with the energies that bring you peace and joy. You are not eliminating pain and suffering, you are shifting your focus to all of the good in your life, and by doing this you soften your pain's power and empower your soul truth.

Autumn: This season represents death and loss. What are you ready to release and let die? Death is a precursor to life. What emotions, beliefs, or physical ailments are no longer serving you? Can you let them be embraced in a cycle of release, so that a new experience may take its place?

Avalanche: There are greater spiritual forces outside of yourself than you are aware of. Sometimes these forces take away what we once dreamed of, and sometimes they create beginnings we never knew were possible.

Avoidant personality disorder (anxious personality disorder): The root cause is a strong desire to be loved. It is fueled by not receiving enough from others while wanting desperately to feel and receive pure and unconditional love. You are not alone in this need. Every human being desires love. But they do not struggle once they come to understand and feel the truth of love. Love is not a commodity. It is not something we earn, we deserve, we run out of, or need to receive. Love is all around you. Love is within you. Love is you. Your basic elemental structure is composed of this love, as is everyone and everything. However, we have lied and denied this truth to give in to the ego (fear). Fear cuts off love and tells us we are not loved and not worthy of love. It is impossible to not be worthy of love, love is what you are. You need to practice disconnecting from fear and the mind, go deeper. Find, feel and know what is within you. Love, unconditional love. Right there, right where it has always been. It's not going anywhere.

Back Pain:

+ Cervical spine (neck and upper back): You are living a contradiction. You want to believe you are worthy of being heard, yet your fear still holds you back from living your life like a champion, from living like a warrior — fearless. Where nothing can stop you from honoring yourself, your purpose, and being authentic. Nothing can stop you from living from a place of flow. Instead you are restricting showing up fully. You are restricting who you are. You know on the inside who you are, but you don't let it out because you are afraid the world will judge you and isn't ready for you. The world is ready, are you?

- Thoracic spine (middle back and chest): You are sheltering your heart. You are protecting yourself from being hurt by others and hurt by the world. You have in fact been sheltering yourself from loving others, loving yourself, and being loved. It is safe to let your walls down and live from your heart. You can experience joy more deeply, instead of holding pain from your past. You can be present to give and receive when you let down the walls.

- Lumbar spine (low back): You want to move forward in life, to grow as a person, and to go after your dreams. But you have been anchored to the ground. Your body is trying to protect you from getting hurt. It is responding to suffering and traumas you have already encountered and it is saying, "Do not change, if we stay put we are safe." It is time to move forward, to break those old chains and step into your power. You can do what your heart desires and the universe is here to support you.

- SI joint (sacral region, hips): The cause is dysfunction of the sexual organs and sexual energy within the body. Looking at your past and your sexual experiences, are there any wounds that need tending to? Wounds that need love, forgiveness, and acceptance? Spread light over any darkness in your divine sexual being, and move forward into freedom. The freedom to express what has been suppressed. Freedom for your inner child to awaken and come out and play. All is safe. You are safe and protected. It is okay to flow and let go of control and of wanting to control your environment and how life unfolds.

Surrender to the divine mystery and sacred flow. Trust that all is unfolding for your benefit and your highest good.

Bad breath (halitosis): It is caused by dis-ease, a lack of ease around how you live and express your life. Are you honoring your truth in this moment? Are you being honest with your heart and its desires? Voice all that you have held back, even if it feels toxic. It is time to rid your body and mind of this heaviness. To expunge the damp, dark shadow self and, in turn, free your light and your love. You are clearing your channel, honoring all truths so that you can go deeper.

Bacterial vaginosis: Step back and take count of your life. In what ways are you allowing negative influences to penetrate your life? There is an overabundance of unsupportive activities, people, and energies. It's time to clear out the junk, and make space for supportive influences to flow in.

Bed bugs: You are being forced out of your comfort zone. It's time to break free and make a run for it. Not running away from life, but running towards it. It's time for a clean slate. The old patterns, the old environment, they're just not serving you anymore and it's pushing you out of your comfort zone. You can stay and scratch the itch, resist, and fight it. Or you can start over, walk a new path, become a new person who is not tied down to their past and thrive.

Bed wetting: It is fighting structure, rules, and foundations. There is a feeling of being stuck between freedom and conformity. Try to find a balance and know that both are beautiful and can coexist simultaneously. Freedom should not be taken from anyone.

Bell's palsy: There is dark and there is light. There is love and there is fear. Both are experiences of life. Both are here. We get to decide what we want to place our conscious awareness on. What we want to focus on, grow, manifest, and what we want to soften our hold on. There are these clear divides in the spectrum for you: Negativity, Neutrality, and Positivity. Where do you wish to be? The choice is yours, it always has been. Bell's palsy is this reminder of the contrasts and that you can focus on the good, you can focus on the bad, or you can simply witness it all from gratitude and love.

Benign prostatic hyperplasia: See prostate gland enlargement

Bile duct cancer (cholangiocarcinoma): What makes you angry? This is driven by passion, by self-love and love for others. Go to the root of your anger and let it be freed through your expression, but rooted in love. See that it is safe to express your potency with force, especially when you are aware that it is an act of love and compassion.

Binge eating: See eating disorder

Bipolar disorder: A pull between two contrasts: one of openness, love and freedom, the other of contraction, suppression and darkness. Your beliefs inspire your reality. Do not give up hope when in the darkness. Know that the darkness was birthed in the light and the light is therefore always present. Even in extreme suffering, love is present, if we choose to see it. Choose to see the light, focus on the light, and empower it. Do not ignore the dark or try to change it, but do not focus on it and empower it. It is simply an energy, an emotion, a thought, a frequency. But at its root, it too holds light and is pushing you towards divine unconditional compassion for yourself and all beings and experiences. The light is there if you choose to see it. The more you focus on it, the softer the darkness becomes as it fades and fades away.

Bladder cancer: Bladder cancer is caused by insufficient efforts and energy in long term care of your self needs. Self-care is not just reading a book and taking a bath. It means going after what your heart desires. It means living your life to its fullest potential and having the courage and self-belief to go after your dreams. It is to live each day in alignment with your truth. Your truth, not the truth of society or family. What is important to you? Have you been living it?

Blood poisoning (sepsis): You are wanting change desperately in your life. Can you sit with the areas of discomfort and allow them to take the time they need for transformation? Instead of rushing to push the old out and make way for the new, slow down, and accept the process.

Blindness: You are open to the deeper truth. By not seeing the physical world, you allow yourself an opportunity to see the deeper truths. You have an ability to connect to spirit, life force, all knowing and the seat of the soul. These are within you as they are within everyone. Your connection is less blocked by the material world than others. The unseen truth comes to light, and you can experience it. With the awareness of this truth you will experience greater joy, love, and peace than all others whose distracted sight/attention gets in the way of their journey.

Body dysmorphic disorder (BDD): You are a tender soul susceptible to deep pain in this universe. The deeper the darkness you have experienced, the greater the light that is available to you. However, you need to make a powerful choice. You need to plant your feet in two cement blocks anchoring you to the earth, showing an unwillingness to bend to the darkness and hatred. The choice is to unconditionally love every part of you. BDD has shown you how powerful your thoughts can be. It's time to go deeper into your soul truth, the most powerful voice within you. From your soul only words and feelings of love come as your soul sees you as divine perfection and love. Stand in this truth with courage and power.

Bone cancer: It is caused by trauma from your life that has not been properly processed or expressed. Revisit times that you have been shaken to the bone through your experiences. The trauma has been held so deeply that it's embedded into your bone tissue. Visit your past and all major and minor traumas. Allow yourself to feel them fully, to express them, and then they can be released.

Borderline personality disorder: Dear soul, you are fighting against yourself and your mind. Raise the white flag and surrender your thoughts. You don't need to fight any longer. Surrender to the universe, to the flow of love that is within and all around you. You are love and you are loved. Let this truth rise from your depths so you can function and relax into this space.

Bowel cancer: Your body is basking in negative energy that needs to be released. Two methods for releasing are needed: The first is acceptance. Accept all that has happened in your life, and all that you are. Accept the "bad and negative" as simply an experience of life. The second is letting them go. Let go of the experiences in your past that caused sadness and suffering. Let go of the beliefs you formed based on your negative experiences that hold you back from living a more fulfilling life.

Bowel incontinence (fecal incontinence): Letting everything flow through you is often a positive quality. It can, however, create a loss in your authenticity and personal power. Stand strong in who you are, soak up the good things in your life, and only release what you want to release. What things have you been letting slip through the cracks that would bring you great joy if you held onto them more tightly?

Brain cancer: Something in your mind has given up and lost hope. It is not functioning in its soul truth (highest and healthiest self). The brain is needing a boost of hope, and of belief. Allow yourself to fully believe and have true hope, the kind that fills your heart with joy. A joy that once again trusts the universe and connects you to source (God/higher power). You need to build or rebuild this connection that was lost to voicing the ego, and giving dominance to your thoughts. You lost your connection to your inner knowing. You need to reconnect those wires so that health, abundance, and optimism can once again flow.

Brain injury: Slow down. You have been overthinking, over-processing, and overworking your brain. Your brain needs a serious break. Connect to a space within the mind that is simply a space of non-thought. Allow your mind to rest within this space. And moving forward, return to this place of peace within the mind daily, to balance your overthinking and processing.

Brain tumor: Something in your mind is not serving you. What belief are you rigidly holding on to that is bringing unnecessary suffering into your life? Can you soften it and release it? What belief can you replace it with that will bring a life of greater joy and ease?

Breast cancer: The root cause is a feeling of emptiness, and of not being whole. It's as if a part of you or a major part of your life is missing. This may be caused by societal beliefs you have chosen to follow, your family lineage, or a self-doubting and critical mind. It is time to accept that feeling that you are not full/whole is not the truth. It is just a story you choose to believe. You are whole. You have always been whole, even when you have felt empty inside. You are always you. And the "not good" qualities are a part of what makes you great, what makes you, you. Accept all of you, and see that every piece has a place; you are not lacking but overflowing. You are abundance and you are a gift.

Broken bone (fracture): Time is of the essence. Time creates pressure and stress on the body until something breaks under pressure. A broken bone or fracture gives you time to settle and realign with what is most important to you. As you are healing and healed, be motivated to use your precious time doing what feeds your soul.

Bronchiectasis: Lungs are the organ that holds sadness. Childhood trauma, being spoken down to and neglected, and being emotionally harmed by adults create sadness in the body. If this sadness is internalized and suppressed, it becomes harmful to you. Can you make space for your inner child to feel loved and heard? Visit the times in your life when you were neglected and offer a warm hug to yourself.

Bronchitis (acute bronchitis, chest cold): Your body has a lot of emotions to process, including current stress and past pains. See if you can allow your body to purge. Release toxic emotions and feelings that are not supportive of your highest self in a safe and gentle way. Spend some time mindfully allowing yourself to feel your emotional pain so that it can release from your body.

Bruxism: See teeth grinding

Bulimia nervosa: See eating disorder

Bullying:

- ◆ Being bullied: Someone who is intentionally causing harm and inflicting emotional pain on you is trying to make you feel unworthy and unloved. It is your greatest blessing. It is your greatest challenge to realize: "This is not true, I am worthy of love. I have and will always be worthy of love." Do not fall to someone else's suffering that they are trying to inflict on you. You are meant to rise to the truth and stand in love, hold the light in a dark room. You are worthy. Your soul knows this. Do you know this?

- ◆ Being a bully: You are in pain, it is deep and hidden. But people who are hurting, hurt others. You need to start healing your wounds. You were unloved and devalued. You created a hard protective shell and said: "Nope, not again. I am tough. I am a great person." But that was a lie to cover your wounds. If you truly loved yourself, you would see that all humans are deserving of that same love. How you treat others is a reflection of how you internally are treating yourself. It's time to step into real love. Let the walls down. You are worthy.

Bunion: Bunions represent being pushed off of your path. How have you allowed the ideas and desires of others to throw you off track from your hopes and dreams?

Burns: Burns are caused by toxic people and toxic emotions. You are in a situation or environment that is not healthy for you. Stand back to reflect on how you can harness healthier relationships with others and yourself until your environment reflects health, peace, and love.

Bursitis: There is too much weight and too much tension on the body, especially on your energetic body. Your mind and emotions are carrying far more than you are capable of holding in a healthy way. How can you lighten your load? Have you done a clearing? An energy clearing, space clearing, mind clearing, heart clearing — all will help you lighten this energetic weight so that your body can thrive and things can begin to move fluidly once again.

Cancer: There is an accumulation of fear. You are holding on to the walls and barriers that have restricted you from feeling and finding love. This may be love for yourself, love for others, or both. Either way, this is a time to do some serious release work, forgiveness, and healing so that you can align with the vibration of love that is within you and all around you. Let go of your past and the hold it has on your present. Be here and do the best that you can now. No one is stopping you but you. You got this.

Canker sore: There is a concentration of "too much" of something. Too much of anything is never healthy. Reflect on areas of imbalance in your health and lifestyle and make improvements to find homeostasis within.

Car accident: The universe is shaking you up. It's time to get on the right track, the track of least resistance and flow. In what ways can you align with your heart-centered path of joy? It's time to "drive around" your obstacles and make your way to a clear path of abundance and peace.

Cardiovascular heart disease: Your heart has stopped functioning in its healthy vibration. There has been a lot of wear and tear in your life. Reflection is needed on the pain you have experienced: Trauma, sadness, anger, and resentment. Allow these emotions to arise, to be felt and processed. It is a cleaning of the pipes as we clean the backed up emotions that have not been felt and honored. Create space for this healing work and allow your heart to regain balance and health.

Carpal tunnel syndrome: Caused by over stimulation, over working, and overachieving. Take a step back; it's time to infuse some down time and rest into your life. Non-action can be one of the most fulfilling actions. Find balance in yin and yang. They are both valuable and essential to health.

Cataracts: When vision is hindered physically, we are called to go inwards. When cataracts develop, it is a powerful time to connect with your inner truth, with the realms of spirit/divine, and the unseen. Are you ready to uncover a deeper truth?

Celiac disease: A part of you feels lost and unloved. You are disconnected from the cord of truth telling you that you are love and you are loved. Let go of the fear that you are not loved, and embrace the love that is connected to your being. Was fear-motivated love gifted to you by your parents? This creates a tethered relationship with fear-based love. To assist your body in healing, reflect on your own boundaries with love and motivations of love. Is it infused with fear, or is it healthy and trusted? Surrender and let go of control, step into divine love, and trust that everything is unfolding for your benefit.

Cerebral palsy: There is a gift in slowing down. It is essential to be able to see the gifts in life, to be able to hold gratitude and connect to greater joy. Cerebral palsy assists you in finding space to detach from the flow of the fast-paced world and to enjoy witnessing all of the gifts it has to offer and see the things that not many others can see. Whether you suffer from cerebral palsy or are a parent with a child with CP, you are being given the space and time to breathe in all the gifts of life.

Cervical cancer: There is an inability to birth your dreams. Have you been suppressing, or holding back in the creation aspect of your life? Are you living your lifestyle, career, and family life in accordance with your heart's desires (soul truth)? Let go of any fears or judgements standing in your way. You can do and be what your heart has been gently guiding you towards if you allow yourself to move forward in a space of trust.

Cheating: See adultery

Childbirth (having a baby, adoption, or surrogacy): This is a joyous time for your soul. Your soul has chosen to accept a new path of love in your life. This new path pushes you to release your deepest fears so that you can allow more love to flow into you and your child's life. You will face great fears and can easily succumb to them. But this is not why your soul chose this path. You chose it to awaken your heart to a new level, a new world. Constantly surrender the fears and allow the love to shine. As you allow more love into your heart through trust (trusting everything will be okay, trusting everything is happening and will happen for the highest good), you allow more love through loving speech and loving action, even when being tested and tempted to give in to anger and fear. You allow more love as you love another human and care for them with a love so powerful you could not imagine its strength. And you realize you must now tend to yourself with greater depths to teach your child what self-love means, and how to live authentically and passionately. What a beautiful journey you have opened yourself up to, as this gives you the biggest opportunity for soul growth.

Chest cold: See bronchitis

Chicken pox: You are learning that you cannot always have what you want in life. Sometimes you will go through a painful experience, and not be able to escape it. But, you will make it through to the other side with a greater appreciation for life.

Child molestation/sexual trauma at a young age: You are whole. You are healthy. It may feel like a part of you has been stripped away, a piece that you can never get back. The trauma you experienced may have been identified with, picked up, and absorbed into your being. You may have been reflecting it every day since the trauma, with a closed heart with a lack of trust in the people of this planet and with a strong barrier of protection. There is a part of you, deep within, that wants to be set free again. To freely trust. To let love in, and to let love out. To do this, the first step is to go back to that vibration of love. To love that younger version of yourself who experienced this trauma. And to have compassion for the hurting adult who forced their pain onto you. Only when you can love and accept these parts can you move back into the space of love. Does this make sense? When you stay strong in your hatred and fear, your heart will not open to its truth. You will only protect and close yourself off from that truth. So to move forward it will take gentleness, it will take support from those you feel you can trust, and it will take as much time as it needs. But know that you are not creating a new sense of trust within you, you are only returning to that of the child's trust, before it was harmed by another. You are taking back what is yours so you can live from that space of full love once again. Beautiful trust and openness to the world is always accessible within you.

Cholangiocarcinoma: See bile duct cancer

Cholecystitis: You are repressing and storing anger in your body — both current anger and anger from your past. How can you express and release the anger that your body carries in a healthy way? Is it by creating healthier boundaries, crying, yelling, telling others that they have hurt you in the past? Whatever it is, make it happen and take these actions so that your body can flow in alignment once again.

Chronic childhood arthritis: See juvenile arthritis

Chronic Fatigue Syndrome: Chronic fatigue is caused by a struggle within to follow your pathway of truth. Your path of love, of self righteous doing (through the eyes of love), and discovering your wisdom platform. Your wise inner knowing knows the path towards soul fulfillment. You must look within to discover this path. Slow down your breath, slow down your mind, until you find silence and stillness. Here is where you will discover your soul's path. You have not been off the path, only distorted and twisted from your path of ease and grace. Come inwards, to the stillness of being, to discover what is being shown to you. Beauty awaits.

Chilblains: You need to get better at protecting yourself with personal boundaries. Overexposure to other people's energy and problems has been leaving you feeling depleted and not in your power. How can you remain pure in your essence of love and compassion while around others who are struggling or negative?

Chronic kidney disease: Your center of fear and judgment have been overworked and are shutting down. It is pushing you to move directly into your heart space. How can you love your shadow self? How can you accept the flow of life more greatly? Stop resisting and degrading it. Invite softness and surrender into your mind and let compassion and gratitude flow through your being.

Chronic obstructive pulmonary disease (COPD): You are battling and fighting your truth. You have been living a lie (possibly unknown to you) for some time. Who are you, really? Have you been honoring your deepest self? Or have you just gotten comfortable being who you think you should be, and who you want others to believe you are?

Cirrhosis: Cirrhosis is caused by long term damage to the solar plexus energy center and the area of self-love within the body. Your body wants more from you in terms of compassionate self-care. It wants to feel more gratitude for all that you do. It wants to feel like you are enough as you are. It wants to feel joy within for being here on planet Earth. But instead, it has faced a feeling of inner rejection, that you are just getting by, and trying to get by as painlessly as possible. I have news for you: You are special. You are a beautiful and wonderful soul. It is time for you to start honoring this and living this truth. Time to see that each day is a gift not only to you, but that you are gifting the planet with who you are by showing up as yourself. Your whole self. Not hiding it, or protecting it. Just being it. Letting your light shine once again.

Cold (common cold): Your body is calling you to strengthen your expression of truth. How can you be stronger in living from your heart? How can you express yourself more freely and authentically?

Cold sores: See herpes simplex

Colorectal cancer: There is a build up or blockage of negative and unsupportive energy. You need an energetic purge, a deep cleanse. To do this it takes vulnerability and fearlessness. Surrender negativity you have been wanting to release for quite some time but still feel attachment to: relationships, memories, emotions, and energies. To release them fully, you must be vulnerable and allow yourself to feel them in their full form. This takes courage, but you can do it. As you clean your history and negative energy, you clean your body and mind.

Comatose/coma: The mind (awake state consciousness) has too much to process, or experienced a heavy trauma. Being in a coma gives the mind rest so that the body can repair and heal, or choose not to repair and heal — whatever is the journey of the soul. The coma takes away the mental and emotional instability that is too much to bear. It allows the body to do what it is trying to do: to heal and return to life, or to surrender and move on to the next plane.

Concussion: Before the concussion happened, the mind was running scattered, exerting too much energy and leading to a burn out. Your mind wants to slow your thoughts, to slow life down, to give you time to rest, refocus, and reprogram, giving you fresh eyes, a new pace and clarity on your path. If you are still feeling scattered from the concussion, the mind wants even more rest, less effort, and more time to heal and to repair, until you are ready to try doing things a little differently, more calmly and always from the heart.

Congenital heart disease: There has been deep suffering of the heart (emotional body) over lifetimes. In this life, it is tasking you with a soul growth opportunity. Do you struggle living with an open heart? Being vulnerable, loving others fully, and allowing yourself to be loved fully? Or, are there walls and restricted access to this special part of you? Can you begin to trust and open yourself to the world? Can you open your heart to yourself, and love yourself to the depths of the ocean, loving every piece and part of you, as you are? You can, and now is the time. For children growing up with heart disease, it is essential to receive affirmations of love and confidence from their parents. It's also essential to instill a growing foundation that allows the child to discover deep self love and worthiness from within.

Conjunctivitis: See pink eye

Constipation: There is a blockage of fear that is holding you back from letting your greatness shine into this world. Have you committed your life to being your truth? Knowing it is the first step, and you have become aware of your true self. But are you letting it out into the world, letting your light shine onto others at its fullest capacity? Or are you compressing it within, for fear of rejection or not being received well by the world? Release your fears and step into the vibration of love. Let your light shine.

Cosmetic surgery: Your soul chose this body before entering the womb. It chose the conditions and illnesses you would experience, it chose each and every detail in your life for a reason. There is beauty in all, especially the parts of you that feel like they are not enough. These are the most beautiful parts because there is soul growth to be found through acceptance. If you change your appearance with plastic surgery, you are creating a new path. If surgery has been completed, the gift you are giving your spirit is a fresh start. The path before surgery offered the gift of true love and acceptance of the self to be discovered. This new path offers love and acceptance for not being able to accept and love the old self. Both paths lead to soul growth, self-love, and compassion.

Couperose: Do you struggle to find your own path and own voice in life? You are not meant to be a follower, but a leader. Your path is a new path destined to be created and walked by you. What is your path? Go for it, and don't worry about people-pleasing. Please you.

Cough: Your body is releasing blockages between your heart and throat (center of love, and expression of that love). It is clearing old beliefs and experiences that have not been serving you in speaking your truth.

Covid-19: Caused by inflammation of the mind and ego. Your life is wanting a huge adjustment. It is time to release old patterns that are no longer a reflection of your truth. You and your truth are love and light. There are many patterns and beliefs that you are feeding that are not serving your highest good. It's time to let them go.

> ♦ Long/post covid: You are clearing out some old clutter in your energy field. Things have been left unaddressed for some time that are ready to be processed and released. You can help support these shifts by reflecting, journaling, and surrendering to the healing and growing process.

Cradle cap: Cradle cap is fueled by a transition and change that one is not prepared for. Talk to your baby intuitively or verbally, let them know they are safe and only good things and love will surround them in their life. Exiting the womb can be very scary as they are birthed into a new world. Help ease their spirit in this transition. For adults, see seborrheic dermatitis.

Crohn's disease: Your body is trying to shift and transcend (transition) to a new being. In this transition, you must embrace death of the old self. Symbolically shed your skin like a snake, and be born anew. The new self is closer to your soul truth. It can be scary to allow death and vast change to take over your being. Trust, surrender, allow, and release. Only beauty awaits you.

Croup: It is time to use and find your voice. Croup is allowing you to discover what does not need to be said, and what is important to say. It gives you a gift of time and reflection to discover how you want to express yourself.

Cutting (self-injuring behavior: burning, causing physical pain): Anger is fueling your desire to inflict hurt. This anger needs to be expressed. Maybe there is a healthier and more satisfying way to release, feel, and express this anger that you hold — anger at the world for making life difficult, anger at God, anger at yourself for not being happy. Your anger is useful. It is telling you this isn't right and you are not happy about it. It's trying to push you to take action, to find and create another path. A path of acceptance and deep love, and of nourishing your needs. Yell, scream, vocalize, express, and write your frustrations. Get them out of the head and into the earth. Mother Earth is ready to hold space for you to release this, so that you can go deeper to find the love that is underneath this pain.

Cyst: A cyst is an energy blockage in the body. The flow of qi has not been moving as freely as it would when the body is in a fully healthy state. To assist you with the healing of cysts, or healing of the energy movement at the very least, a lifestyle practice is needed, one that will allow you to release negative energy. This energy may be formed by your own negativity, or that of others. A daily clearing can help create a freely flowing energy body. When energy flows, health follows. One practice you can do is picturing a waterfall of light cascading down from the top of your head down your toes and into the Earth. This light picks up any heaviness you may feel you are carrying. A physical practice is doing a shaking movement. Shake and vibrate, let everything go, as if you are shaking it off your body and out into the earth. A deep breathing practice: breathing in and having a strong, hard exhale as you release through your breath all that is not supporting you. The goal is to tune into your energy and feel a flow. You can envision it flowing to every part of you, wherever you may have a cyst(s) as well, and bringing health and vitality to your whole being.

Cystic fibrosis: Softness and fluidity are ready to flow into your life. How can you invite softness and fluidity into your way of being/lifestyle? Cystic fibrosis brings about a hardening where you can get stuck physically, mentally, and emotionally. What would your life look like if you were constantly flowing?

Cystitis: Surrender to the flow of life. Allow things to unfold when it feels tough. Savor the juicy enjoyable experiences. Try not to hold onto or resist the natural flow of your life's unfolding.

Dandruff: Dandruff is like snow piling on the top of the head, creating a barrier between the mind and spirit (or God). To clear dandruff, we must clear the blockages holding you back from a strong flowing connection to source (your highest self).

Deaf-blindness: You can make waves in this world. When visual and auditory faculties are compromised, what is left is a dependence on your inner knowing and being. You have a strengthened connection with your deeper self. Live from this space of feeling and intuitive decision-making, let it guide you to an enriched life. Many doors are open to you when you follow your heart's wisdom.

Deafness: You are a gift! So much about you needs to be appreciated and honored. Your partial or total loss of hearing does not make you any lesser or greater than another being. It also does not take away your fundamental right to create and receive meaningful connections with others, to love and be loved. You are gifted with the ability to connect, to love, and live fully without any feeling of loss. You are whole, and you are full, as you are.

Death (grief): We struggle with faith and hope when a loved one passes. We wonder, why do we have to experience such pain? How is it fair that they are not here anymore? Death is the greatest gift to life. Knowing our time is limited so we better be authentic and make the most of it drives us to live with purpose. Grief is the body processing the physical loss. Grief is a useful and powerful emotion that surfaces uniquely to each person. Give your grief the space and time to be processed, as it is just love expressing itself through heartache. The soul is just fine because the soul knows that the one who passed didn't disappear, and that they are back home in love and light. Death teaches us to have gratitude for life.

Deep vein thrombosis: There is an internal pressure that has been building for some time, and an avoidance or inability to cope with it. Soften yourself, and open yourself. Trust that you can handle what you need to process, and allow it through. This will help your body gently heal.

Dehydration: Stop what you are doing. It is time to stop living outwardly and go inwards to take care of your deep and essential needs. Focus on you, recovery, and thriving to be your optimal self.

Déjà vu: You are being shown an intersection of dimensional reality. Time is an irrelevant system. All things have happened and are happening at once. You are everywhere and nowhere. You are you, you are all, you are nothing. You are catching a glimpse of this celestial truth.

Dementia: The soul is still here in its fullness. The mind has begun to drift away onto the next phase of living (non-living). Not a death necessarily, but onto the next step of your journey. This detachment from the mind happens because there has just been too much trauma, and too much pain to process. The mind has been harboring it for your entire lifetime. When left untouched, unopened and unaddressed, it becomes too heavy a load to carry. As this detachment of the mind occurs, it pulls with it the energy of the brain. Prevention is helpful by going to talk therapy, journaling, and feeling your feelings that have been suppressed in the past. If left untouched, they become too much for the mind to continue carrying so the mind slowly gives up. It just does not have the energy to support holding that big of a sacred space for that long. Nothing magically disappears on its own. If we believe we can just tuck things away, slide them to the back in a box, they are occupying precious real estate that can be used to live presently. Instead of carrying the past in a large storage container, don't hold it back, things need to be processed and felt.

If you are already experiencing symptoms of dementia, it can be powerful to gently unfold the layers of your mind and your heart. Take time and make some space to decompress and allow everything to one by one rise to the surface to be felt, accepted and eventually released. This will allow healthy energy to re-enter the mind. And in turn, the mind will not abandon the body before the body has run its course.

Dependent personality disorder: Let go of the hold you have on others. You give them so much power that it is stripping you of your whole self. You are whole, you are powerful, and can accomplish all that you desire. You are your support, and mother Earth is always here to guide you and catch you. Surrender to this truth. Let go of the fear within, underneath it is just love.

Depression: Metastasizing energies of darkness and fear create depression. To cure this cycle of fear, you need to let your body do and create what it must. But, step in with the power and force of a new energy, the energy of love. Create new systems of love, and new connections with love. Nourish the seeds of love. You must understand that the darkness also comes from the space of love and light. When you reject and resent it, you feed the darkness. When you embrace it, and cradle it with love and acceptance, only then will it dissipate as it returns to the light.

Step into a space of courage and strength to begin doing more of what you love and what sparks joy. Even though it can feel impossible at this time, you can do it. Depression is a guide and teacher, in that it is showing you the contrast of how you don't desire to feel. You must go deeper to the light that is hidden underneath the darkness. You must water the seeds of light with loving action and loving thought so that when the seeds begin to grow, they break through the darkness. Be firm in not watering the seeds of darkness (depression). By accepting it, you hold space for it, without encouraging it to grow. It will die as all things in life do, so long as you do not feed negative thoughts and negative action. Depression is motivating you to trust that deeper than this darkness is pure light. It is motivating you to step into your power and do, think, and speak in ways that touch and reflect your light (positivity and love).

Dermatitis: See eczema

Diabetes type 1: There has been insufficient love and a tendency to be hard on yourself. This is a lifelong battle to accept all of you, as you are. Do not reject any part of you, love every little piece. See the dark or bad as a part of what it means to be human. Know that there is no such thing as perfection, unless you accept perfection as being riddled with flaws. As this is your truth. All of your flawed existence is beautiful, purposeful, and in each moment reflects your truth.

Diabetes type 2: Diabetes is caused by lack: lack of love from others and lack of love from yourself. The most important factor is self-love. If this is healthy and strong, the body will flourish. This love must be shown to yourself through loving action and loving words at all times. Once you give in to the inner critic and never being "good enough", it feeds this condition and the actions that feed this belief. Love, love, love yourself. Allow yourself to be loved by others. If you do not have a community or family that appreciates and loves you, it may be time to foster healthier relationships.

Diaper dermatitis: The body is trying to rid itself of negative energy or negative experiences it has had but it is struggling to release this negativity. With intention, without diapers and a nude bottom, invite that negative energy to purge, to release from the body and be absorbed into the earth below. Wait to feel a shift in energy; it will feel lighter and more clear (healthy).

Diarrhea: Energy is being purged from your body. You have absorbed qi from others or held onto toxic qi of your own, and the body is ridding you of that energy before it is absorbed into your organs and tissues. It is a protective mechanism. Drink water, eat whole and healthy simple foods, clear your mind and empty your heart of any unsupportive emotions, thoughts, and energies. This is your time to detoxify and start anew with a healthy intake of physical and vibratory energies that align with your highest self.

Diverticulitis: Your rooted values that emanate from the soul have been abandoned. Have you been living your life in accordance with your beliefs? Are your beliefs in accordance with your soul truth? Reflect on what is most important to you and if you have been in alignment with your soul truth. It may be time to re-analyze what was once thought of to be important and go deeper to the root beliefs that reflect your highest state of being.

Divorce: You are being called to discover the self in a greater way. Change, growth, and strength are all opening on your path. There is a storm before the rainbow appears. Although it may seem too painful or too dark, know that there is beauty on the other side, bridging you and your soul truth in a divine dance of grace.

Down syndrome: There is fatigue in the soul from over-indulging in the consciousness of the mind (overthinking and stressing) in a past life. Your soul wants to be in greater alignment with your emotional consciousness. It is time to enjoy, and to create balance, as you embrace your emotional wisdom in this lifetime, wonderfully welcoming greater simplicity and presence.

Drug abuse/addiction: Every day you are changing, you are healing, and you are growing. Drug addiction and abuse is a resistance to this change and natural growth. It is a fear of letting go of your past and your past self. It is a fear of uncertainty and feeling of undeservedness of who you may become. Let go of the fear. You are deserving of growth and change to find more balance and happiness in your life. Embrace the fires of change. It will feel uncomfortable at first, but the more you resist, the more difficult it becomes. Surrender and allow your physical reality to align with your soul's truth.

Dry mouth: Nourish your needs. Check in with yourself, and ask what is it that your body and mind need at this time to feel nourished and supported? Quench that thirst.

Dyslexia: The mind is fostering an unhealthy residue caused by being overworked. Find ways to calm the brain activity and create clarity. A deep clean of the mind is needed, one that requires trust in a universal force to assist with the cleanse. As you build trust or faith in a divinity, it opens a clear pathway for energy to flow through the mind, and spiritual vortex of the head. This helps remove the blocked energy contributing to dyslexia.

Dysphagia (trouble swallowing): There is a blockage in your throat area, leading to energy being trapped in your mind. Because energy is trapped in the head, it contributes to over-thinking, worry, and anxiety. The energy is not being evenly distributed throughout the body. This blockage in the throat can be softened and even removed with expression practices. These practices are things that encourage free communication, letting your heart sing, and letting your soul speak. Activities can include singing, yelling, and allowing all of your emotions to be properly vocalized. This helps open this passageway and clear the energetic blockage in this area.

Dystonia: Life is constantly stopping and going, flowing and halting. You need to stay open and accept this wavering flow. How can you not get caught in obstacles on your path, and instead allow and surrender to their unfolding?

Ear infections: You have listened to the world, to your family, friends, and society. You have listened to your own thoughts and inner voice. What you have been receiving and listening to has been overly negative. This negative energy has sparked an infection in your ear canal. You need a deep release of these energies. Create a fresh start by being present in this moment and create a strong gratitude practice. This will help switch the wavelengths of what you absorb from negative to positive and in turn clear up the infection.

Ear problems: The ears are a vessel that energy flows into and out of your body. The energy that flows in is what you are absorbing from your outer world. Are you grateful and feeling supported by your environment? Or are you feeling unsupported and negatively impacted by your environment? It is time to create a filter for the negative experiences and energies, while also creating a magnet to pull positivity towards you. You can create this magnet for positivity by using powerful intentions like: "The magnetic force within my ears attracts and absorbs all of the good experiences, and energies surrounding me." This does not completely change your environment, but does change your perspective on feeling supported and grateful for what is around you. Even if there is a negative energy or person around, you will always find light and positivity to be absorbed from the situation.

The energy that comes out of the ears is your ability to be there for others. To hold space and listen is the deepest gift of love you can share with another human. If it feels draining to show this love through listening to another, change your conscious perspective. See that giving love to another only fills your heart with more love and energizes you as you are in your highest vibration when you do this soul work.

Earwax buildup: Life can be stressful and too much to handle at times. Your body is trying to go inwards and close yourself off from the world. It is trying to close you off from other people's problems, work stress, and society's struggles. Closing yourself off does not encourage growth, it does not allow you to show up and contribute your essence to the world. How can you stay open and not feel overwhelmed? How can you show up and contribute without picking up everyone's heaviness?

Earthquake: The earth is opening up. It is a time to connect with this doorway/opening to mother Earth. Feel her life-blood, and allow her vulnerability to connect with yours. Release what no longer serves you to the fires of the Earth. Ask the Earth to support you with your dreams and desires for self growth. Feel her energy rise through your feet, legs and pelvis. The Earth is here to infuse life force into you, and to create powerful action.

Eating disorders: Eating disorders are a disassociation with the truth that you are love, and you are loved. You are worthy of self-love because you are important, just as important as every being on the planet. You can lose your connection to this truth and feed the truth of not being worthy as if something within you is just not good enough, and not deserving. It's time to stop feeding those lies. It's time to start feeding the deepest truth:

You are love, and you are loved. Your soul loves you; and your mind needs to accept this truth. As you accept and honor this truth, you can begin to nourish your health (mental, physical and emotional), since you have been harming yourself for some time. Now is the time to give yourself what you truly deserve: love.

Ebola: Great fear comes with great transition. You are transitioning through the fires of ultimate transformation.

Eclipse: When dark and light come together, you are left in a space of balance. How can you embrace the contrasts in your life, and create space for them to co-exist even if it seems impossible or unlikely?

Ectopic pregnancy: Things are not in alignment. Trust in divine timing and that greatness is still on its way. The stars will align and bring you greatness when the time is right. Soften and surrender to the journey.

Eczema: There are parts of you, or things in your life that you are having trouble accepting. You constantly irritate these pieces of yourself by "scratching the itch". You are wanting it gone so badly because you view these parts as undesirable. The thoughts, actions, and feelings you hold towards these unwanted parts are only empowering and strengthening them. You must lovingly accept and allow them to be there. This allows your body and life to heal, to die, and be reborn. Know that everything changes, and everything dies. You must give it space, accept it and let go, and stop clinging to it (by not wanting it). Trust and allow. You will come to where you wish to be once you let go.

Edema: See swelling

Edwards syndrome: It is time to release your fears and your worries. Time to be present with each moment and to experience the joy in it. Know that there is beauty here, always. Do not get pulled by the mind to panic or fear of the future. Take a deep breath and just be with what is.

Elements: The elements are all needed for us to find balance. How can you balance these elements within yourself?

- Water: Your emotional body. What does your heart need?
- Fire: Your energy body. What does your soul desire?
- Wind/Air: Your mind. What does your intuition want to share?
- Earth: Your physical body. How can you live and act with potency and truth?
- Metal: Change and flexibility. Where are you too rigid? Where are you too malleable?
- Wood: Growth and planning. Are your life plans aligned with your spirit and heart?
- Space: Awareness. Are you able to be a participant and a witness to your life?

EMF sensitivity: You and nature are one. Your soul beckons you to be outside with nature as often as possible. Being around electromagnetic frequencies is a very different vibration from that of your natural frequency. EMF is not negative, but it is a large contrast from your own frequency. If you want to be unencumbered by these vibrations, tune in to your truth. Stand in the power of your vibration. Not even the largest satellite can shake you, you have all the power of the universe at your disposal. Choose mind over matter, as it really is energy above all else. If you are struggling with EMF, go outside and recharge. Your body thrives when it is outside, as nature is calling you.

Endometriosis: There is inflammation of the mind, and of your thoughts. Over-analyzing and overthinking does not allow your womb to be open, clear, and healthy for birthing energy. This over-abundance of your thoughts holds you back from truly connecting to your inner wisdom and your soul's voice. Your soul wants to guide you and plant seeds for growth in all aspects of your life. The logical mind has been so over-filled that there is just no room. This creates an overgrowth of cells. Cut back on the mind's chatter. Surrender and let go of wanting to control everything. Create space and see if you can begin to trust your soul truth to guide you and make things happen.

Epilepsy: Your brain is shaking things up. It's trying to assist you in clearing the channel of your truth center, where you speak your truth and create your truth through your actions. There are some blockages holding you back from fully expressing yourself. It is time to actively release the trauma, fear, and pain that is standing in your way of letting your heart and soul shine into this world. Seeking talk therapy, professional counseling, energy healing and physical therapy can all assist you in releasing what your mind and body are holding on to. You can then step into a more grounded and balanced way of life.

Erectile dysfunction: There is a loss of vitality in your sacral energy. Your body wants to free your inner child. It is time to be more playful and silly. Engage in creative projects with no pressure, doing them simply for pleasure (music, art, writing, etc.). Let your inner child out and be free to express your creative juices. This will result in fun, freedom, and a new flow of vitality to your sacral energy. Stop adulting all the time, loosen up. Be free like you once were as a child.

Escherichia Coli (E.coli): Large changes are ready to happen in your life. Who do you want to be? What do you need to let go of to be this person? Now is the time to stand in your power and be that which you desire. Stay focused as you are easily pulled off-course.

Esophageal cancer: You are being directed to follow your spiritual path. There has been resistance in living through your heart center. You have fallen into a comfortable pattern of continuing to do what is easiest. What is your heart calling you to do? How is your heart calling you to live? Do it, be it — only you are holding yourself back.

Ewing sarcoma: Transitions can be difficult to accept in life. Things are not always easy, but there is beauty in all. Even with the really hard stuff, there is beauty to be found here. Step back from your situation and see what gifts this is offering you at this time.

Eye cancer: You have an inner knowing that is wanting to guide you through the world. Do not take things at face value, go deeper. Your inner knowing is showing you that everything is connected, everything has a purpose, and there is a gift in every experience. Allow your inner knowing to take hold of your consciousness and shake out the worry and fear.

Eye problems: Your eyes connect you to the physical and material plane. But as you know there is so much more than the eye can see — your emotional being, the world of energy, and deeper into the world of your soul's truth. Eye problems can be an expression from the soul to stop looking outside of yourself. Activate your 3rd eye and look within yourself. The answers are here. Peace is here. Rest your physical eyes and look within.

Fall: See autumn

Falling: When you trip or fall, you are brought down to a lower level. Have you been blissfully ignorant of what is going on around you? Stuck in the clouds, or in your own thoughts? There is an opposing viewpoint that is being missed. Where can you be more mindful and aware of the other side of your experiences and perspectives?

Fatty liver disease: See nonalcoholic fatty liver disease

Febrile seizures: Life has ups and downs, and it throws in some scary experiences at times. Stay grounded and know that you are safe, and everything is going to be okay. Arrive in the present moment, don't hold onto these traumatic events. Everything is okay in this present moment.

Fecal incontinence: See bowel incontinence

Fetal alcohol syndrome: A beautiful gift is wanting to be revealed for the parent and child. The gift is that of appreciation for all of your gifts. You are a beautiful soul, talented and unique in many ways. Can you appreciate all of your gifts? All of your positive aspects and attributes? When you step into full appreciation of self, self-love flows and gives you greater access to a joy filled life.

Fibroid: A fibroid is caused by a mass of energy that has been collected and trapped. There is an imbalance in the body, and your energy has not been flowing freely. It has been getting pulled to certain areas and creating a blockage. Reflect on the area it has been pulled to (where the fibroid lives) and ask your body what it is holding onto. What can it do to step into a state of greater flow and balance?

Fibromyalgia: Your mind is chronically fatigued and this is creating unnecessary stress in the body. Your world and environment are constantly shifting. There are always cycles of life and death. Let go and surrender to these changes, and things that are outside of your control. Turn inwards and find solace with the one constant in your life: You and your truth, your love and your inner light. Rest here, find ease and gratitude. Life is beautiful because you are alive and living. Even though it feels stressful and tiresome at times, it is always a gift. See the gifts in all experiences. And do not stress over what is not in your control, accept it and let your attachment to it go. It will free you.

Fire (forest fire, home fire): It is time for ultimate change and transformation. You must move forward on a completely new path. Contemplate and intuitively discover where your new path is guiding you.

Fired (getting fired, job loss): This transition marks a growth period for you. Can you step out of anger and resentment and move forward into the vibration you wish to manifest? Have gratitude for this experience as it is marking a path that was not the right one, and bringing you closer to the path that is.

Flatulence (gassy): You need to work on grounding yourself. Being an airy person (a person who is constantly in their mind thinking, or constantly dreaming and imagining), you need to come back down to Earth. How can you be more present with what is?

Flood: It is time for a movement in your life. You have been staying too long in a situation that just doesn't feel right. What sparks joy? Take steps, real steps towards it. Now is the time, head for high ground, and be rock solid and intentional with your creations.

Flu: Time is slowing down. It is time for deep self-care and self-love as you nourish and take care of your health. Have you been prioritizing other things before your health both physical and mental? The flu is a reminder to rest; as you have been attentively focusing your energy elsewhere. It is time to heal and recharge. Begin anew, but this time with a focus on your needs so you can be healthy and complete. Your body has been triggered for a while, it is exhausted and expending too much energy on things that are not of the utmost importance to you. Take a look at your priorities. Are they a reflection of your deepest self? It may be time to expend your energy in more efficient ways. Taking time to rest and fill your reservoir is essential. Then when creating action, ensure you act on what is in alignment with you and your core values.

Food poisoning: It is time for a fresh start. You have picked up some negative energies and unhealthy habits. Now with a clean slate, what direction are you ready to move towards? What areas are you ready to empower? What are you ready to release? The process is not fun, just like food poisoning. You will feel refreshed at the end of your purge.

Fracture: See broken bone

Frostbite: A wound is being created, this wound is creating a painful release. A part of you is being removed. Healing will take time, but it is forming a healthier version of you. This piece may be a habit or heaviness that has only been serving your ego.

Frozen Shoulder:

+ Right shoulder: You are being called to freeze, hit pause. Something is not in alignment with you anymore. The actions you have been taking, the energy you have been giving, it is a misuse of your power. This pause is meant to realign you with a new pathway that is more in alignment with your heart.

+ Left Shoulder: There are wounds and emotional trauma that need tending to now. Now is the perfect time to hold space and feel your feelings. Feel what you have pushed down over the years, your body needs to empty the heart vessel to make space for enrichment and love. Take your time, and move piece by piece. Love each emotion, express it, and send it off. Your heart will thank you.

Full moon: Now is a time of fullness. You are full and whole! When you use gratitude as a practice, can you connect to all of the beauty in your life and all of the beauty that you are? You are radiant, you are powerful, you are whole.

Fungal infection: Do you let your environment affect you easily? Are you easily brought down by another's mood and what they are going through? Check in with your center/soul, who are you? Be you. You are here to be you, not to take on the pain and struggle of the planet and everyone on it.

Gallbladder cancer: There is something from your past that is creating disease in your body. When trauma goes unprocessed and left to fester in the body, it creates cancer. In the gallbladder it is a trauma that has been left in your subconscious mind, hidden unbeknownst to you. Through reflection, see what small or large events in your past (especially childhood) affect who you are today in a negative way. Pull those memories up and bring them to a space of love and acceptance. Try to see the gifts within them, and how they are encouraging you to grow as a person.

Gallbladder disease & gallstones: Gallbladder issues are caused by an overabundance of egoic thoughts. Have you been focusing greatly on thoughts and actions from your head and not your heart? Gallstones are a solid formation of too much emphasis on your shadow self or dark side. Although this is important and a part of who you are, your body is reflecting to you that it's time to reel it in. Time to get in touch with your heart and soul's truth, and to bring that truth forward into your thoughts, actions, and words. Time to let excessive fear-based and ego energies be released.

Ganglion cyst: Time to check in with your path/journey. Are you doing the things you wish to be doing? Are you walking the path and creating the dreams that make your heart sing? Or are you doing things that dehydrate your heart? It is time to make your heart happy.

Gastroenteritis (stomach flu): Your body is purging and releasing what is not in alignment with you. What is your intuition telling you to let go of? The stomach flu is related to emotional and personal energy. Make space to softly and gently surrender what is not supporting you.

Gastroesophageal reflux disease (GERD): You are having issues stomaching life, especially what you have expressed, said, or done in your present and past. It is leaving a bad taste in your mouth. You can't "stomach it" because your body doesn't want to accept it. It is time to create acceptance and unconditional love and allow all that you have spoken and expressed to be a part of who you are. Know that you are imperfect and that is beautiful and okay. Is there something you have been holding back from expressing that feels toxic, or rotten and is eating you up inside? In this case, let it out. It is still a part of your truth. Don't judge it. Free it from your body and soul.

Genital herpes: See herpes simplex

Genital warts: There is an imbalance of serotonin in the body, you are missing that joy factor. Have you been taking time to do joyful activities and reflecting on your inner joy? With an open mind connect to the inner joy within you. Dedicate yourself and your beliefs to accessing it, trust you can experience it. You are worthy of this self-love practice.

Germ cell tumor: What dreams are you holding back on in your life? The seeds of dreams need to germinate with healthy love. Have you been allowing yourself to create the life of your dreams? Or have you been hesitating, and fulfilling goals that don't bring you joy?

Gingivitis: The small things matter. Has something seemingly unimportant gone unnoticed? How can you tend to a healthy you, and express your truest self? Don't speak ill will towards yourself, filter your thoughts and find gratitude and praise.

Glandular fever: See Mono (infectious mononucleosis)

Glaucoma: Have you missed out on enjoying the simple pleasures in your life? Do you place a lot of pressure on wanting more, or something better? Energetically, glaucoma reflects a desire to release that pressure, and finally see all of the beauty that is happening right now. To accept the beauty in the small things, and know that is not what you hoped for, it is even better.

Glomerulonephritis (kidney disease): The kidneys are composed of tiny filters energetically and physically. They are filtering negativity and fear based thoughts and energies from the body.

When there is an overabundance of things to filter, they get backlogged and cannot function. A major overhaul is needed to "clean the pipes." Let go of unnecessary and unsupportive energies. What thoughts are you having and what actions are you taking that are not aligned with your highest self? Are there memories, traumas, relationships, or energies that are negative and unsupportive? Take action to purge these energies and help the kidneys by clearing out what is toxic for you by no longer accepting it in your field. This will help reinstate balance and flow in the kidneys.

Golfer's elbow (medial epicondylitis): It is time to come inwards. You have been connecting a lot with your outer world and community. Your body wants more reflective, creative and self-nurturing activities. Do activities that are just for you.

Gonorrhea: There is a lack of an emotional connection between you and your partner(s). Open up to them, and open yourself. Be vulnerable and trust — it will nourish your heart.

Gout: Reflect on your relationships and your lifestyle habits. Are they optimal for your health? Have you surrounded yourself with healthy relationships that nourish and support you in a balanced way? Are you being compassionate to your health and only taking in food, drink and activities that are pure and supportive? This is a self-love gift, calling you to divine self loving action.

Greed: Greed is caused by loneliness and not feeling whole. There is insufficient awareness of the truth that you are not alone. You may feel alone in your journey and you don't feel supported. There is divine support, family support, friendships, and inner support. Greed is the incessant desire to find fullness, to fill a hole and to become whole. There is a feeling of lack of, in some way in your life. Greed is the incessant thoughts of "I am not enough, I need more (money, love, etc.)", when the truth is that you are enough. What happens when you stop your momentum, pause and take a moment to reflect on all that you are grateful for? How do you feel? Do you feel whole, even just for a moment? This feeling is within you. This wholeness is not outside of you. You cannot fill your wholeness with things, money, or relationships. Realize the gift that you are, that you are whole and full right now. There is so much beauty in your life right now and so much to be grateful for.

It's time to become aware of the truth of your enoughness. Don't be afraid of losing drive and purpose in your work and projects. Your passions will not die out without the fuel of wanting more material wealth. They will only grow with pleasure as you connect to the source of why you are doing what you are doing. Find a deeper purpose, and act out of love for yourself and others, act out of joy. Once you realize you are enough, everything else is just a bonus. Drop the lack-of mentality, and step into abundance. You are abundant, right now. How does it feel to feel abundant? To be enough? To not need experiences to bring you joy and love?

Grief: See death

Gum disease: You have been suppressing your full truth for a long time. It has been held back, and creates disturbance within the gums. Let your full truth flow. Don't hold back at the last second. People will understand and appreciate you when you speak and act from your heart.

Gynecomastia: There is suppressed and imbalanced feminine energy. Have you been honoring both your masculine and feminine self? Have you been creating, thinking, and doing what you desire? Have you been resting, reflecting, and allowing your emotions to flow? Find balance in the yin and the yang within you.

Hairy cell leukemia: Are you constantly on the defense? How can you soften your shields and allow the universe to unfold with trust that everything is happening for your greater good?

Halitosis: See bad breath

Hand, foot and mouth disease: Pause, and check in with the direction of your life. Some things are not in alignment with joy and soul growth. Some things are causing more harm than good. What can you bring into your life that will bring you an abundance of joy and positive growth?

Hashimoto: This is caused by a "lack of" mindset, and struggling to process life. The "lack of" mentality of not being enough, not having enough and not feeling like you are enough, creates excessive stress on the body. It is constantly trying to produce more, to be more, to catch up to your expectations of how you wish for your life to be. These dreams and visions of more are powerful and can be positive. However, they need to be balanced with gratitude for all that you are, and all that you have. You are already in a beautiful space, and have created many beautiful things in your life. Work from this space of abundance, and not lack. You are abundant. You are powerful, healthy and happy in many ways, and more is on the way. The heightened processing of life seeks to be softened and accepted. There is a constant push to rid your life of the negative, to let go of all things toxic in your life. This gives your body extra work as it is constantly processing life, and working to deliver to you what you are focusing on. If you are focusing solely on ridding the negative, more negative is what will be attracted. Shift your focus to your desired state, to the positive that you wish to emanate in your life, and that is what you will attract and be.

Hay fever (allergic rhinitis): Empower your truth of who you are. Stand in any environment and have a forcefield of your unique vibration be impenetrable due to its density.

Headache: Slow down and take some deep breaths. It's time to relax and move slowly. There is too much pressure (self-imposed and environmental) that is creating this tension. It's time to start actively creating space and releasing this pressure — pressure to perform, responsibilities, to be your best self for yourself and for others. It's time to honor and appreciate yourself as you are. Time to nurture yourself with rest and care.

Head and neck cancers: Have you been allowing your thoughts, dreams and goals to be vocalized and created? Or have you been holding back, letting them swirl within your mind for years? Now is the time for you to free your dreams and create the reality that you desire.

Hearing impairment: It feels like your outer world and external environment are constantly grabbing your attention. What happens when you sit in silence, and listen to what is going on within you? There is a space of blissful peace that awaits your discovery. Take time to connect with it, and eventually live from this space.

Heart attack (myocardial infarction): Your heart is speaking to you, yelling at you, in fact. It has had enough. Your heart holds love, love for yourself and all others. It also holds pain, pain of the times when you did not receive the love you were deserving of. Pain from times you did not or do not love yourself. Your heart is saying no more. These wounds must be healed from your entire lifetime, as they have been held onto for too long and you need to step into greater love. Forgive, accept, and love. Love all people, all experiences and especially yourself, no matter what you have been through, because love is in alignment with you and the vibration of health. Resisting or blocking that love creates dysfunction. Putting up walls of protection only traps your love. Free your heart. Free your love. Open, open, open.

Heartbreak: Your heart jumped out of your body and left with another soul. It feels like a piece was taken from you that you can never get back. Will you ever love with the same intensity again? Absolutely. Your heart is rebuilding. It may feel small and weak right now. But it will return and shine insurmountable love on another once again. This time, however, it will be stronger and resist the urge to give itself away to another. Your heart will stay with you, as you have learned and are learning from this current heartbreak. It is building you a stronger, wiser, and more loving heart.

Heartburn: An emotion has been eating away at your heart. It is time to vocalize and express it. Share your wounds.

Heart failure (chronic heart failure): There is pain in your heart, in your emotional center that holds love from relationships to others, and your relationship to yourself. Only love can heal and free this pain that has created this imbalance. Go deeper than the emotional disturbances of the love you have not received, or when love was desolate, or ripped away from you. Go deeper than the wounds to find that love is here and has always been here. Allow this love to take precedence over the pain you have felt, and to hold space for those wounds. Love those wounds, only love can heal them.

Heat exhaustion: You are unprepared to take on what is in front of you, whether that's responsibilities, new projects, or even self-care. Reflect on upcoming events and internal self-growth that you may have been pushing aside or not feeling ready to handle. Ask yourself what needs to be done to help prepare you for the task(s).

Heat stroke: There is an entire system shut down because things have gone too far. It's time to look inwards at what has been burning away at your insides. It's time to heal these internal emotional and mental wounds so that you can move forward.

Hemorrhoids: Anal hemorrhoids are caused by fissures in the mind. There is a leakage of unsupportive thoughts, or negative habits that is taking place. They are toxic yet they are being heard, received, and even fed (supported and nurtured). It is time to allow your deeper truth to flow into your thoughts. Connect to love and to your higher self. Nurture those supportive thoughts, and allow them to flow.

Hepatitis: You have been lying to yourself, and not respecting yourself. It is time to align with the soul truth. Let go of fear-based action and fear-based thought. You are not alone, the universe is supporting you and you are a being of love. All that you need is here within you. Stop seeking outside of yourself for joy, peace, and love. It is all right here, right now, within you. Nothing is needed for you to feel a desired way. How you desire to feel can be accessed only when looking within.

Herniated discs & hernias: Something unsupportive has been needing to be released for a very long time. The level of the herniation shows which area of the body it is most closely related to (check Chapter 11: Anatomy of Energy). Reflect on what you have been holding onto that is deeply unsupportive of your truest self, whether it be emotions, thoughts, experiences or memories. It's time to let go and let flow.

Herpes simplex (cold sores and genital herpes): It is caused by trauma to your emotional body. When you are undergoing extreme stress and ignoring the self-care that is needed, you are creating emotional trauma for yourself. You are saying you are not worthy or good enough to be cared for and that you are not deserving of time for rest and play. You allow yourself to experience anxiety and stress that is harmful to your being. When you have an outbreak, that is your body reflecting its pain and warning you to take a chill pill. Go inwards. Make space for your needs and nourishment. Unwind.

High blood pressure: There is a fear of letting go of your past. You are afraid because your past has helped you make decisions in the present and for your future. It has helped to keep you safe, protected and comfortable. Your soul is calling you to step out of your comfort zone as it is compressing your light and your truth. Let go of your past so you can listen to the wisdom of your open heart in the here and now and flow with the river of life in abundance and joy. It is time to let go of fear and stop resisting divine will. You are holding yourself back from greatness.

High cholesterol: Stop ignoring your issues and problems. It is time to face them. Take a hard look at what is not serving you, shift it, step into your personal power and fight for what you know is right.

Histrionic personality disorder: You are afraid you are not good enough. There is nothing you can do or say to others to prove you are worthy of love. Your viewpoint is the only one that matters. Self-love and appreciation of all of you is needed now and every day. You are deserving. There is nothing to prove.

HIV: The communication center of your body is not in alignment. It is too dominant in one aspect and not honoring the others. Communication is how you show up in this world through your actions and words. You can communicate from: ego, fear, your mind, your heart, your intuition, and your soul. Which areas have you been expressing yourself from into this planet? How can you align with your deepest truth in your expression?

Hives: There is non-acceptance of a trigger. It is not just physical, they are mental and emotional triggers. Are there things that trigger you (create turmoil within)? Is there a way to learn or receive from these triggers? How can they ignite growth within you?

Hodgkin lymphoma: Be true to who you are. Don't get pulled into your environment of stress and worry. Live from your heart and from your truth, let it penetrate your cells and your lymph. Let your love flow from the inside out. Nothing can hold you back from being the beautiful soul that you are.

Huntington's disease: The gift of this disease is acceptance. Accept yourself and your body as you are. If you can bring full acceptance to the table, it improves your quality of life and slows the progression of the disease. What does acceptance feel like in your body?

Hurricane: A hurricane is a force of God, the same primordial energy that you are. A big message is being delivered to you now: Stop, turn around and look back at the life you've lived and created. What is going right? What is wasteful and neglectful? It is time to be extremely intentional in your life path. What are the next steps for you?

Hyperglycemia (high blood sugar): You are multi-faceted, there are so many different parts of you. Your soul growth has been trying to align you with the many beautiful aspects of self you carry. It can feel hard to define all of you, it can feel confusing in expressing and being your authentic and true self. Your truest self is being all of you at once. Being love, being fear, being fight, being calm. All of it=all of you. Like a beautiful rainbow, you are not one color, but many. Embrace the rainbow that you are.

Hyperhidrosis: This is a beautiful gift in that you are constantly purging. It can feel uncomfortable when you release what is toxic to you (thoughts, emotions, etc.), but the process brings you to a space of greater clarity and empowerment. When you feel uncomfortable with your body's constant state of releasing, try to soften into it. Allow things to flow with ease and grace, and your body will react with greater ease and flow.

Hypersexuality: See sex addiction

Hypertension: See high blood pressure

Hyperthyroidism: There is an inability to produce and create from your heart space. There is an over accentuation of the mind and your thoughts. You give so much power to your protective mind, guarding you from loss and hurt, trying to keep you safe. But your heart knows what will bring you satisfaction; it wants to guide you to what you truly seek — more love, connection, peace, joy, and abundance. Pass the microphone to your heart; listen to its sage advice through the language of feeling. As you turn down the volume dial of the brain, go inwards to feel your path and your truth.

Hypoglycemia: How can you show up in your life in a more balanced and sustainable way where you don't feel drained and fatigued, but feel energized? How can you maintain your energy level so that you do not burn out? This is referring to the energy of your essence, your uniqueness and personality.

Hypotension: See low blood pressure

Hypothyroidism: It is no surprise that your body is imbalanced. It is expressing to you a deep sadness, a yearning for something more. It craves balance and health. Reflect upon your lifestyle and habits. Reflect upon your dedication to self-care and connection to others. Is everything optimal? Or are there aspects you can improve upon but have been holding back? Now is the time to put in energy and effort to give your emotional body space to breathe. Give your physical body a detoxification and cleansing. Give your thoughts a filter of mindfulness so you can be more aware of the messages you are thinking. Nourish your spirit: give yourself some soul food. Find and create balance in all aspects of your life. Not just one or two, but all of you as a whole, you are deserving. The body will thank you.

Impetigo: There is difficulty in accepting your situation. It's time to accept and receive. Everything goes just as it comes, have patience and endure what is present now as tomorrow you will be in a new place.

Indigestion: You are having trouble absorbing the nourishment from not only food, but also life. Are you engaging in the healthiest lifestyle and actions? Or are you nourishing yourself with low nutrient content and creation? How can you align with a scrumptious take on life that fills you with joy and vitality?

Infertility: There is an inability to address what is fundamental to your existence: your happiness, your path to happiness in the future, and to receive happiness now in this moment. What is holding you back from living your life in accordance with the emotions of joy, contentment, and peace, and to take action on what makes you feel really good? Focus on feeding your soul and allowing yourself to be a true reflection of your highest self. Reflect on thoughts and actions that can assist you in connecting with your inner joy right now. This brings your body into alignment and allows you to move forward in birthing. You may be birthing children, birthing projects, or whatever you wish to create, as long as you allow yourself to go through your own rebirth and align with your highest self.

Infection: You are stronger than you know. You can fight back by realizing your power. This is a time where your confidence and empowerment are ready to blossom into full bloom.

Influenza: See flu

Ingrown toenail: Something that seems small has been bugging you and getting on your nerves. What this situation needs is compassion and acceptance. How can you accept the small annoyances in life so that your mental health can thrive and be at peace?

Insomnia: Your monsters are getting into bed with you. What are your monsters? Unhealthy and unsupportive thoughts? Unnecessary worry? Fears? You can tackle your fears and thoughts by challenging them, or you can accept them. What feels best to you, and what do you have the energy to do? Embrace your monsters with love, or spend time figuring out how to defeat them. Your body is calling you to work with your inner monsters so that your mind can truly rest.

Iron-deficiency: See anemia

Irregular periods: Your life is craving more balance. It is feeling an inconsistency in your lifestyle. It wants a balance going inward and going outward — a balance of being playful and fun, and focused and serious. A balance of action and non-action. A balance of exercise and rest. You need a balance of thinking and non-thinking (meditating or simplifying life). Take some time to reflect on ways you may be too extreme, ways you may be low and not fueling some of your needs. See if you can begin to integrate more balance into your life.

Irritable bowel syndrome (IBS): IBS is a rejection of what is being absorbed into your being. Not only food, but also energy. The energy of experiences, relationships, information, and self-awareness. Your body is struggling to process everything because there is too much toxicity. Too many unhealthy and unsupportive aspects in your life are making it difficult to absorb and eliminate in a healthy and balanced way. A cleansing energetic purge is needed. It is needed to help calm your system and bring you into a state of rest and peace. It is time to simplify and surround yourself with supportive energies. Embracing positive thoughts, healthy relationships, work that feels balanced and joyful, and lifestyle adjustments that reflect a healthy body. Intake healthy foods, activities, and energies that support and nourish you so that your body can heal. Once healed, continue to implement these changes. When you are wanting to digest or experience something that is harder to process (in moderation), your body will have the foundational energy it needs to support you.

Irritable hip: Irritable hip brings a life lesson to the flow of life. You can't always move forward at a fast pace and freely. At times, you need to have patience and come to a stop. All things will return to a state of flow once again, you simply need to trust the process.

IMS (irritable male syndrome): This time in your life is a time of transition. Embrace changes that are a reflection of your deeper truth. Create space to release old habits and ways of thinking and being that are not for your highest good. As you release these old vibrations, you may have a period of discomfort. You are undergoing a spiritual detoxification.

Irritability & excessive anger: There are seeds within you of anger that have grown over time. They have not been tended to, at least not at their root cause. It is safe to feel what you once did not feel safe to feel, especially the suppressed anger from your past and the hurt that was caused. Allow it to rise and be felt, to be heard and be processed. As it releases, you are pulling the roots to your irritation so that you can be present with love and acceptance.

Itching: Something is trying to break free from your being. Can you resist the urge to scratch it and rush its release? Sit with the discomfort and allow it to move in its own time, trusting your transition.

Itchy bottom: Resist the urge to scratch what feels uncomfortable in your life. Allow it to move in its own natural rhythm. Health and balance will return when you surrender and accept.

Jaundice: Self criticism and harmful thoughts are ready to leave your body. They can't stay any longer, it's time to let them go. Toxic thoughts are not serving you, and doubt is hindering you constantly. What would happen if you truly believed in yourself? How would you be different if you were in your full power?

Jealousy: Your shadow self is taking over. Your ego is creating a toxic environment and holding you back from growth and self love. This toxicity takes over your aura and can be felt in your relationship to your community. You need to turn inwards, into your solar plexus. It is time for a self love renovation. Deeply loving thoughts and words need to be gifted to yourself at this time. You need to rebuild the trust in yourself and your gifts. Your inner critic and judgmental thoughts have been telling you that you aren't good enough. It's time to fight back and appreciate all of the richness of your soul.

Joint pain: The universe is trying to slow you down. Are you constantly doing, or overthinking? Is there a go, go, go feeling within you? Time to nurture the sacred feminine yin energy within you. Press pause. Relax. Breathe. Reflect. Go inwards.

Judgment: Judgment is heavy on the heart dear soul. Judgment tears apart the beautiful vibration of love and joy, and brings chaos and pain. When you judge yourself and you judge others, you are only rejecting the self. Even when it is judgment towards others, you are still rejecting yourself. Because we are all one, you are reflected in all beings of the planet. It does not matter what we are judging someone for, judgment is always the same vibration, the same feeling and thought process. It is the "shouldn't" mindset. It is the "not good enough, not right, you need to change or be better" mindset. You cannot erase this mindset completely and instantly because often you guilt yourself for having it in the first place. Guilt is still in that fear vibration, so the judgment cannot heal. When you have a judgment toward yourself or another, pause, love and accept it. You don't have to like it or agree with it to your core, but accept that there is a part of you feeling this judgment.

The heart and the soul do not judge. They only love. Let's not judge our judgements (feed fire with fire). Whenever judgment is present, be aware that it is from the humanness of your being, from the ego of the self. Accept that your ego has a right to have a feeling or thought, then go deeper to the heart and to the soul. Find the view of the soul which stems from love, and bring your focus there. For example, if you have a judgmental thought towards yourself such as "I am not good enough", discover where it comes from — usually, the ego. Accept that this thought is present and coming from your ego. Then ask yourself, what does my heart believe? What does my soul want to say about my worthiness? You will receive an answer from love, "I am worthy, I am enough, I am love." Then carry on. This is a powerful way to interrupt the judgment process stemming from fear and also bring to light the deeper truths of love. Go through this process when all judgements arise for yourself and others. Be gentle with yourself, accept and know that in time you will learn to tune into the heart awareness naturally.

Juvenile arthritis (chronic childhood arthritis): A separation from soul truth is occurring, either following ego, or getting caught up in your environment. A pulling away from the self is happening. Juvenile arthritis is trying to pull the body and soul back together, back to wholeness and oneness in order to create strength and a solid foundation in preparation for adulthood. Practices like meditation, art, and embracing imagination or intuition can help alleviate the symptoms of pain and discomfort.

Juvenile diabetes: It is a gift to be cared for and tended to as a child. It allows us to feel extra love and embrace. JD gives us more support from our family. This creates a stronger feeling of being worthy of love, which helps us in adulthood find ourselves and live passionately, authentically, and be fearless. For more information see Diabetes Type 1.

Kaposi's sarcoma: Fears and traumas are bubbling up to the surface. They are ready to be released from your being. Can you make space for this transition? This often means you need to feel these uncomfortable feelings once again from your past, but it is a final farewell if you send them off with love.

Kidney cancer: In what ways has fear run your life? Fear can be a healthy and useful emotion when it comes to survival. However, when fear is used for making everyday decisions it creates illness in the kidneys. What fears are not serving you? Can you release them and step into greater trust and positivity?

Kidney disease and dysfunction: See glomerulonephritis and nephropathy

Kidney stones: You are not taking yourself seriously enough. What are you going after? Have you been focused and using your heart to guide you on your path? Or have you been stressing out, diverting your energy and efforts all over the place? It is time to create a clear path to what you desire in your inner and outer world. Release and surrender distractions and things that are not supporting you on your path. You got this.

Kleptomania (stealing): You want to feel fuller. You want to feel bigger, more important, special and loved. The love you are receiving doesn't feel like enough, or there was a major lack of love at a time when you needed it in life and it created a void. Stealing is a way of trying to fill those holes, to feel worthy, to feel special and important. All of the love that you need is ready to embrace you, it is within yourself. Look into the mirror, and gaze into those beautiful eyes. Tell yourself you are loved, you are enough, you are special. Feel the truth of those words. And if you can't feel it, you need to spend some time looking in the mirror and facing all of the lies that are blocking this truth.

Knee tears (meniscus, MCL/LCL/ACL): The tiny details are important. Some things have been put off for too long, made to feel unimportant and unprioritized. It's time to look at those small things and realize that they are more essential to your health and thriving than you thought. Go inwards on a healing journey of tending to the needs that you have not made time for. Now is the time.

Labrynthitis: You are being thrown off the course of your soul's journey. You need to be headstrong in what your purpose is, what your path is. What is your purpose and your path? Believe it, see it, stay on track, and go for it. Don't be deterred by obstacles and distractions.

Lactose intolerance: Your body wants you to be in alignment with what is healthy for you. What habits are not supportive of your health and wellness? Can you take the actions you need to so that you can step out of these unhealthy habits with strength? Your body craves balance. Being in a state of balance is when bliss flows throughout your being.

Langerhans cell histiocytosis: Have you been protecting a piece of you that feels broken? You have been harboring this broken piece within. It has the potential to explode and create chaos in your mind and heart. Now is the time to slowly and safely unpack this piece of you. See if you can wrap it in acceptance and love.

Laryngitis: Take notice of what you are expressing to the world. Do you speak to make conversation and connections? Or do you let your truth resonate from your core? How can you align with your heart when you express yourself?

Leaky gut: You have too much mental stress. Your mind is working very hard at digesting the unfolding of your life. It is trying to process everything that is occurring, has occurred, and is preparing you for what is to come. It is time to step back, soften the reigns of the mind, and allow the universe to interject your path with beauty and grace. Allow your life to unfold like a flowing river, and to stop fighting the current. This will heal the mind and the over-processing. Your intestinal walls can finally rebuild, as they are not being overworked by the constant stress of trying to process, digest, and absorb life. Instead they can be nourished by the beauty and trust of all that is.

Leukemia: Acceptance and gratitude is the gift. Leukemia tests us and can push us to live in a state of fear. To hold space for gratitude is powerful and assists in healing the body. Gratitude creates flow and ease on your path. Have a gratitude journal. Create a gratitude practice to assist you in stepping out of the fear vibration. This will help create acceptance of life, and of the universe's plan, whatever that may be. Accept and allow it to flow and unfold from a space of trust. Trust that everything is happening as it is meant to unfold. Acceptance means shining love on all of your life, and all of yourself, as you are.

Lewy body dementia: Life has shown you stress, fatigue, and discomfort. The mind has built a blockage to begin disconnecting you from your harsh reality, and go into a state of hibernation. On your path to healing and ease, acceptance is key. Acceptance of life as it is, accepting that there are difficulties, but that there are also beauties waiting to be discovered. Enjoy this ride for the time you have left, hold it in gratitude in your heart. Complete your journey from a place of love and optimism.

Lice: Have you been honoring your mind (your logical self)? Have you been listening to your thoughts? Or have you been caught up in the flow of life, constantly being pulled to the next thing? Slow down, there are some powerful messages to be heard, received, and processed from your own beautiful mind. Create space to honor this part of you, so that your mind doesn't get carried away and overworked or underworked and not utilized. Check in with yourself. There are things that wish to arise.

Lichen planus: Your body is releasing toxic pent-up fears and emotions that are not supporting you. Reflect on what you are ready to release in your life, and let it go. Stop scratching the itches of unhealthy lifestyle patterns and beliefs. Soften their grip by surrendering and allowing them to move out of your life and out of your system.

Lightning: Heaven is touching Earth. Now is a time to connect with your higher self and receive deep insights on your path. You may also receive healing, abundance, and positivity if you remain open. Lightning is a powerful force of energy that can destroy and create. Lightning sparks a fire and after the fire comes rebirth. What are you ready to burn in the fire and what are you ready to give birth to in your life?

Limp (crooked gait/walk): Sometimes it may feel like you are behind others in your progress, in your actions, and in your drive. The truth is you have the ability to be more focused than others. You are capable of major creations, progress, and extreme self-growth in your life. It is okay to go slow and be behind the pack. It gives you more time to be clear in your direction, to see all the possible routes, and to know: "Yes, this is the path for me." Instead of running in circles and never getting anywhere, slow down, assess your path, and know that you have the power to create any future and growth that you desire. Know that getting to that goal and dream is done so much faster when you move slowly.

Lisp: Impatience will be a soulful challenge for you to overcome in your life's journey. There is no rush to get things done, or to get your point across. Every moment is precious and enough, just as it is. When you rush in life, you don't savor the small juicy moments, and miss out on many of the gifts laid before you.

Liver cancer: Let your emotions be held in love and freely expressed. Don't hold in or hold back from letting your feelings out into the world. What have you been holding on to that isn't healthy? Can you make space for it to be expressed through love now?

Liver tumor: Anger has taken over internally. You need to step back and review your lifetime of felt emotions. Those you have suppressed and those you have expressed. The emotions not fully processed (especially anger) are wanting to be freed from your body. Now is the time to express yourself and let them go.

Loneliness: A numb void is being felt in your life. It is time to ignite passion within. Passion for your goals and desires, and passion for living from your heart. Bring the warmth back internally, then love from others will be drawn like a moth to a flame. Love and embrace will flow with ease and grace.

Low blood pressure: It's time to push yourself out of your comfort zone. Life has been getting predictable and boring. This creates a slow moving un-interesting flow. Follow your desires, follow your imagination, see what artwork you can create through your life. Have fun and be spontaneous — beautiful things will happen.

Low libido/low sex drive: It is time to let go of the old fears of not being good enough. Relinquish the high standards and ideals comparing you to others. This goes for your sexual energy as well; to heal, you must begin with acceptance, not with a comparison of your past, of others, or the way you believe you "should" be. Accept the way you are in this moment, and be okay with it. Only then can you heal, grow, and find happiness and value within. Let's drop the labels of good and bad, and just be with what is and hold it as being enough. Then create change from that space of love by showering yourself with gratitude for all that you are. Only from gratitude do you grow and change. When you are hard on yourself, full of judgment and self-deprecation, you compress the sunlight that allows you to flower. Nurture the seeds of compassion within you to grow a compassionate flower. Sexual energy, loving energy, physical love for yourself, your health and your life — it is all interconnected. Begin with love and it will spread to all aspects of your life.

Lung cancer: You are holding sadness and fear from your past, about yourself, about others and about the world. Sadness is dwelling within your body. It is safe to feel your sadness. Let the river flow, don't create a dam and block yourself off. Step out of the fear vibration and let love in.

Lupus (systemic lupus erythematosus): The body is attacking itself. It is trying to stop you in your tracks and sway your direction. Some part of you or your life is not in alignment with love, and with compassion. There have been self-destructive behaviors and patterns for some time now. It is time to reflect on the areas you have allowed to slide to the back burner, to bring them forward, and let your heart instead of your head guide the way. You can go your whole life without addressing these misalignments, but that will lead to more physical stress and harm in the body. Your body and soul want you to align with truth, health, and happiness in all areas of your life.

Lyme disease: When you give too much power to your thoughts and your mind, it discombobulates your path. It can make it difficult to live with a clear intention of your life's purpose. You can feel shaken around and uncertain on your path. Pave your path forward using choice and heart. Purpose driven by the heart always leads to success and joy. Purpose led by the mind spins you in circles. Reflect on the questions: Who am I? What gifts can I share with this world? What direction does my heart lead me to? Clarity and focus are needed on your path. Find this not from thinking, but from feeling.

Lymphedema: How can you live a more balanced life? Is there an area in your lifestyle that goes untended? Create balance in your health, wellness, actions and non-actions. Find balance in your relationships to others and relationship to yourself. Do not leave any small facet of your life unattended to. Every piece of you is deserving of love and attention.

Malaria: Have you been overpowered or made to feel lesser than others? It is time to step into your power and to hold your ground. Know your strength and don't be afraid to embody it.

Male menopause (andropause): There is resistance to growth. Not the growth of building and strengthening, but the growth of shedding your skin like a snake. The growth of letting go of the old self so you can transition into who you are today. Allow a deeper level of truth and self-awareness untainted by experiences from your lifetime to enter your being. This is a rebirth of your truest and highest self. Resistance to this transition and release can create pain and illness in the process.

Malnutrition: In which areas of your life are you placing too much energy and attention? In which areas of your life are you depleting yourself of energy and attention? Find the balance and create full body/soul health by not over or under focusing on each area of your life.

Marriage: You are committing your devotion to another being. You will be pushed to release your ego when your relationship struggles, so that you can choose the path of love — the path of honoring your highest self and honoring your partner's highest self. You are ready to divert a lot of your vital energy to support another and trust that they will do the same. You are awakening to great trust in another and trust within yourself to be there for them and the relationship, all while honoring your heart on the journey.

Measles: What belief system is not supporting you and is hindering you? Don't get stuck in the stubbornness of old patterns. Progression and growth can feel difficult, but it will lead to a greater sense of freedom and love in the end.

Memory loss: You need to stay focused on your soul path. Don't get too comfortable in a space of misalignment. Stay on your path of purpose, and be motivated by what brings you joy. As you veer off the path, you lose connection to your full brainpower because your energy is being dispersed trying to pull you back on track.

Meniere's disease: Center and ground yourself. Life throws curve balls and multi-directional distractions on your path. Take one step at a time in the direction you dream to create. Don't get distorted because you can not see the end of the path, trust that each small action you take will get you to where you want to be.

Meningitis: How do you handle your beliefs and values being questioned by the outside world? Stand strong and own the beauty of your mind. You are intelligent. You are right and justified to have your own opinions. You are intuitive. Don't be discouraged or traumatized if others oppose you. Own your truth. There is only one you, no one in the whole world will agree with you completely.

Menopause: It's time to shut down the system and rest. Now you will need time and space to embrace this soul transition in your life. Your body, habits, mind and emotions are shifting closer to your soul truth. This transition can feel difficult and uncomfortable (especially when resisted). The more space and gentleness you infuse into your life, the easier and smoother this blossoming will occur.

Menstrual cramps: Breathe. Embrace the changes constantly flowing into your life. Embrace your menstrual cramps with this same acceptance, as they are representing the growth and death you experience. Nurture them with remedies that help ease the transition period. The more you surrender and accept your cramps, the easier the challenges, growth, and change will flow into your life. All of the changes you are experiencing are bringing you closer and closer to your highest potential of self.

Mesothelioma: There is an imbalance in your energy. Are you constantly trying to please others and not giving yourself the energy, self-love, and self-care you are deserving of? It's time to put your needs first. Find joy, love and peace within and in your environment. Do what feels good!

Migraine: Have you been focusing, working hard, or stressing out? Migraines are a gift reminding you to slow down; sometimes you need to "turn off" completely. You need deep rest and relaxation. You need peaceful activities where your mind and focus relinquish their power to your inner peace.

Miscarriage: Trust in divine timing. Know that there is a greater force at work always looking out for you in all aspects of your life. The hardships and suffering offer you strength to find real joy and happiness within yourself. Strength to allow for deep growth and alignment with the vibration of love. This is not always easy to see or understand. When you don't understand it, surrender and trust that there is a positive force infused into all of life and death.

Misophonia (sound sensitivity): You are a hyper-sensitive being. You are greatly and deeply affected by others. You are affected by vibration, and by sound. This condition is here to empower you and to tell you: You need to strengthen yourself. You need to strengthen your energy. Your energy is love, and you are pulled into the fear (anger) vibration too easily. Stand strong in your love, your truth, your essence. Be empowered. Be firm in your light, your joy, in yourself, so that you are not being harmed by others. However, you can assist them by holding space for them, a space of love and acceptance. This is an empathic gift; you are sensitive and an empath, which means you are a healer. You just need to learn your strengths in healing and not take on everyone else's pain.

Mold in home/environment: It is time to leave the old behind. It has become toxic and unhealthy. There are patterns that are only pulling you down and creating disharmony in your life. It requires immediate change, it is serious. It is your mental health, your energy, and your vitality. It is all being affected by holding a space for what is not supporting you anymore. To clear the past and the old unsupportive energies, do a purge. Maybe it is a symbolic or literal purge for you. Release old photos, old thoughts, old, old, old, so that you can step into the new healthier and happier you.

Monkeypox: There is chaos around you. It's time to focus, simplify, and move with intention.

Mono (infectious mononucleosis): You need to stop and take a good look at your path. Have your decisions and actions been in alignment with your soul truth? Or have you been venturing off of this path? Let your outer world reflect your inner world.

Monsoon: This is a time to connect with your heart center. How can you align with your heart's desires, and live from this space with greater ease? Monsoon also has the energy of working towards powerful releases in ancestral clearing, or individual healing.

Motor neuron disease (MND): Motion in your outer world has been classified as essential to survival. What about motion in your inner world? Now is the time for you to explore the inner realm of your existence, living from the heart space, accessing your inner knowing (intuition), and spirituality. How can you slow down the reliance on outer motion, and find the beauty and ability to harness your inner motion?

Multiple myeloma: Strength is within you, not something you create. You can be strong in thoughts of fear, or strong in thoughts of love. Where are you on the spectrum? You can be strong in being true to who you are, strong in embracing life, and strong in making challenges opportunities. Are you ready to rise to your inner strengths?

Multiple sclerosis (MS): Go after what you truly desire and live life to its fullest. MS is showing you not to take anything for granted. Know that every moment is an opportunity for your soul to shine and for you to be in alignment with your truth and live your life in accordance with the truth of this present moment.

Mumps: You can do anything! Believe in yourself. Don't let people's views hold you back from going after your wild and silly dreams. You can do anything, if you let yourself believe it.

Murder: Experiencing murder in your circle brings a feeling of fear and darkness. You may begin to believe that the nature of humanity is bad, and that people are untrustworthy. It causes you to close your heart. It pushes you into a state of darkness. It is really giving you an opportunity to step into the greatest love, trust, and hope for all beings and discover real unconditional love. This means loving all beings as they are and knowing everyone is deserving of compassion. To know what real true love is, you must experience seeing a human being in darkness, inflicting suffering on others. This gives you an opportunity to be unconditional in your love, to actually experience the fullest of love, instead of falling into the dark. The darkness (hate, suffering) is a cousin of love. It gives you an opportunity to utilize love's true potential, and apply it unconditionally.

Muscle cramps: Disengage. Take some deep breaths and create space for your mind and body to relax. Find balance.

Muscle pain: You are so dominant in your thoughts that it has spread to the body and is creating pain. Meditate, breathe, and create space just to be.

Myocardial infarction: See heart attack

Nail biting: You need an outlet to release pent up energy, stress, excitement, and anxiety. Are you engaging in physical activities that get your heart pumping, your sweat flowing and endorphins generating? And if so, are you engaging in these activities enough? This can help release that excessive energy you are carrying. Create a vision board, set goals, organize your priorities, let your mind have an outlet to express all of its vibrancy.

Narcissistic personality disorder: Do you fear being vulnerable and being hurt by others? You are protecting your inner child by stepping into a protective bubble of self-assurance that is manufactured. It is time to release that bubble, and discover that you never needed to build or become anyone. You always were, will be, and are worthy of love.

Narcolepsy: This gift has been trying to slow you down. It has been attempting to show you that you can relax and rest in acceptance. There is no need to struggle trying to prove your worthiness in this world. You are worthy. You are loved. Let go of unnecessary efforts so that you can begin to just be as you are. Start to observe and enjoy witnessing your life unfold, instead of struggling to show up in it. Witness your effortless part in the flow of life. Witness your body speaking to you in how it feels moment to moment. Witness all of the gifts that are in every situation. Take these moments to witness the constant stream of love and support that is all around you. The universe is gently holding a space for you to flourish and grow.

Nasal and sinus cancer: The face is symbolic of something you need to face head on. What have you been ignorant of embracing or releasing on your path? What excuses have you been making to avoid what is truly important to you? It is time to go for it and get it done. Release your resistance and blocking beliefs. Charge forward on your path with power.

Nasal and sinus congestion: Clarity is needed on your path. How can you be more focused in delivering your message to the world? Can you do it in a non-forceful and compassionate way? Let go of the pressure to deliver a strong message and to impress your circle. Just be your authentic truth, and let it flow with ease and specificity.

Nasopharyngeal cancer: Many areas of your life are in balance. How can you maintain your state of balance by holding firmer boundaries? Boundaries are a healthy way of expressing self-love and care, by creating an ideal atmosphere for you to thrive.

Neck Pain: Speak your truth, don't hold back, but check that it's coming from your soul and not your ego. Do the things that make your heart sing. You are worthy. For more details, see back pain.

Nephropathy (kidney disease): You are holding on to deep-seated fears. These fears have established a home in the body. They feel like a part of you. But they are villains in disguise, robbing you of your potential — the potential to experience more love, joy, peace, and abundance. What fears are holding you back from living fully? What would your life look like without these fears?

Neuroblastoma: When you are slowed down in life, it becomes easier to see the gifts. Presence and gratitude for each moment are an essential skill. Neuroblastoma causes you and your family to slow down and to take a moment to process life.

Neuroendocrine tumors: You are not helping others connect with you when you are constantly defending and protecting yourself. How can you let down your walls and expose your vulnerable heart? Soften the sharp edges and realize there is nothing that needs to be defended. You are love itself, and cannot be diminished or made to feel small. You are made of the same material as everyone else: love. Transfer your power from fear to love and embody it. What does it feel like?

New moon: You are in a time of new beginnings. Where are you inspired to create change in your life? What are you ready to release? Now is the time to let your inspiration move from fantasy to reality.

Nightmare: Your inner fears are poking into your consciousness. What is the feeling in the nightmare? How can you interpret it as a challenge you are ready to face?

Nonalcoholic fatty liver disease: Your liver is holding on to painful emotions of sadness. Take your time to heal these wounds from your past. Spend as much time as you need with each painful memory and embrace it in love. Let yourself know that you are loved, even when your inner child was hurt and made to feel small. Visualize your younger self being wrapped in a loving hug from yourself now. Feel how that love softens each blow of hardship that you have encountered. Hold yourself today in this comforting love. Let all of your shadows and unwanted aspects of self be held in tender compassion. This is what your body needs to heal.

Non-Hodgkin lymphoma: Toxicities need to be released from your body. What toxic energies have you been holding on to? Negativity, judgment, and fear have filled your being and suppressed your loving and healthy energy from flowing. Can you surrender your attachment to your toxic thoughts, memories, and feelings that do not support your health and wellness? Now is the time. Find a way that works best for you: therapy, journaling, art, movement, etc.

Norovirus: Do you feel pulled in multiple directions? The uncertainty and confusion on your path are being caused by depending on your mind. It is time to step out of the traditional formula of using your brain to figure out your next steps. Step into your heart and intuition to feel the way. The way will spark joy within you, it will call to you. Follow your inner compass, and stop trying to figure everything out. There is a part of you that knows — feel this inner knowing.

Nose bleed: Your vitality, strength, and life force are leaving your body. Your energy is feeling misdirected. It wants to be utilized in a way that serves your deepest truth, not just floating by in life, or comfortably stagnant in where you are. But to be utilized fully, living through your heart and being fueled by passion. Take action towards your dreams and believe in yourself. You have the capacity. Stop wasting energy, thoughts, and actions towards things that are not really serving you.

Nose picking: It is time to be more present. Shake off stress, worry, and living in the future. Arrive here in this moment. How can you live with greater intention and mindfulness?

Obesity: You are special and you are important. There is nothing that needs to be proved or deserved. You are worthy of love and acceptance from yourself and others as you are. Honor yourself for all that you are.

Obsessive compulsive disorder (OCD): Surrender and open yourself to the sensation of freedom as you release control. Be free. Be present. Be open. Let go.

Obstructive sleep apnea: See sleep apnea

Oral thrush: Your wants can't be clearly communicated and met. Discomfort is sometimes inevitable in life. How can you take the extra steps to bring comfort in other ways? How can you support yourself and use self-care as a tool to bring more ease and enjoyment into your day?

Organ transplant:

- ♦ For the receiver: You are being given a rare opportunity at a new life. This new beginning is a gift. How do you want to show up differently in the world? Now is the time for ultimate changes and soul growth on your path. For the specific energy of the organ, refer to Chapter 11: Anatomy of Energy.

- ♦ For the giver: You are being challenged in your belief systems to know that you are much more than your body. You are energy and you are love. When you donate an organ, you are removing a piece of yourself and your functionality. However, you can replace it with an abundance of loving energy. Do this with intention and positive thoughts. After you donate an organ, you can heal and come to a place of greater health than before.

Osteoarthritis: There is anxiety to be free of old unsupportive ways. There is an urgency to let go and to surrender. You have been carrying out old patterns and ways of living that are just not useful to your growth and your purpose. It's time to let them go and step into your new self with love.

Osteomyelitis: You are overthinking and giving your mind too much to process, this creates inflammation for the bones. Surrender, surrender, surrender. Surrender the mind. You have given it too much power and control; it is time to discover what happens when the mind is at peace.

Osteoporosis: Silence the mind and your thoughts. Create space and freedom in the body by freeing the mind. Your thoughts have weighed you down and exhausted your body. This will be a hard practice, but it is attainable through effort in releasing effort.

Osteosarcoma: There are many gifts in slowing down. For some time you will be called to slow down, to step back, and have a greater perspective on life. Osteosarcoma gives you an opportunity to access your inner wisdom and move through life at a different pace. Over time you will come back to feeling invigorated and energized. You will have gained valuable insight into living a more balanced life.

Otitis externa (swimmer's ear): Your inner voice wants to be heard. Spend some time in silence and see what comes up for you. Contemplate important questions, reflect on what is important to you, and align with your deeper truth.

Ovarian cancer: There is an infection of fear that has spread to the ovaries. Your ovary energy houses the energy related to sex, your visions and dreams, inner child, and connection to the world. There is an imbalance here that needs to be addressed.

Can you truly let go of what is not serving you and step into the vibration of love as you step out of fear? Now is the time.

Ovarian cyst: Life will always have obstacles on your path holding you back from going after your dreams and from dreaming itself. How can you see your obstacles and soften their power? Don't let them tell you that you can't do something. See them for what they are, something to overcome or accept. Your obstacles have been holding you back from dreaming, from creating goals that bring the deepest joy to you. When you accept or release your obstacles, what dreams become accessible to you?

Overeating: A hole or void is trying to be filled. A piece of you feels empty, unloved, and unheard. Food is something that helps to temporarily fill this hole, but it is insatiable and unending. It is not food your body wants. It's love, self-love. Once that is achieved and topped up, then you can open to love from others. Another person cannot fill this hole for you. It must come from you, and only you know how. You do know. Food is a distraction from facing the self. Spend some time looking into a mirror, staring at your soul through your eyes. And ask: What does my soul need to feel loved? What do I want to feel loved?

Paget's disease of the bone: Bigger is not always better. In what areas of your life can you focus and zoom in? How can you create greater potency and power by staying focused on what is important to you? Staying small in this case will bring about the greatest results. This can relate to beliefs, lifestyle, work, or relationships.

Paget's disease of the nipple/breast: Two things are wanting your attention: 1. Things that need to be changed. 2. Things that need to be appreciated and accepted. Spend some time reflecting on what areas you can improve upon in your life with powerful action and change. Also reflect on the things that you cannot change, or would be difficult to change, and grant yourself the courage to accept them.

Pain: Something is off or not in balance. Pain is your body's way of drawing attention to an area of your body and life that needs attention. Refer to the symbolic references in Chapter 11: Anatomy of Energy and check the meaning on which area of the body you are feeling your pain. Pain can also be guiding you on your path. Sometimes your pain may prevent you from doing an activity for example; this may be because you need rest. Pain can let you know when you need to slow down and do self-care. It can take your mind off of life and teach you invaluable lessons on presence and acceptance. Tune into your pain and ask it, "Dear pain, what do you want me to know?"

Pancreatic cancer: What simple things in life bring you joy? How can you go deeper into an awareness of gratitude to see all of the gifts in this moment? Live from this moment, see the richness and beauty constantly unfolding. Nothing more is needed, not riches, extravagance, fame, glory, just you and this moment is abundance itself.

Pancreatitis: Now is a good time to reassess your lifestyle. Are you living with a lifestyle that is in accordance with your wisdom? If not, it's time to make it happen.

Panic attack: Breathe. Be aware that you have given yourself over to your thoughts. You have placed all your power and being in the mind and in your outer world. You need some detachment or, rather, attachment to your inner truth, to the peace that lies within, the soul truth. It is always present, even when it feels like your world is falling to pieces. You simply must breathe, and you will be connected with the deeper meaning. Everything is okay. You are okay. You are alive. Peace is here.

Panic disorder: Everything will be okay. Imagine accepting this mantra and living from a place of acceptance. Panic attacks, stress, fear — they do not need to vanquish from your life. They can be present and you can still be okay. A panic disorder brings a beautiful gift of unconditional love and trust in your heart consciousness to take care of you. On the outside, it may look like you have a mental health condition and that things are not okay. But, when you live from your heart center, you realize from within that everything is okay just as it is. Sit with this mantra, "everything is okay." See what resistance comes up and try to hold space for it in your heart.

Paralysis: Surrender dear one. Surrender to your greatest truth: You are not your body, you are not your mind, you are love. You are a whole, loving, and beautiful soul. No matter what has been taken from you, you are whole; your soul cannot be taken. You can live from this greater truth at all times. You can live with more passion and purpose, with more joy and peace than anyone, if you surrender to these truths within you.

Paranoid personality disorder: Trust in yourself. Find the space of love and compassion within you. There is pure love in your heart. Once you feel and know this, open your heart to the world around you. Those with an open heart will be drawn to you, connect, love and support you. Live in awareness and truth of your heart. You are deserving of being deeply loved not only by yourself, but also by others.

Parkinson's disease: Are you getting caught up in your chosen beliefs? You have chosen to create your reality based upon what you see. You are getting stuck on a superficial level of reality. You must see deeper, to where there is so much more. There is love and there is light. There is an interconnectedness between all beings. It is time to connect to your soul's truth and shake off old belief systems to experience your deepest truth.

Parvovirus infection: Listen to your body and what it is telling you. If you are nervous and acting out, take a moment to close your eyes and discover what is bugging you. Your feelings, actions, thoughts, and body are always communicating what is going on at a deeper layer. Parvovirus calls for greater reflection to understand what your body and soul are needing.

Pelvic organ prolapse: Your spirit is feeling deflated and not full. How can you build strength in your core of being and increase your potency? You are being challenged to stand strong in your power (your unique self) against all odds and currents.

Penile cancer: What are you injecting into the world? Are you in alignment with who you are, and in turn reflecting that through your creations? It is time to reflect and turn inwards to rediscover your "why" and your "what."

Penis enlargement: You have a want to constantly be creating. There is an overabundance of yang energy/masculine energy. You have feminine yin and masculine yang within you, regardless of gender. It is time to balance your active mind and "go, go" lifestyle with rest, reflection, and going inwards. It's not all about being productive. You must have balance. Just as you need sleep at night to balance your awake state, you need yin energy in your life.

Peptic ulcer (stomach ulcer): Stress has been eating away at you. You need to create times of silence. Silence is needed so that your mind can process the unfolding of your life. Give yourself space to digest this life and how it chooses to unfold. Begin to pull the nutrients from every situation and experience. There is beauty in all, but when you are not paying attention (or your mind is too full), you will never see it. See that every moment has been enriched with something positive just for you.

Peripheral neuropathy: Your mind is in need of intensive care. Can you create the space to dive deep through your thoughts, underneath your beliefs, and arrive at your inner knowing? This inner knowing in your mind has been restricted and blocked by habitual and chosen thought patterns. Your inner knowing is waiting to share a calm awareness with you that will bring more flow, ease and presence into your life.

Peripheral vascular disease: There is so much love within you. Are there greater ways you can share this love with the world? Through loving action, acts of kindness or words of compassion? This love wants to be manifested into your reality, into your outer world in a powerful way. It is not just meant to be internal, but also external. Expand, grow, and share.

Personality disorder: There is a lack of love for yourself. Reflect inwardly to discover the treasures and soul beauty that you hold. You are a fierce god/goddess. You need to feel this, know this, and be this. As you step into this truth, you connect with the god and goddess in everyone. You are worthy of living heaven on Earth.

Pervasive developmental disorder: Things have been slowed down tremendously, as if time has come to a standstill. This gift allows you to be more present, to be more aware of each moment and take it all in. For parents of children with PDD, you are being gifted with an opportunity to learn presence and acceptance of this moment. For those with PDD, you are exactly where you are meant to be. Have gratitude for all that you are. You are a gift to this world in so many ways. Reflect on all of your gifts. Feel them, know them. This is your truth.

Peyronie's disease: Your self-love, self-care and self-appreciation is speaking out to you. Honor yourself and know that you are worthy. You are a powerful and incredible human being. Commit to more self-care practices as you honor yourself and your worthiness. Step into more self-love and empowerment. When your inner strength shines, your outer world reflects this.

Pets: When an animal gets sick, injured or is struggling it is similar to humans as they have a spirit, energy body, physical, emotional and mental body as well. I have not channeled specifically for pets in this book, as it is too much information to include, but I will share a bit of information to help you with their health. When your pet is struggling, there is healing being offered to the pet and to you. Reflect on the gift or challenge that this is bringing you. Reflect on the possible gift or challenge this is bringing your pet. You can ask your intuition for more details to connect with the guidance of the condition.

Phlegm: Things that are ready to leave your body are sticking: Toxins, negative energy, and old behaviors. They are clinging for dear life to you. It is a more painful process than it needs to be. It's time to invite in some softness and flow to your releasing process. You can do this simply with intention: "I release all that no longer serves me with ease and grace." This will help combat the inner struggle as the body resists releasing stagnant unsupportive energy.

Phobia: There is trauma being held in your nervous system and it is reflected through your phobia(s). Reflect on your small and great struggles in life. Is there any anxiety in these reflections? If so, healing work is needed. Self-healing, talk therapy, meditation, whatever you feel will assist you in finding peace with your past traumas.

Pink eye (conjunctivitis): Your physical eyes are putting up a wall. It is time to look deep within yourself and align with the truth of your inner world. Sometimes we need to stop looking outside of ourselves at the world, so we can more clearly see the truth that lies within.

Pleurisy: There is a wall or barrier restricting you from expanding your heart consciousness. Your ability to love fully and wildly is being restricted by your environment (societal beliefs, social community, etc). What would it feel like if you let your heart be free? Your actions and words would stem from pure love, and an interconnectedness between you, the universe, and everything in between becomes real.

Pneumonia: It may feel like life is attacking you at this time. Physically but also emotionally and mentally. Surrender to the higher power within you. The space of divine peace that is always present in your being.

Poliomyelitis (polio): A part of you or pieces of you may feel like they are missing or have been taken. Your physical body may not feel optimal. But your soul, that is full and whole. Polio guides you to finding your fullness inside, no matter what is going on externally. You are always whole.

Polycystic ovary syndrome: Energy is stuck in the lower abdomen, and change is required to free this energy to maintain health and balance. Release your fears of personal growth and allow yourself to align with your deeper truth. Take action with a healthy lifestyle and reflect your kindness and beauty of your soul (who you are) into the world. See your beauty. Now let the world see it.

Polymyalgia rheumatica: Do you feel restricted? You may feel like your world is pre-planned and you are taking the practical and predictable steps. How can you break the mold and dance through life?

Polyps: Your body is holding onto unhealthy emotions in the area of your polyp(s). In Chapter 11: Anatomy of Energy, look at the area that your polyps have developed and see the connection to which emotion is being held there. Allow these emotions/areas of your life to lift to the surface and be revisited. Surrender the pain that is being suppressed and carried. Feel the feelings that want to arise, and let them release with acceptance.

Post-nasal drip: You may be, or have been for some time, facing a resistance to speak your truth and be your authentic self. This resistance may be internal, external, or both. Step into your power with clarity and specificity of who you are, and what you desire. You are unstoppable.

Post-traumatic stress disorder (PTSD): You are getting stuck, unable to process, absorb and excrete your trauma. Softening is needed and vulnerability is essential. When you are present, you know that you are safe. In this moment, you are safe. It is safe to let down your walls gently, with ease, integrate with your trauma, and feel your pain. To feel this pain fully and express it can be very scary. But know that as you feel it, you are processing it. When you hold it through the eyes of love, or simply as a witness, it shifts. When you hold it through the eyes of fear, you cling to it. After you process and feel, only then can you release and surrender that pain. Once processed through love you can be emotionally present in the vibration of unguarded love once again. You got this. Take your time. It will unfold if you allow it to unfold.

Puking (vomiting): Your body is energetically purging the lies you have been expressing. Who are you at your core? Have you been authentic and truthful in sharing this with others, or even with yourself? Let go of old patterns of masking your true self, and shine through in your words and how you carry yourself.

Predominantly inattentive type ADHD (formerly ADD): You are being guided to move your awareness away from your mind and into your heart space. When you are living life through the mind, it may seem as if everything is of equal importance. When you are living through your heart, it is easy to focus on what is really important, and live with greater purpose and effectiveness.

Pregnancy: New life is awakening within you in more ways than you can imagine. Physical birth also creates a spiritual birth for the mother. It is a time of new beginnings and a new awareness. In what ways are you ready to charge into a new arena of your life? Now is the time. Let this beautiful energy within you symbolize your own birth (into your improved version of self). Heavy sickness and pregnancy discomfort offers you an opportunity to shed the old. See it as a symbolic purge of what doesn't serve you anymore (beliefs, lifestyle, etc). The discomfort and body pains offer you a gift of acceptance, accepting this present moment, and that nothing lasts forever. Even if it feels uncomfortable, it is still a gift calling you to be present with this moment.

Preterm birth: This child is excited to enter this world. For the parents: your preterm baby has many gifts they are going to offer you. Gifts for your own personal growth, with unexpected challenges (opportunities) to align with your highest self.

Premenstrual syndrome (PMS): Things are not in alignment. Your body is speaking to you and letting you know changes need to be made. Reflect on: your diet, exercise, work, relationships, mindset, and past. When PMS is heightened, reflect on these areas currently and see if you are in alignment with your healthiest self. If not, what steps can you take to assist you with alignment?

Prostate cancer: There is friction in your growth. There are aspects of yourself awaiting deep transformation. Are you clearing the path and allowing this transformation to occur? Or are you consciously or unconsciously resisting and blocking these big changes? Surrender and allow, as the transformation can be scary but beautiful like a caterpillar to a butterfly. Freedom awaits on the other side.

Prostate gland enlargement (benign prostatic hyperplasia): You have been operating out of the fear consciousness in aspects of your life. You are coming from your ego, because you have a fear of being judged by others and you judge yourself. It is time to accept and honor your gifts and your natural state of being. Step into your authenticity more strongly, by softening the inner pressure and fear of striving for perfection and appeasement. It is time to accept and just be you. Just do you. You got this!

Psoriasis: Can you let go of pressure? Can you surrender your control to the universe? Psoriasis is a reflection of the body feeling trapped by your perception of your environment. Can you let go and allow things to flow? This will assist the skin in its natural capacity to heal.

Psoriatic arthritis: Do not focus on what you cannot do, instead focus on what you can do. You may feel slowed down and restricted at times. Focusing on the negatives only intensifies their power and potency. What positives can you divert all of your attention to? How does your life improve when you come in with an abundant and grateful mindset?

Psychosis: Come inwards, into your being. Ground yourself. Connect with the earth beneath you and around you. You are here now, even though there is a lot going on around you pulling at your attention. How can you focus and prioritize the essentials? By simplifying your attention, your world will also become clearer.

Rabies: The body and mind have been in an erratic state of fight or flight. Contracting rabies is a serious message to center yourself, breathe, and find calmness within you.

Rain: Washes away thoughts and impurities.

Rainbow: Joy is shining into your life. There is beauty in every moment, every action, and every reaction. Take a moment to feel gratitude for all the areas of abundance that you currently have access to. You are a being of light, you can access more energy and power than you know. You are powerful, and have the tools to create your dreams.

Rape: Experiencing rape is the ultimate challenge. It challenges you to find deep worthiness, self-love, and inner knowing. Step into your self love and own it, be empowered by it. Know you are love, it is your truth, it is you. Although your love was once taken or crushed by another, that is not your truth. That was an experience. That was a reflection of someone else's pain and fear body. It is not your job to take it on. It is not your truth. Come deep inside yourself, deeper than the trauma, to find your soul truth. Your soul truth is the part of you that is constant and never affected, it never changes. It is love, always love. Let it shine into all the corners of your body, all of your being. Let it shine brighter and brighter, until you shine more brightly with love than ever before. This is an opportunity to realize your truth.

Raynaud's disease: Your actions and direction are not in alignment with your passion. The fire that burns within you, the core essence of who you are, are you acting and creating from this space? Or are you being pulled in multiple directions?

Reactive arthritis: Your outer world reflects your inner world. Your body is calling you to go deep within and discover pieces that feel broken or unwanted and ready for a change. Are you ready to confront your inner demons from a loving perspective? Only love births the optimal environment for change and growth. Once you harness the ability to step into your heart, you are ready for anything!

Reactive-attachment disorder: Trust needs to be established. Endless and unconditional love must be shown and given consistently, until the walls of your heart are ready to come down. The built up walls can lead to issues with tormented self-love in adulthood. A new pattern needs to be established, and can be done through loving affirmations such as "I am love." Your heart knows it will always have love flowing from others on the other side of those walls.

Renal failure: The universe is shutting you down, trying to impede your path so that you can rest, maybe even move backwards before going forwards. It is time to lose unnecessary attachments and just be. Be as you are in this moment. Soak it all up. This moment is a gift, as is every moment before it and every moment that follows. Find softness and stillness by not needing forward motion.

Renovations: Home or office renovations are a wonderful time of transformation. What other areas of your life are you ready to upgrade and enhance? Reflect on doing a personal renovation, and tackle it with enthusiasm and hope.

Restless legs syndrome: You are always on the go. Constantly in motion physically or mentally, or both. Find value in non-action, non-movement, and non-thought. Stillness is a virtue, it is time for you to experience it.

Retinoblastoma: See eye cancer

Rhabdomyosarcoma: You cannot control everything in life. There are moments of peace, moments of joy, and moments of suffering. All of these moments are gifts as they give you an opportunity to access compassion and presence. How can you find greater compassion (loving acceptance and gratitude), and presence now, while suffering?

Rheumatoid arthritis: RA is caused by an inability to shed light on what is going well in your life. Are you able to truly appreciate all that you are? To have gratitude for all of life's blessings and gifts and for all that you have done, all you have created? Or are you constantly seeking more? It's easy for you to fall into the "not enough" mentality. Never having enough, never being enough, and always wanting more. This fear-based energy creates blockages at the joints and creates an imbalance in the flow of life. It is safe to dream and have goals, but do not get pulled into the future. Be here with all that you are and have right now. Joy is here now if you can only see all of the beauty in creation.

Rheumatic fever: A blockage has become deeply lodged in your heart (in your emotional body). It may have been lingering for some time, but now it must be addressed. You must surrender and allow this pain to rise so it can transition away from your body and into the light.

Ringworm: Have you been susceptible to other's energy? Have you been easily affected by pain that your family, friends, or even strangers have been processing? Your system or field of energy is weak and vulnerable. It is time to strengthen your essence and hold space for you. Hold space for a candle to illuminate a dark room and not be overcome by the darkness. We can do this with ritualistic self-care. Consistently fill your needs of the heart, mind, body, and spirit. As you help to fill any energy depletions, you can stay strong and not be suppressed in who you are when you are around others, so that you no longer absorb their pain.

Rosacea: You have difficulty in releasing energies that do not serve you — whether it is past experiences, emotional wounds, physical ailments, or negativity. It is very important for you to consistently and mindfully let go. Let go of all that is not supporting your highest good. Affirm: "I release all that does not serve me." Feel it leave your being until you can feel your truth of peace and wholeness.

Rotator cuff injuries and dysfunctions: The body is slowing you down with your energy input (left side) and output (right side). It is time to reflect and go inwards. Time to align you with your soul's desired truth, so that you may attract and share your highest vibrations as you transcend old vibrations.

Scabies: Surrender to the itch. Your body is releasing pent up and unhelpful energies. It is a time of transition. Sit back and allow what needs to move through you to move. Calmness is always within, if you reach for the peace within you.

Scarlet fever: Don't procrastinate in life. If something is important to you, put it first and make it happen. The longer you wait, the harder it becomes to correct or improve. Nip it in the bud.

Scars: This is an area of vulnerability at first, then it transforms into an area of strength. You can have healthy scar tissue, or restrictive scar tissue. If it is restrictive, you are feeding too powerfully into modes of protection and boundaries. If it is a healthy scar, you are balanced. If it is flaccid, you are too flexible in your personal boundaries.

Schizoid personality disorder: There are beautiful self-discoveries to be made. The distance you feel between others is a blessing at this time because it allows you to discover the depths of yourself. Dive into the light and the dark with love and acceptance of who you are. Once you sit in the seat of acceptance, your desire for connection will change and flow as your deepest self is present.

Schizophrenia: You are a multidimensional being. A part of you is in this physical reality. Your mind, however, is completely open to the multiverse of dimensions, dreams, and fears. It can seem difficult to be a part of this world of structure. Know that you are special and the gifts you hold are simply not integrated as acceptable to society yet. You are born ahead of your time. Moving forward, try to work with honoring and accepting yourself as you are, not fearing or rejecting your soul's truth, but embracing the loving being that you are. Nourish loving thoughts and let them blossom into flowers.

Sciatica: Sciatica is caused by energy being trapped in the lower spine and sacral region. You are clinging tightly to your fears. They are stopping the flow of energy and abundance into your life. Reflect on your fears and see if it is time to soften and surrender them. Can you begin to trust that everything is divinely unfolding for you as it is meant to?

Scoliosis: It can feel like you are being pulled constantly by your environment and by those around you. Everyone wants you to walk the path they have in mind for you. But it is your right to walk your own path, to choose your line, and not veer from it for anyone. You are strong. Whatever you desire, you can do it, it is within you. You just need to believe in yourself and take your steps one by one, even if you are constantly being pulled in opposite directions, stay steady on your path and you will arrive.

Sensitivity: See Allergies/food allergies and sensitivities

Severe acute respiratory syndrome (SARS): Extreme sadness is wanting to be felt and released from the body. It may be sadness with the structure of your life and how it is unfolding. It may be pent up sadness that has overfilled your reservoir and flowed into the lungs, resisting and fighting to hold in emotion. Create space to let it all out.

Seasonal Affective Disorder: Like the yin and the yang, there is darkness and there is light. All things perfectly balance one another. Accept your time of darkness. Cradle it like a child; find gratitude for its gifts. Do not resist it and fight it, instead be with it. Know it is not who you are, it is an experience you are having at this time.

Seasons: See autumn, winter, spring, summer, monsoon

Seborrheic dermatitis: Fueled by transition and change that you are not prepared for. Softly surrender and allow your body to move forward into its new desires and lifestyle. Release the old patterns and beliefs that are not serving you anymore. Allow your radiance to shine through.

Sepsis/septic shock: See blood poisoning

Sex addiction (hypersexuality): You are expending a lot of energy, and needing outlets for this energy. This energy is actually carrying sadness that needs to be loved, held, and expressed. It is sadness from your past (and past traumas). Take time to sit with your sadness and to give it a voice. It wants to be heard. You are deserving of freeing it from your being.

Sexually transmitted disease (STD): You are enthralled in a beautiful picture, a picture you want to believe is your truth but is in fact just a picture. You must tear through it to come to the naked truth. At this time it may feel like an ugly truth. There are some deep rooted fears and fear-based patterns you have not been addressing. You've been stuck in your imaginary world, trying to see it through rose-colored glasses. You must look at all of your truth. Accept it and move forward, destroying what is not supportive, and empowering what is supportive.

Shingles: Shingles are caused by a feeling of not being in control. There is a feeling that your outer world has control over you, your life and your health. A feeling you are fighting a battle that you have no chance of winning. It's time to step out of the battle and the mental fighting. It is time to step into love and interconnectedness. Know that you are a divine being, and you have a say in what comes your way through your heart and your mind. The thoughts you think and emotions you hold are constantly creating your environment. You have the power to create the life, the health, and the abundance you desire. You can create the relationships you crave and the soul growth you have dreamed of. It is not just by having a positive intention, but by having positive thoughts and emotions that are in alignment with the way you wish to live. Your outer world will respond to the signal you put out into it. So keep your thoughts in check, are they in alignment with your deepest desires? Or are they being fed by fear? Check in with your emotions; is your heart singing with joy? Or is it holding sadness and anger? Come back to the joy and the love deep within you. When you hold that vibration, the world will match it.

Shin splints: Foundation is important for you. In what ways can you encourage greater solidity to your life? How can you feel more supported and balanced moving forward?

Shopaholic: A part of you is trying to be filled and find fullness, wanting to feel deserving, special and important. You are not seeking joy in a soulful longevity kind of way, but through quick egoic ways that do not last. The fullness you seek is a lack of self-love, of feeling worthy and like you are enough. You are enough. You are worthy of love and true acceptance. This is not something you can earn, reward, or create. It is already here, as you are, unconditionally. You must release the attachments to everything in the way of that truth. Everything you have chosen to believe, so you can experience the truth.

Shortness of breath: Are you feeling contracted and small as there is not enough room for you to breathe (to take up space for what you need)? How can you make space for yourself right now and put your needs first? Now is the time, because you are just as valuable as everyone around you.

Sickle cell disease: Things don't always flow with ease. Patience helps to let life unwind in its own divine time. Gentle nudges support you on your path when you are feeling stuck. Find a balance between acceptance and action so that you can create your own unique flow.

Sigmatism: See lisp

Sinusitis: Emotions are being blocked or held within the body. You need to allow full expression of your emotions. If you are holding anger, express it. Express it in your face, your eyes, your mouth, speak it with the passion of anger in its fullness. Let your body language allow the anger to take over. This goes for sadness, joy, grief, and any emotions that you have not allowed yourself true expression of. Let it seep from your pores, out of your body and into the universe. Your emotions are not meant to be suppressed. They are a reflection of you, a piece of you. If you resent your emotions, you are not honoring yourself.

Sjogren's syndrome: Don't be afraid to ask for help or support when you need it. Life has many gifts and tools to bring you more comfort and deeper self care. Reach out and try new activities that bring joy and ease into your life. You deserve to have blissful comforts that activate greater joy and health within you.

Skin cancer: There is a toxic energy you are living in. Your body is speaking to you. It is telling you it is time to create major change. It is time to surrender and release this toxic energy. This toxic energy may be your thought patterns, actions, beliefs you hold, words you speak, or the past you hold on to. Maybe it is all of them combined. Now is the time to realign with the love within you and expel these fear-based vibrations.

Skin rash: Your body is speaking to you. It is trying to expel negative energies from your being. There are fearful thought patterns and vibrations you have been hoarding within, and your inner truth has had enough. Your body is purging these patterns. Can you allow this detoxification to flow with grace? Can you assist it by mentally and physically feeding only vibrations of love as you stop nourishing your fear? Or will you resist these shifts, scratch the itch and continue holding on to that which no longer serves you?

Slapped-cheek syndrome: See parvovirus infection

Sleep apnea: This relates to the flow of universal qi. The cessation of breathing is a disturbance to the flow of life. Qi is life and vitality. Can you open and surrender to a higher power, to a space of trust that the universe is here to support you? Because it is. It (God/source energy) wants to give you all that you need, to fill you with support and life. But you must open yourself up to this divine flow. Realize you are not alone. Receive the help, and love from spirit that is essential to your well-being.

Sleeping disorders: There is a part of you that wants to be awake. This part of you is struggling with time (valuing time too highly). You are wanting to accomplish a lot of things and feel a pressure within to create and to live life more fully. Sleep is a reflection of our death. It is a time for non-action, a time for rest and non-productivity. Do you struggle with the fact that you and your life will die? That there is an end? Does it create an inner pressure to live more vibrantly? This struggle with your timeline and life impacts your thoughts by forcing them to jump ahead. It creates worry about the future, and your physical and emotional body follow suit as your fight or flight response gets turned on. Because you live in worry of the future, you need to accept the yin and the yang, the light and the dark. Just as you live, you will die. As you are awake, you will sleep. Be present and allow yourself to accept the constant "death" of life each night. The contrast is needed for you to find balance.

Smallpox: Smallpox is representing a misguided step that has led to misfortune and fear-based vibrations (negative energy). Retrace your steps as of recently, and reflect on the steps to come. Are you on track with the guidance of your heart? Can you alter your course to align you with your heart's path? If not, can you accept the consequences and energy currently surrounding you? Accept what is and realign with your heart to align you with the path of love.

Snoring: There is an imbalance in what you are receiving. Are you receiving self-love by doing self-care work that nourishes and pampers you? Are you receiving enough love from those you care for, that you feel valued and honored? Are you receiving abundance from the universe that helps to support you and your desires? If any of these are lacking, you need a shift in consciousness. Know that you are deserving of high quality love and energy in all aspects of your life. If you have this awareness, do your actions reflect this truth? Snoring is a want for more, to fill a part of you that is low. Resistance is in the breath, because there is a misalignment with receiving.

Snow: Light, spirit and purity.

Social anxiety disorder: Know your power. True power can never be taken from you, because it is a truth you have aligned with. The truth that you are exactly who you are meant to be. That you are worthy and divine when you allow yourself to be as you are. Your gift to the world is to be natural. Let go of non-acceptance and feelings of unworthiness. Accept your value, integrate it, stand in it, be it. It is yours.

Sociopath: See antisocial personality disorder.

Soft tissue sarcoma: Simplicity and nurturing are needed in your life. How can you embody your healthiest and happiest self? What self-care actions and lifestyle changes bring ease and joy to you? How can you simplify your life to the bare bones and only focus on what is of the utmost importance to you? Now is the time to do this work of simplifying.

Sore throat: Take some deep breaths and bring your awareness to them. Slow down and find gratitude for this moment. There is beauty all around, but it is only seen and felt when you are present and attentive with it.

Sound sensitivity: See misophonia

Speech impediment: Slow down and find clarity on your path. Find clarity in what you wish to say, express and create. This world full of vast experiences can be too much for the brain to process as it tries to convey your truth to the world. Do not filter yourself or hold back, pause more often to check in with yourself before expressing your vibrant self to the world. You have so much beauty to share, do not worry if it does not come out "perfectly." You are perfect as you are, and the world will understand your message clearly through your intention and energy.

Spider veins: You are very connected to others and your environment. You are a sensitive and empathic soul. How can you create healthy boundaries for yourself? How can you empower your vibrancy and your potency so that you are not as affected by others' struggles?

Spondylosis: See osteoarthritis

Sprain: Your momentum has been too strong in life. Slow it down and come inwards. Make sure each step you are taking feels good to you. Check in with how you are feeling with every step and action. Do you feel good? Calm? Excited? Or is there stress, anxiety, and fear? Do some self-discovery to align with that inner calmness and excitement about your path. Live it passionately, and in a healthy way.

Spring: The time for new beginnings is now. What are you ready to begin working towards? What seeds can you plant in your life that you are ready to blossom into beautiful new beginnings?

Staphylococcus aureus (staph infection): Have you been critical of yourself and your life, wanting more, or wanting to be more? There is an essential piece missing and that piece is gratitude. You are so gifted as a human and need to shake off the critical lenses so you can see all of your beauty. See all that you offer this world by being you. There are many things to be grateful for, you need to spend time honoring them. Gratitude brings you health and joy. Express and feel your gratitude so that you can step into presence.

Stillbirth: Through death, new life emerges. Grief is a powerful emotion that needs to be fully honored and experienced. Grief is love at its roots. With this death, new life has an opportunity to emerge within you. An opportunity for deeper love, joy, and peace awaits you when you are ready. Can you see the old beliefs and patterns you can shed that are not supporting you? This death of unsupportive thoughts is also awaiting your action. The action could mean infusing loving and positive thoughts, or maybe it is taking loving actions. Do what feels best for you at this time.

Stomach ache/abdominal pain: Your body and spirit go through energetic transformations daily. They are constantly shedding old toxic experiences and energies. At times, this shedding creates discomfort emotionally, mentally, and physically. The best way to support this transition is to intake healthy foods, thoughts, and actions. How can you support yourself with rest, exercise, food, etc., right now? This will ease the journey of your unsupportive energy.

Stomach cancer: You are energetically unsettled in life and with yourself. There is an inner rejection of the way life is or has been unfolding for you. Deep gratitude for the goodness and richness needs to be realized. Not forced, but realized. Then the body, the stomach especially, can process and "stomach" (or break down) your reality as something desired and wonderful. Instead, your reality is being rejected and feels unpleasant. To find this gratitude, look within to see that all you are seeking, including the emotional aspects, are already here. They can be accessed at all times. As you begin to access the emotions you desire: love, peace, freedom, and whatever else you desire. The physical world will reflect these good feelings more and more. You will not have to wait or drastically change your life to discover what your soul wants you to align with. You get to access it now in the present moment.

Stomach ulcer: See peptic ulcer

Strain (muscular tear): You are stretching yourself too far and too thin. You are extending your energy to your projects, loved ones, and work in a way that is not serving your needs. It is in fact causing harm to you. Pull it back in, bringing the love and energy you have been exerting outside of yourself towards yourself. It is time to go inwards, to rest, repair, and nourish your needs. Once the reservoir that was depleted feels full again, move back into giving outwardly in a more balanced way, a way in which you serve your needs as well as others.

Streptococcal pharyngitis (strep throat): You have been feeling strangled or compressed by others (people, society, and the world). Compressing how you show up, how you can speak your truth and take action derived from your heart. Truthfully, the compression or resistance of allowing yourself freedom of expression is self-imposed. Only you can stop you from being your truth. Take time for recovery and then slowly begin breaking down your walls to set yourself free and to really show up in the world.

Stress: Your body is speaking to you. Change needs to happen right now. How can you prioritize you right now? What can you let go of? What can you bring in?

Stroke: The mind has had too much. It is incapable of allowing your life to unfold in the same way it has been moving for some time. It wants to tell you: "You need to stop the unhealthy patterns and unhealthy thoughts. Stop all of the unsupportive, over-usage of your mind and body." It is time to get fully on track with your deepest self. That means no more ignoring the voice inside you that says: "I want to do this, I shouldn't do that, I don't feel good about this, I wish I could live my life in this way." It is time to listen, as your body will not take anymore excuses or distractions. Only you know what that inner voice has been calling you towards, and if you are uncertain as to which direction and path it is, it is time to create a serious check in with yourself to create a safe space to listen to your heart's desires. No one and no thing is stopping you from living your dreams, except for you.

Stutter: You have a very high frequency that moves faster than most. This is beautiful because you have lots of powerful energy that you can use towards helping others and helping the planet. It can affect your speech and your nerves if it is not utilized in a healthy way. It's time to find some outlets that support you and your beautiful energy. It is bursting from you at the seams. Maybe it's finding things you are passionate about, ways you can be more playful, or just good old exercise. Tune in to see what ways you can pour your powerful energy into your environment that feel good to you.

Sudden infant death syndrome (SIDS): The cessation of life reflects a time of inner death within oneself, especially a death of emotions. You may find a numbness being felt as there is a death of the heart, or heart break. A piece of you and your world has died. From death comes new life. Death is essential in all systems of life, and is needed for soul growth. To lose a child is the deepest and most painful death one can experience. It signifies the beginning of the deepest soul growth, initiating a birth of hope, of finding complete trust in the universe. A birth of emotional strength that most will never come near accessing. It births a deep connection to trust in your divine plan. Trust that there is purpose, even when you face pure darkness. Trust that light is always present. It gives you an opportunity to step into the light instead of succumbing to the darkness.

Suicide: Some pain feels too heavy to bear. There is an inner knowing that on the other side there is no more pain. No more getting stuck in the vibration of fear (darkness), only love (light). This is true. But this love, this light, does exist here on the Earth plane and in your life. The darkness has just been in its power, blocking you from your truth: that you are love. That love exists within all things, and all beings. We can only reach out and grab it when we have trust that it is there. Trust that what you seek is here, in this physical life for you, even if it does not feel accessible at this moment. If you can trust it is here, you are already accessing your light.

Summer: Now is the time to shine! What insights and growth have you experienced in the last year? They are ready to be utilized and enjoyed. It is time to move from processing, creating and reflecting to being.

Sunburn: Listen to the subtle ways in which your body speaks to you. Your outer world is always tugging at your attention. Never lose the awareness of the self and its needs.

Swelling (edema): Too much of something is never healthy. In what areas of your life are you doing too much, wanting too much, or being too much? How can you come to a space of greater balance, acceptance, and gratitude? For a more specific description of which area of "too much" your swelling is affecting, look at Chapter 11: Anatomy of Energy and the specific area of your body being affected.

Swollen glands: Your truth needs to be voiced right now, whether through a whisper or a scream. How have you been suppressing your desires and needs? Have you been showing up fully with friends, coworkers, and others? Speaking your truth comes from your heart, the space of love. It also comes from ego and the mind. All of these thoughts and emotions are your truth. Have you been holding back?

Syphilis: Refer to STD

Systemic lupus erythematosus: See Lupus

Technology addiction: You are distracting yourself from some very important things that want to be addressed. You are filling your mind and your time with noise so that you don't have to listen to your soul's voice which has been itching to be heard. It wants to tell you that now is the time to live passionately and purposefully. Now is the time to heal your past and your present. Now is the moment to live. How do you want to live? Be that and do that. You reflect whatever you wish to reflect. Your heart and soul want to be honored in your actions.

Teeth grinding: Your energy is being pulled in multiple directions. How can you balance your actions and live by your word? What is most important to you? Are you able to put that first? When you disperse your energy into too many people or projects, you find yourself feeling over-stimulated. It is time to focus and simplify.

Temporomandibular joint dysfunction (TMJD): You have done a lot of work to get where you are in life. However, there are some big steps that still need to be taken. You are holding back and not going all the way. In what areas of your life are you not fully expressing your needs?

Tennis elbow: It is time to embrace your connection with others and community. Time to step outside your inner world and give and receive love from others. Find balance in inward activity and outward activity. Rest in the middle.

Termination of pregnancy: See abortion

Testicular cancer: Your desires, dreams, and actions (that are in alignment with your truth) have not been allowed to unfold. You have been resisting allowing these truths to come forward. You have been separating your dreams from your reality. Your dreams have had enough and are wanting to burst into your reality. Action and courage are needed to allow yourself to move and create from your heart space, and from your soul, instead of your body and mind. Allow these seeds to be planted. Water them with positive thoughts and loving action. Give them a chance to grow and for you to grow.

Thirst: A dry throat and thirst shows that you are seeking more. In what ways are you not nourishing yourself now? Are you holding back expressing yourself? Are you not tending to your needs and basic care? Tune in and see where you can water your life with greater abundance.

Threadworms (pinworms): It is important to have your defenses up when you are in an environment that is toxic or harmful to you. Are you good at standing in your power when around dominating or aggressive personalities? How can you hold space for your wellness and not let others rub off on you? If you feel drained by another person, clear that energy and let it go. This can be done by energy sweeping. Sweep your body (auric field) with your hands, doing meditation/visualization or by sitting alone in nature.

Thrush: See oral thrush

Thunder: Something is coming, something big. Take heed, remain open and accepting to the universe's delivery of your gift.

Thyroid cancer: Due to the thyroid's proximity to the throat center, thyroid cancer is intertwined with self expression. What have you been holding back from the world? Your words and actions need to reflect your deepest self at all times. If you are holding back, you are creating dysfunction.

Tinnitus: Your celestial hearing is opening to the universe. Your inner truth wants you to connect and receive its whispers of wisdom. You are being guided on a new path. Useful advice and guidance awaits you when you are able to listen to your soul speak. It is guiding you towards expansive love.

TMJD: See temporomandibular joint dysfunction

Tonsillitis: Something in your environment is not healthy for you. Reflect on what it might be that is out of alignment, and remove it from your life. Not everything can be won by fighting through it, sometimes we need to welcome greater ease by physically removing obstacles.

Toothache: One aspect of your life is needing your attention and is becoming angry from your avoidance. Reflect on your self-care, work, relationships, and lifestyle. See what aspect has been unattended to and needs an infusion of your focus and action.

Tooth decay: You have not been completely clear in expressing your truth to the world. Your pain body and fear vibration have been decaying and muddying your truth. Let out, spit out, do an oil pull, or any practice to release the untrue and toxic patterns you have been expressing. Once you have gotten it out of your system, create a clear and clean path for your deepest truth to flow freely from you.

Tornado: It is time for a fresh start. Your life is being lifted, tossed, and turned, and then returned to you in what feels like a mess. Now is the time to take small steps. Life can feel overwhelming and chaotic. Choose one small task each day to bring you closer to living your highest potential. Before you know it, everything will be exactly where you wish.

Tourette syndrome: This syndrome is catapulting you into confidence. You are worthy of being heard and seen. Stand strong in your worthiness, no matter how you present yourself. You are just as worthy as everyone else. You are enough. Know this, be this, you got this.

Transient ischemic attack (mini stroke): Your mind is struggling with its health. How can you have a calm and clear conscience moving forward? It is time to be stern with your thoughts and energy. No more wasting precious space on what ifs. It is time to be with what is and to enjoy it!

Trigeminal neuralgia: The energy of the face is about how you present yourself to the world. Are you accepting of your flaws? Or, are you having a hard time and hiding parts of yourself from others? It is time to show up as you are, beautiful and flawed. Where is acceptance needed in your life?

Tsunami: The ocean is returning to you a piece of your soul that has been misplaced or stolen. Keep your heart open. Can you love your inner child that was hurt or broken? Can you hold it in your heart for the rest of your life with tender love and care? This is a return to fullness and wholeness. It can feel difficult and vulnerable, but in the end you will return to a space of greater love.

Tuberculosis (TB): Even when your health may seem depleted, the world is still unfolding around you. Beauty is here and gratitude is within. Your inner world is healthy, calm, and balanced. You can access this space within you at any time, the space of peace and balance. You can see the gifts outside of you, the beauty in your outer world. There are endless gifts. No matter what is happening in your physical reality, gratitude can still be found and felt. Balance can be accessed. Simply look deeper.

Tummy ache: See stomach ache/abdominal pain

Tumor: Toxic energy has been trapped here within your body. It is an internal toxin, not external, meaning it is created from within. This negative energy needs first to be accepted and loved, instead of feared. Fear does not help it release, diminish, and soften; it only strengthens and empowers it. Love helps the tumor to soften and release its grip. Then you can take the next step, which is to clean your body energetically. There are things that need to be released: old memories, habits, and beliefs that are not supporting you. Some of these things may have been under the radar for some time. Do a deep purge of unsupportive energies through consciously shifting your awareness to the new truths that you are ready to live. Surrender the old. This will help your body and tumor(s) heal. Refer to Chapter 11: Anatomy of Energy for the meaning of the specific area that the tumor has grown.

Type 1 & 2 Diabetes: See diabetes

Ulcer: See peptic ulcer

Ulcerative colitis: What have you not been letting go of? Sometimes we need to let go of our past, habits, or thoughts, to move into our best version of self. Have you been slowing down or resisting your inner deaths? Take time to reflect on what is not serving you anymore, and when you are ready release it with ease.

Urinary incontinence: Strength and calmness are waiting to be utilized in a grander way. How can you be stronger (in your power), and calmer at the same time?

Urinary tract infection (UTI): What support can you bring in to help you with your elimination of negativity and toxicity? Negative thoughts and emotions are having a difficult journey out of your energy field. How can you support their release? Therapy, vitamins, water, healthy foods, journaling, etc.

Urticaria: See hives

Uterus cancer: See womb cancer

Vaginal cancer: What are you afraid of creating? The life of your dreams? The dream job, relationship, or health? Don't resist your opportunity to shine brightly in this lifetime. How can you open yourself to your own creator energy and feel excited yet calm about it?

Vaginal yeast infection: There is inflammation and disconnection from feeling grounded, safe, and present. This imbalance can feel like you are cut off from mother earth. In what ways can you arrive in your body at this moment? How can you ground your mind to only be aware of what is relevant? Going outside is helpful for the Earth energy to connect and clear this blockage.

Varicose veins: Connection to the Earth is vital. Mother Earth supports you with all of your basic needs: health, wealth, shelter, and relationships. She makes sure you are supported. You must lean into her, allowing her to flow. Let the goodness flow all around you and bring balance to your physical world.

She also takes away the old and what is not supporting you: habits, thoughts, or whatever you need to detox from your life. Varicose veins show a disconnection in energy flow with that of mother Earth. You have not been trusting and feeling supported by her qi. You have been holding on to toxic qi that you want to release. Open these gates, connect to the planet and become one, as you support her with your life and she supports your living. You are not alone.

Vegan/vegetarian: You are a lightworker. This means you are a healer. You cannot stand for unnecessary suffering. You care for the planet and animals, even if it means you are not going to be accepted by others. You are stepping into your power, the power of love. You are a peaceful warrior of love and light.

Venous leg ulcer: You need to take extra care of yourself — protect yourself, heal yourself and tend to your inner wounds. What have you left unattended in your heart? Now is the time to nurture and love it.

Vertigo: You need to center your awareness and focus on the truth. What is most important to you above all else? Be that truth. Everything else can wait; it does not require your energy. But your truth does. If you are unaware of what this deep truth is, spend some time with your hand on your heart until you feel it. It is right there always.

Volcanic eruption: An explosion of new life is flowing into your reality. A birthing of dreams and hopes is ready to be birthed through fire to create a new world. What are you ready to move forward in? Now is the time. Doubts and fears will be burned, leaving confidence and power for you to stand in your truth.

Vulvar cancer: Your vagina is the energy of creation. The vulva holds the energy of seeing your creation through. You need a final push to make your dreams the reality you have wished into being. You have been taking lots of positive action, but at times procrastinating. It is time to hit it home and use your strength to make it happen.

Wart: Warts symbolize resistance to your soul path. You are getting distracted by your ego and outer world. Come back in and be driven by your heart. How does your heart wish to live? What thoughts does your heart inspire?

Whooping cough: Can you remain calm in a tense situation? Whooping cough is a great symbolic test of feeling your body jerking, but having your mind remain calm.

Williams syndrome: You are a gift out of this world. You offer a connection to the divine. You speak through love and honesty, teaching others to find their own truth. You are an angelic human who gifts us with presence, patience, and unconditional true love.

Wilms tumor: Humor, laughter, and fun are the best medicine. Be playful, and see that laughter really is the best medicine.

Winter: Winter is a wonderful time for reflection and inner work. What do you need to feel nourished? Whether it is rest or productivity, do what feels supportive for you in each moment. The energy of winter is wonderful for gaining clarity and perspective. In your spiritual journey, can you take time to go deeper and tune into your soul self?

Womb cancer (uterus cancer): Have you felt worthy to listen to your intuitive dreams? Or, have you held back and thought that you are somehow not enough to create the joyous life that you are passionate about? You are worthy! Everyone is worthy of living their best life. What would your dreams be if you had no fears?

Workaholic: Have you been ignoring your problems, and ignoring your soul as it cries and speaks to you? It asks you for self-love. It asks you to be your truth. To stop running and hiding from what needs to get done: the real work, the soul work. Now is the time. You are ready.

Wrinkles: All of life leaves an impression on you. Wrinkles are one way your experiences are imprinted into your physical body. If you view your wrinkles with disdain, you are viewing your experiences through the lens of regret. If you view your wrinkles with acceptance and joy, you have accepted and found gifts in all of your experiences in life.

Yellow fever: Let go of the old fear-based thoughts and vibrations you have allowed yourself to get stuck in. Surrender and release them. Come to a space of trust and move forward. Trust in this moment that everything will be okay.

Zika virus: Sometimes your body must become dirty to become clean, like a pig bathes in the mud. Now is the time to do a soul cleanse. Release all that is not aligned with your heart and your spirit.

ACKNOWLEDGEMENTS

Over four years I've encountered blistered fingers from writing, countless revisions, moments of despair, and knee trembling joy. To my patient and loving husband Degju, I thank you deeply for your support as I wrote this book. You were there watching me skip with joy as I finished each chapter, and you were there watching me fight off a panic attack as I faced another rejection letter from another agent or publisher. Thank you for keeping me grounded and believing in me and this project, as well as supporting me with my final editing.

Claudia-Sam Cataford Sauvé, my dear friend and soul sister, thank you for not only supporting me with editing, but being an inspiration in following your dreams. You are a wonderful example to me of being a woman in a leadership role who is not afraid to share her heart wisdom with the world.

To another soul sister: Evie Gravino, you wild woman. Thank you for filling me with a little extra confidence and encouragement as I wrote this book, as well as supporting me with editing. You constantly remind me to color outside of the lines.

A very special thank you to each client and friend who shared their story with me to use in this book. I am so happy that your story gets to be a part of someone else's healing journey. I know it takes vulnerability in sharing your story. Now through your own healing, you are a healer for others, just by sharing your healing story. Thank you.

Thank you to my family and friends for supporting me when I needed your help, and for being my cheerleaders!

When deciding to write this book, I faced a skyscraper of doubt that I was worthy of sharing my story and my gifts with others. I chose to honor the quiet voice within me that does believe in myself, my value, and the equal value of all others. I hope that when you face your own skyscrapers of doubt, you are able to listen to the loving words of encouragement shining through from your higher self.

Soul Alignment Exercises:

BIBLIOGRAPHY

Works Cited

BAKER, SUE. "Exiled Tibetans say 1.2 million killed during Chinese rule." *UPI*, 17 September 1984, *https://www.upi.com/Archives/1984/09/17/Exiled-Tibetans-say-12-million-killed-during-Chinese-rule/9452464241600/*. Accessed 17 May 2022.

Hanh, Thich Nhat. *You are Here: Discovering the Magic of the Present Moment.* Edited by Melvin McLeod, Shambhala, 2009.

Hoge, Elizabeth, et al. "Randomized Controlled Trial of Mindfulness Meditation for Generalized Anxiety Disorder: Effects on Anxiety and Stress Reactivity." *The Journal Of Clinical Psychiatry*, vol. 74, no. 8, 2013, pp. 786-792. *National Center for Biotechnology Information.*

Kaptchuk, Ted. "The power of the placebo effect." *Harvard Health*, 13 December 2021, *https://www.health.harvard.edu/mental-health/the-power-of-the-placebo-effect.* Accessed 8 May 2022.

Long, Jeffrey. "Near-Death Experiences Evidence for Their Reality." *Missouri Medicine*, vol. 111, no. 5, 2014, p. 372. *National Library Of Medicine*, https://www.ncbi.nlm.nih.gov/pmc/articles/PMC6172100/.

McManus, David E. "Reiki Is Better Than Placebo and Has Broad Potential as a Complementary Health Therapy." *National Center For Biotechnology Information*, vol. 22, no. 4, 2017, pp. 1051-1057. *National Library Of Medicine*, *https://www.ncbi.nlm.nih.gov/pmc/articles/PMC5871310/.*

"NIMH » Mental Illness." *National Institute of Mental Health,* *https://www.nimh.nih.gov/health/statistics/mental-illness.* Accessed 2 July 2022.

Raghupathi, Wullianallur, and Viju Raghupathi. "An Empirical Study of Chronic Diseases in the United States: A Visual Analytics Approach to Public Health." *National Library Of Medicine: A Visual Analytics Approach,* vol. 1, no. 15, 2018, p. 431, *https://www.ncbi.nlm.nih.gov/pmc/articles/PMC5876976/.*

Sherman, Harold, and Ingo Swann. "An Experimental Psychic Probe Of The Planet Jupiter." *Central Intelligence Agency,* vol. NSA-RDP96X00790R000100040010, no. 3, 2008, p. 14.

Wager, Tor Dessart, et al. "Attenuating neural threat expression with imagination." *Neuron,* vol. 100, no. 4, 2018, p. 17. *The Cell, https://www.cell.com/neuron/fulltext/S0896-6273(18)30955-3.*

Made in the USA
Monee, IL
31 March 2023

30993978R00169